The Cost of Business

edited
by

SHANE BORROWMAN

and

MAUREEN McBRIDE
Associate Editor
University of Nevada, Reno

Longman
Boston   Columbus   Indianapolis   New York   San Francisco
Upper Saddle River   Amsterdam   Cape Town   Dubai   London   Madrid   Milan
Munich   Paris   Montreal   Toronto Delhi   Mexico City   Sao Paulo   Sydney
Hong Kong   Seoul   Singapore   Taipei   Tokyo

Senior Acquisitions Editor: Lauren A. Finn
Senior Marketing Manager: Sandra McGuire
Production Manager: Stacey Kulig
**Project Coordination, Text Design, and
    Electronic Page Makeup:** PreMediaGlobal
Cover Design Manager: Wendy Ann Fredericks
Cover Image: © John-Marshall Mantel/Corbis
Senior Manufacturing Buyer: Roy Pickering
Printer and Binder: Courier Corporation
Cover Printer: Demand Production Center

For permission to use copyrighted material, grateful acknowledgment
is made to the copyright holders on pp. 209–211, which are hereby
made part of this copyright page.

Library of Congress Cataloging-in-Publication Data
The cost of business / edited by Shane Borrowman and Maureen
McBride.—1st ed.
    p. cm.
  ISBN-13: 978-0-205-56294-7
  ISBN-10: 0-205-56294-9
  1. Economics—Study and teaching.   2. Civil society—Study and
teaching.   3. Entrepreneurship—United States—Case studies.
  4. United States—Economic conditions—21st century.
  I. Borrowman, Shane.   II. McBride, Maureen.
  HB71.C667   2010
  338.5—dc22   2010028830

1 2 3 4 5 6 7 8 9 10—CRW—14   13   12   11   10

Longman
is an imprint of

www.pearsonhighered.com   ISBN-13: 978-0-205-56294-7
                          ISBN-10:   0-205-56294-9

TABLE OF CONTENTS

v

THEME AND APPROACH

Across centuries of use, the word "cost" has gathered to itself a range of meanings, from an Old Norse word for "quality" to a Gothic term for "trial," from an Old English expression meaning "to try" to a similarly used Greek word signifying the more specific activity "to taste." Out of its rich etymological heritage, the modern meanings of "expense charged" and "amount paid" arise, and it is to these, primarily but not exclusively, that we have turned throughout *The Cost of Business*. What costs do we pay, we wondered, for living within a capitalist economy? As importantly, we also wondered, what benefits are we paid by virtue of our lives within this system? The readings that follow consider a range of issues across the payment/profit spectrum.

The intent of *The Cost of Business* is neither to sing the praises of late-market capitalism nor to decry its failings. Instead, the readings in this text represent a range of opinions, with a diversity of rhetorical choices and authorial voices. This range and diversity rarely includes consideration of "both" sides of an issue, for only the most simple and unimportant topics can legitimately be said to have only two possible views. The writers whose works fill this book understand, in all cases, that black-and-white approaches fail when applied to gray areas.

Despite the (sometimes literal) life-and-death seriousness of many economic issues, the following readings often take surprising turns. Divided into five broad chapters, *The Cost of Business* begins with the economics of entertainment and ends with the economic realities of class and race. Between these two areas, which are not as separate as they may appear, the readings focus on the ups and downs of big business practices, from the largest of retail stores to the smallest of check-cashing outlets, from the significance of "green" practices to the ubiquitous place of advertising in modern culture. (For a more detailed consideration of the topics covered within each chapter, see the summaries provided in the introduction that follows.)

For teachers, *The Cost of Business* offers a range of interconnected readings on topics from illegal immigration in professional boxing to intellectual property and the use of FaceBook. These readings offer enough depth to inform students about issues both known and strange, and, more importantly, they serve as places where both further scholarly research and civic awareness can begin.

Students, mired in the economic realities of school and work, tuition payments, and insurance costs, will see their lives reflected in the readings that follow. Like the editors of *The Cost of Business*, these student readers bring to the book their own contexts, their own concerns, and their own histories. The readings that follow, combined with the structure of the editorial apparatus of the book itself, offer new perspectives—and both affirmation and refutation of old ones.

FEATURES AND STRUCTURE

The chapters and their individual readings have been chosen because of their ability to stand both alone and in conjunction with one another. Teachers who choose to take the readings in their front-to-back order will find clear and meaningful benefits, as the readings within each chapter build upon one another and one chapter builds to the next. Teachers who choose to take the chapters out of their present order—or who choose to pick and choose readings from across chapters—will find themselves particularly well supported by the questions that surround each text.

- Readings on topics that are fundamental to how our society and economy works are particularly relevant to the discussions we see and hear on the news, among our friends, from our members of government, and from those in business. We ask both students and teachers to remain aware of the interconnectedness of one issue with another. Whether the US economy is in a time of boom or bust, ascension or recession, there are no easy answers, no complicated questions, and no simple solutions to multifaceted problems. The readings are to help us consider the decisions we make when we shop for food at whatever outlets are available to us, work at whatever employment will support us, live within the race/class/gender that defines the frame of our lives, and more.
- Chapter introductions provide just enough detail to help students consider why the chapter topic is worthy of study, and

how the chapter's readings introduce thought-provoking issues and perspectives within each topic.

- A prereading question before each reading helps students preview a key idea in the reading and serves to launch either discussion or informal writing as needed.
- Questions that follow each reading begin by pushing students to consider the rhetorical and structural work of a specific reading. They then move to connect the reading to a similar/dissimilar reading elsewhere in *The Cost of Business*, either within the same chapter or across the book.

ACKNOWLEDGMENTS

No book arises *ex nihilo*, and *The Cost of Business* is certainly no exception. The editorial act of creation, like the process of writing itself, is both collaborative and contextual. We proposed, constructed, and revised *The Cost of Business* within the larger frame of our shared lived-experience as teachers, parents, and citizens; we proposed, constructed, and revised *The Cost of Business* within the smaller frame of our experiences in the American economic recessions of the 1970s and 2000s. These were our contexts for creation, and they guided our editorial decisions at every turn, in ways both clear and still concealed.

Our collaborators were many and varied and too numerous to thank directly.

We owe a debt to our families for their love and support, even when they were uncertain of our project.

We owe a debt to our friends and colleagues for the feedback they provided free of charge.

We owe a debt to our students across decades of teaching, students whose cares and concerns made *The Cost of Business* a multivoiced collection that reflects multigenerational concerns.

And we owe the publishing professionals who made *The Cost of Business* a reality, especially our editor Lauren Finn.

Lastly we owe our manuscript reviewers for their many suggestions of vital topics, current readings, and effective questions: Stephen Bauer, Babson College; Terry Benton, Youngstown State University; Joe Calabrese, University of Nevada, Reno; Maureen Goldman, Bentley College; Keith Gumery, Temple University; Patrick McGuire, University of Wisconsin-Parkside; Chris Roush, University of North Carolina-Chapel Hill; and Eileen Seifert, DePaul University.

In a cliché likely as old as the nation itself, the argument is advanced that "the business of America is business." This assertion is true in good times—the Roaring Twenties, the boom in the housing market after World War II, the rapid rise of the Dot-Com economy in the 1990s. This assertion is true in hard times—the Great Depression of the 1930s, the economic recession in the late 1970s and into the 1980s, the "Great Recession" of the new millennium. In the history of America, there are times of boom and times of bust. The business of America is, was, and possibly always will be the business of business.

In the pages that follow, you will be challenged by readings that take stands both in favor of and in opposition to the various models of American business—in both the old and new economies, in the real world and the virtual. You will be asked to consider the costs and benefits of business as usual—for individuals, for racial groups, for social classes. In a world dominated by massive international corporations that function within national economies driven by small business engines, you will consider your own experiences—and those described in the readings—in these shifting economic and social contexts.

As the last years of the first decade of the new millennium unwound—and the U.S. economy walked a tightrope stretched taut between economic recession and another great depression—Americans found themselves thinking about business in a worried-yet-optimistic way recognizable to their parents and grandparents, who watched this same economic ebb and flow before. Suddenly, Americans were called upon to be a lot more savvy about the workings of business, from issues affecting family budgets and the price of a gallon of gasoline to political budgetary machinations and the relative merits of military versus infrastructure spending. None of the issues were—or likely are—simple. All of the decisions that had to be made had consequences—good and bad, predictable and unforeseen.

Consider these findings by the Federal Reserve Bank of San Francisco: Between 1980 and 1994, the personal saving rate (the percentage of average income saved rather than spent) was in the neighborhood of 8%. It fell steadily as the 1990s ran to their end, and, by 2002, the PSR among U.S. citizens had reached 1%, compared with double-digit savings by citizens in Japan, Germany, and France, to name only three similarly developed economies. This virtual elimination of saved capital, concurrent with a rising dependency on credit, concerned economists and political pundits.

Americans were not saving money, and this was a problem for the economy.

Beginning late in 2008, as the U.S. economy experienced what is sometimes dubbed the greatest drop in its history since the Great Depression, Americans began to save their money. Statistics for these savings vary and carry only confused connections with numbers from preceding decades. With double-digit unemployment in some areas of the nation, circa 60% loss of value in the stock market, and inflation at its highest point since the recession of the late 1970s, everyone was worried . . . including those same economists and pundits who bemoaned the low PSR among American consumers. Americans who had money kept it. Investments were down. Consumer spending was down.

Americans were saving more money than at any point since the 1980s, and this was a problem for the economy.

In a situation where saving money and not saving money were both bad courses of action, individuals were left to consider the evidence of their own experiences, left to research what they could as best they could, and left to act—knowing that actions have consequences.

At its heart *The Cost of Business* is built around a form of argumentation more than two thousand years old, a pattern of argumentation so effective that Aristotle listed it in his *Rhetoric* (a sort of combination of lecture notes and a handbook for engaged and active Athenian citizens) as one of the twenty-eight common ways to organize a persuasive speech: cause and effect, action and reaction, antecedent and consequence. In a world of contradictory evidence and conflicting conclusions, we must riddle out our own ideas of cause and effect, our own ideas about how things got to be the way they are and how they're going to be after we make our own contributions.

Perhaps the simplest way to express a cause and effect argument is through an "If/Then" pattern that develops a clear (if incomplete) chain of causation between one event and another, between an action and its possible ramifications. Consider the following example:

> *If McDonald's aggressively markets its products to toddlers, then those toddlers are more likely to develop unhealthy eating habits.*

The argument is straightforward enough and certainly (or at least superficially) sounds logical and reasonable. Of course, it dodges important aspects of good argumentation: the definition of aggressive marketing, the definition of toddlers, and the slippery issue of arguing "more likely" rather than the certainty of "will." Still, it's a good place for an argument to start and shows much promise. The chain of cause and effect can be further extended:

> *If McDonald's aggressively markets its products to toddlers, then those toddlers are more likely to develop unhealthy eating habits. Children with unhealthy eating habits become unhealthy adults, and adults who are unhealthy in ways that can be avoided put an enormous strain on the healthcare system in America. The overburdened healthcare system causes the costs of healthcare to rise sharply, a cost that insurance companies pass along to their policy holders. When insurance prices rise, employers must find ways to cut costs in order to remain in business, and one way of cutting costs is to reduce the size of the U.S. workforce: firing employees and/or outsourcing work to other nations.*

Obviously this example is straining the chain of causation, pulling on it hard enough to cause a logical break in the weak links. In the most literal reading of this passage, the choice by McDonald's to market to toddlers becomes responsible for the loss of American jobs, the cost of health insurance, and the failures of the overworked U.S. healthcare system. Even the least discerning reader, uninformed on all of the issues raised, knows that this is weak argumentation, argumentation that works only when it's not held up for critical inspection.

Any part of this causal relationship can be argued persuasively, but all of it together makes the kind of flashy antagonistic show that plays well on MSNBC or Fox News but poorly in the realm of reasoned debate among reasonable women and men. At some point—a point fairly early on, possibly—the argument becomes absurd. It's an argument ready-made for talk radio and ready-made for a critically minded academic beating.

But this argument about causation is also, in many ways, the lived experience of millions of Americans—at least in part.

McDonald's *does* market aggressively to toddlers (with its clown spokesperson and ubiquitous Happy Meal toys), and studies *do* show that these toddlers frequently develop habits that lead to health issues, including diabetes and obesity. U.S. employers *are* facing rising insurance costs, and they *are*, in some cases, beating the cost by taking their business beyond America's borders—to places such as Latin America and Southeast Asia, where wages are low and health insurance is not a benefit of employment.

Such a chain of causation was verbally forged by President Barack Obama in his first State of the Union address, early in 2009. He argued:

> I took a trip to Elkhart, Indiana, today. Elkhart is a place that has lost jobs faster than anywhere else in America. In one year, the unemployment rate went from 4.7 percent to 15.3 percent. Companies that have sustained this community for years are shedding jobs at an alarming speed, and the people who've lost them have no idea what to do or who to turn to. They can't pay their bills and they've stopped spending money. And because they've stopped spending money, more businesses have been forced to lay off more workers. In fact, local TV stations have started running public service announcements that tell people where to find food banks, even as the food banks don't have enough to meet the demand.

The picture painted by such a terrible collage of causation is a grim one, and President Obama used this argument to launch the most sweeping reform of the American economy ever attempted—a simultaneous investment in infrastructure and renewable energy, social programs, and national defense in a post-Cold War world.

The readings in *The Cost of Business* exist where the issues raised above intersect: arguments from cause and effect, issues facing U.S. businesses both at home and abroad, and the lived experience of Americans (citizens and noncitizens alike). Topics range across a broad spectrum and have been loosely divided into five frequently overlapping chapters, all geared toward offering enough information to build a foundation from which you can launch your own research.

CHAPTER 1: THE BUSINESS OF ENTERTAINMENT

The readings in Chapter 1 touch upon a range of issues within the entertainment industrial complex in America, from online gaming and adult filmmaking to boxing and golf. But the issues go well beyond simple entertainment to include major figures such as Tiger Woods and minor figures such as boxers forced to cross the U.S.–Mexico border illegally in order to fight in bouts that pay well enough to allow them to live.

CHAPTER 2: BIG IDEAS LAUNCHING BIGGER BUSINESSES

Big ideas aren't necessarily good (or bad) ideas, and the readings in Chapter 2 explore this shifting transitional space between ideas and their execution. Topics considered here range from the complexity of student loans, which allow generations of Americans access to education while also making some corporations fabulously wealthy, to tough drug enforcement laws and mandatory minimum sentences that had a measurable effect on crime in some areas while allowing large corporations to exploit the pool of imprisoned labor to achieve great financial advantage. Within Chapter 2 two other major threads of American business are unwound—the wildly successful trade in gourmet coffee and the unprecedented growth and financial success of Wal-Mart.

CHAPTER 3: BUSINESS PRACTICES

The readings in Chapter 3 consider fast food and fast finance, Facebook and phone systems. Automation and mass production have repeatedly changed the face of American business, while franchising has changed both the way Americans eat and the way they cover their monthly bills. Business practices, ethical and otherwise, abound.

CHAPTER 4: BUSINESS ECONOMIES

While the readings in Chapters 1, 2, and 3 of *The Cost of Business* have overtly considered a range of business practices and their effects on (and beyond) individual consumers, Chapter 4 builds upon this focus to consider both the real-world and virtual-world economies. We begin with a consideration of one small California town's economy and end by considering the U.S. economy in an ever-more interconnected (and sometimes unreal) world.

CHAPTER 5: BUSINESS OF/AND CLASS

Extending the focus begun in Chapter 4, the readings in Chapter 5 focus on issues within and beyond the U.S. economy—particularly in relation to issues of socioeconomic class, from the hiring of low-income workers to perform menial tasks in the home to the competition between classes in developed nations. While the business of America is business, according to the cliché with which we began, the poorly hidden secret of American society is its often rigid hierarchical division by class—a poorly defined but real factor in the economic lives of all citizens, regardless of race or religion.

In brief, these are the issues raised within *The Cost of Business*, and the ways in which they are argued range along the spectrum from straight narration to researched and reasoned argumentation. These are issues about the costs of business, about the prices we all pay for the lives we lead, about cause and effect and connections between and among disparate experiences.

I offer a final extended example, a personal example, of the lived experience that exists when economic and social forces combine with business practices to form a strained and strange chain of causation:

Anaconda, Montana, my hometown, was the child of the Anaconda Company, one of the primary players in the environmentally unsound copper mining boom of the late 1800s. Marcus Daly and the other copper kings dug their mines and imported the workers to keep them running. Butte's "Richest Hill on Earth" became one of the largest copper-producing sites in the world. Later it became the most polluted pit on the planet, not counting Chernobyl in the former Soviet Union. Butte copper was smelted in Anaconda, and my father worked at this smelter virtually from the beginning of his working life. My grandfather worked there. My great-grandfather worked there. The jobs were steady and sure and offered some overtime and room for advancement.

The best jobs in Anaconda were, without doubt, at the smelter.

When the smelter closed in 1980, Anaconda died. Slowly. The smelter stopped giving out its reasonably large paychecks, and suddenly there was less money being spent at the bars, the Washoe Theatre, the grocery stores. The bartending jobs went from full- to part-time, like the jobs stocking store shelves and standing at a cash register. The lines got shorter at the grocery stores and longer at the places that dispensed government commodities—"welfare food"—like rice and cheese. Then most of the part-time jobs went away, too, and families moved on. Classes got smaller in the schools, sometimes smaller to the point that a new teacher wasn't needed any more at the high school—or an entire school wasn't needed anymore.

I attended Beaver Dam Elementary—literally across the street from my home—until the Anaconda Company closed its Anaconda smelting plant. Suddenly I had to catch a bus that would take me ten miles to another school, the only elementary school left in town. The high school, formerly housed in two enormous WPA-era buildings, was reduced to a single building, and even that survivor was sparsely populated.

It was like watching a town die of financial cancer.

Suddenly, it seemed, the best jobs were at the prison in Deer Lodge or the mental hospital at Warm Springs, where one of my uncles had an inmate's thumb jammed into his eye all the way to the knuckle. Men who could get these jobs took them. Men, like my grandfather, who could retire did. Other men, lacking the skills and motivation to do better, turned to thievery. My great-grandfather, for example, never had a steady income again but always had new things—rifles, stereos, and cameras, especially.

Some men found good jobs at the Hanford nuclear site in Washington; jobs even better than what they'd done before, sometimes. Eventually, my own father would work as security at Hanford, competing with men ten or more years younger than himself. Later, he'd work as manager of a tank farm, monitoring one tiny part of the toxic waste that regularly made national news programs like *60 Minutes*. But that work would come later, after he spent long years working as a welder and pipefitter in places like Colstrip, Montana, and Pocatello, Idaho.

When the smelter closed, no one saw it coming or understood the reasons. In retrospect the causes were clear and unavoidable and distant from western Montana. The causes, in fact, can be found in Asia and Latin America.

In the late 1970s and early 1980s, Japanese copper flooded the world market, driving the price to sixty cents per pound. It was suddenly cheaper to buy internationally than to mine domestically. This radical market fluctuation was especially devastating to the Anaconda Company, which had lost roughly 70% of its production capability in 1971, when Chile's newly inaugurated President Salvador Allende ordered all foreign-owned copper mines seized in the name of the Chilean people. These distant economic quakes in Chile and Japan sent shockwaves through western Montana. They caused the ultimate collapse of the world copper market. They stripped my hometown of its only viable industry. They stripped my childhood of my father.

There are other arguments to explain what happened, but this chain of causation is mine; it is my lived experience, my argument about what caused the world I inhabit to be as it is. In the pages that follow, other writers present arguments of their own, and you will be encouraged to consider the story that you live—and the costs that you pay.

CHAPTER 1

The Business of Entertainment

Pleasure is profit. This is one of the most fundamental tenets of late-market capitalism. Even in the worst of times—the Great Depression of the 1930s or the recessions of the late twentieth century, for example—some professions are safe (at least relatively) from poverty and need: bartenders and brewers, prostitutes and gamblers, musicians and moviemakers. Throughout the 1930s and into the 1940s, as America struggled against economic collapse and then the sudden need to mobilize and militarize, as many as 90 million people are estimated to have attended one or more movies per week—out of a total population of less than 150 million. Breadlines were long. So were the lines at the theatres.

In the 1980s, prices frequently rose much faster than did the buying power of an average worker's wages, yet the Hollywood industrial complex continued to maker larger and larger profits, a condition that continues into the twenty-first century. And, at the same time, the computer gaming industry grew to become an entertainment behemoth that made more money annually than all of the major Hollywood studios combined. New technology has created unprecedented opportunities for financial gain—just as new technology always has. Computer gaming, in fact, has steadily increased its hold on the U.S. economy since the early 1980s, with games such as Halo and World of Warcraft entering the mainstream of society and catapulting the gaming industry well ahead of the movie industry in annual profits—with gaming drawing in more than $25 billion in 2005, for example, compared to Hollywood's major studio earnings of ca. $20 billion for the same period, a number inflated to that level only by the fact that DVD sales alone account for more than 50% of film profits.

No matter how lean and mean the family budget may be, people always find ways to pay for entertainment. The readings in Chapter 1 challenge you to consider your own sense of the ethics of entertainment, and the issues are complex, while our personal responses are often contradictory. The readings in Chapter 1 range across the entertainment spectrum, from considerations of professional boxing and its connections to illegal immigration to the advertising campaigns that now take place entirely online, with ads for everything from real-world products such as Pizza Hut and straight-to-video DVD releases suddenly appearing beside the unreal roads of cyberspace. In between these topics, consideration is made of Tiger Woods, a man famous for being among the greatest golfers of all time, at the pinnacle of an empire including everything from Cadillac endorsements to a line of video games. The adult film industry—with annual growth as high as 40% and annual profits topping $10 billion—is considered by two doctors worried about the spread of disease rather than possible immorality, and the psychological benefits of games such as The Sims are measured.

In the end, these readings argue that, on some level, pleasure is always profitable for someone. This is a simple foundation for much of the American economy, legal and illegal.

Everything beyond this maxim is complicated.

A Fist Full of Dollars

TIM STRUBY

Tim Struby is a frequent contributor to sports publications such as ESPN: The Magazine, *but his writing has appeared in publications from* Esquire *to the* Chicago Sun-Times. *While he writes on business topics, his passion seems to come through most clearly when he writes about boxing. In "A Fist Full of Dollars," Struby describes the difficulties faced by Mexican boxers who must come to the United States to take part in high-profile bouts but must enter the country illegally because post-9/11 paperwork often moves too slowly to allow them to cross the border legally.*

Prereading Question

The sport of boxing has always been mired in scandal, from charges of corrupt referees to charges of steroid abuse, and boxers themselves often must labor under perceptions that they are stupid, criminal, or both. Even the character of Rocky Balboa in the films by Sylvester Stallone was a petty criminal in the first films and no Rhodes Scholar in any film. Why is boxing, more than other sports, stuck with such a vicious stereotype?

◆

It's a cold December evening in Ciudad, Juárez, and Kirino Garcia is waiting for the blood. It always flows heavy on fight night in this Mexican border city, a golf-ball-drive distance across the Rio Grande from El Paso, Texas.

During Garcia's 40 hometown bouts, more than a few drops of his own have stained the canvas, but tonight he's just a spectator. Perched high up in the bleachers of the Poliforo Juan Gabriel arena, the former gang member turned local boxing legend is one of 5,000 fight fans here to watch the seven bouts culminating in "La Revancha" (the Revenge), the featherweight rematch between former world title contender Cesar "Cobrita" Soto (56-17-13, 40 KOs) and Juárez's own undefeated Miguel "Mickey" Roman (18-0, 13 KOs).

A cross between New York's Felt Forum in the 1930s and the Mad Max Thunderdome, fight night in Juárez is a brutal throwback to boxing days of old. Steep rows of seats ascend from the ring. Thick plumes of cigarette and cigar smoke fill the air. Men wearing cowboy hats, snakeskin boots, and gold chains guzzle Big

Gulp-size cups of Tecate. Women strut the arena in tight jeans, high heels, and crimson lipstick.

The raucous crowd sometimes expresses its displeasure with lackluster fights by showering the ring with full cups of beer and urine, bottle caps, peanut shells, and trash. At the Poliforo, boxers who fight like garbage usually end up covered in it.

Yet the Poliforo fights aren't merely a colorful reflection of boxing's past—they also represent the sport's future. Boxing has always been a ticket out of the slum. The first prizefighters were primarily Irish and Italian immigrants. Then it was poor black kids from the ghettos of New York, Detroit, and Philadelphia. Today boxing belongs to Hispanics. More than 40 percent of all televised fights are on Spanish-language networks. Twenty-six of the 35 fighters in Oscar De La Hoya's Golden Boy Promotions stable are of Latin descent.

Top Rank Promotions boss Bob Arum estimates that *85 percent* of his fight cards (he promoted 51 in 2006) are geared toward Hispanic audiences. "There's no question that it's a tremendous opportunity for Mexican fighters," says Arum, who has been promoting the sport since 1966. "There's been a monumental increase in Hispanics living in the United States. They're loyal fans, and they want to see good bouts. Hispanics, and particularly Mexicans, tend to fight in a much more crowd-pleasing, blood-guts-and brawling style. It's the future of boxing."

Such opportunity lures young Mexican men to boxing gyms in burned-out barrios like Juárez. But the chance of making a better life comes with a price. It means surviving Mexico's most dangerous city—a sprawling industrial wasteland of nearly two million, rife with violence, poverty, and drugs. It demands crowd-pleasing action at the Poliforo. Sometimes it means illegally crossing the Rio Grande on an inner tube to fight in the States. Sleeping in the desert. Going hungry. "When you want something bad enough," says Garcia as the lights begin to dim for the night's first bout, "you do what you must."

THE ROAD TO THE PROMISED LAND

Two days before the Poliforo card, Garcia parks his Chevy Suburban in front of the Miguel Auza Preto boxing gym. Any Juárez brawler who dreams of fighting stateside starts here. Outside the sidewalks are dotted with prostitutes as decrepit as the neighborhood's apartments. Inside the air reeks of body odor and urine.

There are no showers or locker rooms; the fighters change on the gym floor and carry home their sweat-soaked clothes in plastic bags. There's not even a timer—trainers use their wristwatches to keep track of rounds. Yet the 100 or so amateurs and pros who pay 30 pesos a week to train here don't complain. This is the best boxing gym in town.

As the light-heavyweight Garcia changes his shirt and reveals a mosaic of crude tattoos—Jesus on the cross, the Virgin of Guadalupe, his mother, a dragon—he nods to some of the other fighters: two eight-year-olds, a pair of sparring teenagers, and 34-year-old welterweight Mauro "Puños de Oro" (Fists of Gold) Lucero (42-11-1), a 15-year professional veteran who, in 1998, fought fellow Juárez boxer Cesar Bazan for the WBC lightweight world title.

The goal of every fighter in the Miguel Preto gym is to make the 10-minute walk across the Sante Fe Bridge, one of five legal land routes to *el norte*. Last year 15.5 million cars and 8.5 million pedestrians crossed from Juárez to El Paso, and that has translated into a booming boxing business in neighboring states like California, Texas, and Arizona. Not only are there more opportunities and better exposure (Juárez hosts only a half-dozen pro cards a year), but where six rounds in the Poliforo earns a fighter $300, he'll make almost four times that amount across the border.

And tough sluggers are always in demand. "I love Mexican fighters because they are so hungry," says Golden Boy Promotions matchmaker Eric Gomez, "You can call on them at any time for a fight and they'll be ready to go." Basically, they're cheap labor.

Raised in the gritty Colonia Guadalajara barrio, Garcia grew up in a patchwork house of cardboard and corrugated iron. As a teen he ran with La Playa Azul, one of Juárez's estimated 200 gangs. "Back then there weren't too many guns," says Garcia. "You proved yourself with your fists." He earned the respect of his fellow cholos, but gangbanging also garnered him two stab wounds and jail time.

Then, in 1990, at the age of 21, Garcia got a call that changed his life. "I boxed a little bit, but not seriously." he says. "Then a guy offered me a pro fight in the States." But Garcia didn't have the proper papers to cross the Sante Fe Bridge. He was directed to the notoriously Negro neighborhood, where he gave two men a dollar to float him across the Rio Grande on an inner tube. Once he reached the American side, Garcia jumped a wall and was met by men who drove him to the fight in Tucson. Garcia lasted three rounds against a 2-0 fighter named Bobby Gunn. He earned $85 and a hot meal.

For four years Garcia crossed the river illegally, fighting in Albuquerque, Reno, Tucson, Denver, Las Vegas, and Biloxi, Mississippi. "The first few times were scary," says Garcia. "But then it was no problem." The Arizona desert was his bedroom. He went days without food. He fought at 150 pounds. He fought at 170 pounds. By January 1994, he was 0-18. "Fun? No," says the fighter, "I only did it for the money. But in a way I was lucky, because so many of my friends who stayed in the gangs got killed or wound up in jail."

Yet Garcia's career prospects improved dramatically later that year after he approached Oswaldo Kuchle of Promociones del Pueblo. "He wanted to fight for me," says the promoter. "I told him he had a terrible record, but he insisted, and so I put him against a pretty tough guy from Mexico City. After watching Kirino KO the guy, I realized he had a punch, a chin, and a personality. He just hadn't been given any proper training."

Formal training paid off, and Garcia went 14-0-1 in his next 15 bouts. He floored opponents. He filled seats. He was a regular on local TV. He became Juárez's boxing hero, a cholo gone good. He started earning $10,000 a fight, headlining Juárez shows against quality boxers like former world champion Meldrick Taylor (35-6-1) and Simon Brown (47-8). He bought a small grocery store. And although he stayed in his barrio, he expanded his house to fit his six children. Most importantly, he never had to swim across the Rio Grande again.

Yet most Juárez fighters are not as lucky as Garcia. Promoter Kuchle's Promociones del Pueblo is the only show in town, and his stable rarely tops a dozen. Once a fighter is signed, the promoter demands gutty performances. "My boxers don't just have to win," says Kuchle. "They have to fight their asses off. Go head to head. They have to leave everything in the ring."

Even if Kuchle arranges a stateside fight, crossing the border is not easy. Pre-9/11, a few friendly Juárez border guards circumvented the paperwork requirement, but today heightened security makes it impossible. A six-month tourist visa (approximately $4,000) requires a mountain of paperwork—letters from the promoters, proof of residence, proof of family (an indication that the fighter will not stay in the U.S.). And even then, according to Kuchle, since 9/11 the chance of landing a visa has fallen from 60 to 32 percent.

BORDER BLUES

Across the gym from Garcia, Mauro Lucero winds down his workout and explains how his luck has run out. Although "Puños del Oro" began his career 19-0, and more than 20 percent of his professional bouts were held in American cities like El Paso, Dallas, Pomona, and Las Vegas, the former Mexican light-welterweight champion is not part of the Promociones del Pueblo stable. He talks of last-minute bouts, unfair decisions, and shady promoters. "My biggest purse was supposed to be when I fought Cesar Bazan for the WBC lightweight title," he says. "But I didn't get what they promised. The money got wings, I guess."

Then, in a hushed voice, he speaks of his most recent experience—a $25,000 offer to face the highly touted Paul Williams (32-0) in Las Vegas on the undercard of the November 2006 Floyd Mayweather Jr.–Carlos Baldomir pay-per-view battle. "I wasn't nervous about the fight," says Lucero. "I was nervous about getting there." Days before the bout, Lucero discovered his temporary visa had expired. A trip to the embassy proved fruitless. Through a Tijuana connection Lucero was flown to Mexico City, then driven to Mexicali. He hopped a wall at the border, crawled through a 300-foot tunnel, and popped out into the California sunlight.

"The border patrol was right there," he recalls, "so I just ran back to Mexico." Four hours later he tried the same route. This time, no *federales*. According to the boxer's version of events, associates of the American promoter picked Lucero up, drove him to San Diego, and flew him to Las Vegas. Yet when he arrived on Friday, he was not only five hours late but also 25 pounds overweight. "I didn't get paid anything," Lucero says. "They didn't even give me a ticket to watch the fight."

By Monday Lucero was back home in Juárez, tending to the small grocery store he opened with his boxing earnings and shedding pounds in the gym. Scheduled to fight in California in a couple of weeks, Lucero is uncertain whether he'll once again be getting there on all fours. "I m supposed to be getting a visa, but I don't know if I can legally make it in time," he explains matter-of-factly. "Either way, I have to get there."

MEXICAN STANDOFF

Around 1:30 A.M., fight night at the Poliforo comes to a close. Garcia and his two dozen amigos laugh it up. It has been a typically entertaining Juárez card. There's been action, disappointment, controversy, and, of course, blood. A six-round bout between junior lightweights Oscar "Ceviche" Ibarra (10-1, 4 KOs) and Arturo "La Sombra" Murillo (4-4-1) proved to be a classic Mexican war—vicious body shots, knockdowns, faces smeared with red. In another bout, Juárez's Oscar "Zurdo de Oro" Olivas (10-3, 3 KOs) lost to Mexico City's Aldo "El Pato" Valtierra (23-7, 13 KOs). A devastated Olivas cried in the dressing room, and according to his promoter, Kuchle, the fighter will soon be back packing groceries for 45 pesos a week.

In La Revancha—the main event—César Soto's speed and experience appeared to be too much for the 21-year-old Miguel Roman, but Roman, the pride of Kuchle's stable, earned a hometown victory. The announcement incited a cacophony of boos and hisses, as well as a shower of beer cups and trash.

On his way out Garcia is stopped by friends, fans, even security guards. They want to know if the rumors of his retirement are true. Juárez's most beloved warrior says he is not thinking about it right now. This weekend, in honor of his 38th birthday, Garcia will drink with his friends and eat with his family. He will celebrate the better life he has made.

But not for long. Despite Garcia's out-of-the-ring earnings—the private boxing lessons he gives, his starring role as a gang member in the movie *Que Barrio?!*—he understands that fighting is the best way to support his wife and six children. So on Monday he will be back in the gym. Juárez boxers do not take vacations. There are too many hungry fighters from the barrio right behind them. Too many fighters willing to bleed at the Poliforo or cross the Rio Grande in the dead of night. No one knows that better than Garcia. "I still have what it takes," he says, heading out into the evening air. "And I'll fight anywhere, anytime."

Discussion and Writing Questions

1. Struby's article originally appeared in *Maxim* magazine, which targets an audience comprised primarily of men between fifteen and forty years old. How does he write his article for this audience? What details and examples would this audience respond to most positively, and why?

2. Traditionally, the Mexican economy has been weak, especially against the economy of the United States—its powerful neighbor to the north. How is the plight of Mexican boxers described by Struby as an economic tragedy? Is this description persuasive? Why? In an essay, explain your own thoughts about boxing and illegal immigration—and offer your own answer to the "economic tragedy" question.

Intertextual Question

3. How is Struby's description of the difficulties faced by Mexican boxers similar to/different from Steve Albini's description of the difficulties faced by musicians (in his essay "The Problem with Music")?

The Sims: Suburban Rhapsody
CLIVE THOMPSON

Clive Thompson writes on issues of science and technology as they intersect in the swirling maelstrom of American culture, often focusing upon video games (as in his March 2009 article "Teleportation, the Last Battle, and the Creator Talks: How the World Ends Inside an Online Game," which is available on his blog. He writes for both Wired *and the* New York Times Magazine. *In the following article from* Psychology Today, *Thompson considers the reality and virtual reality of the wildly popular game The Sims, which has since its launch spawned many sequels, updates, and competitors.*

Prereading Question

In your opinion, what effect do violent video games have on gamers under eighteen? Do violent games have similar effects on gamers over eighteen? Regardless of the potential effects, why are violent video games traditionally the most popular?

———————— ◆ ————————

Lisa Anne Craig knew she was in trouble when the social worker knocked on her door.

Halfway through her first pregnancy, Craig decided to take a high-tech approach to parenthood. She bought a copy of The Sims, the hugely popular computer game that lets you create and direct a household and a family—building a suburban home, finding jobs for the parents and scrambling to keep everyone happy and healthy. She fired it up, selecting a young professional couple with a newborn. Hey, it was a game. How hard could it be?

Whoops. "You know what? The babies cry a lot in that game," she says. "So it's crying while I'm trying to juggle everything else, like getting the parents to work and making sure they clean the house." After a few hours of domestic chaos, her virtual baby was whisked away by a digital caseworker. "I was devastated! I was sure that I wouldn't be able to handle a real baby," Craig says with a laugh. She kept playing though, and by the time her actual baby arrived, she felt like a pro. "My family thought I was nuts, but I swear it got me through the pregnancy," she says.

At first glance, The Sims is an unlikely hit. It doesn't shred your dendrites with cutting-edge 3-D graphics. You don't blast aliens with plasma guns, drive high-speed race cars or get to play basketball against the Knicks. Yet in 2003 it became the best-selling computer game in history, with more than 29 million fanatic players. It's popular not just with twitchy teenage boys but among people who typically never touch the stuff: women, professionals—even forty- and fifty-somethings.

Maybe that's because playing The Sims is almost exactly like coping with everyday suburban life. To begin, you build a home, choosing details down to the pattern of tiles on the kitchen floor and the shape of the backyard pool. Then you help your Sims along as they stumble along through existence.

Unlike nearly every other game, there's no winning or losing. You're just trying to keep your Sims happy and entertained. And as Lisa Anne Craig found out, although you may be the puppet master, the Sims play by their own rules. Leave a bunch of Sims teenagers unsupervised for a while as they try to make pizza? They just might burn the house down. Forget to send them to the bathroom? Eventually, they'll pee on the floor. Perhaps most eerily, your Sims have emotions: Their "happiness meter" will drop if they get hungry, or if you don't give them someone to fall in love with. Neglect them too much? They'll die.

These lifelike stakes give The Sims a genuinely existential edge, and therein lies the allure of the game. By toying with a virtual version of ordinary life, you can grapple with a very real question: What makes a person happy?

To understand the appeal of The Sims, it helps to understand a bit about Will Wright, the game's creator and co-founder of the game company Maxis. Wright is widely known as the philosopher king of the computer-game world, equally at home in the library as in the arcade. His games may be mass-market hits, but they're based on some very brainy theories about behavior, economics and humanistic psychology.

Wright's intellectual path is about as eclectic as possible: He attended three different colleges but never graduated, sampling courses from computer science, architecture and mechanical engineering to aviation.

One of the first games he designed, SimAnt, was inspired by evolutionary biologist Edward O. Wilson's famous studies of ant colonies. Wright became fascinated by Wilson's explorations of "emergent complexity"—the idea that individual creatures operating with very simple goals can collectively produce incredibly complex behaviors. In the game, SimAnt players assemble an anthill and then marvel as it seems to grow a mind of its own. "Each ant is only doing a few simple things, but when you put tons of them together you suddenly have these really surprising results," he notes, including unusually complex ways of gathering and moving resources around.

When Wright began designing The Sims in the late '90s, though, he faced a more challenging task: How do you get virtual people to act the way real ones do? Ants are relatively easy to simulate, since their behavior isn't too complicated. But what are the fundamental building blocks of human behavior?

Wright boned up on psychologist Abraham Maslow's *Motivation and Personality*, including his famous theory of the hierarchy of needs. Maslow argued in the '40s and '50s that human behavior could best be explained as a quest to satisfy primal needs such as hunger and safety before addressing demands such as love or self-actualization. The Sims are programmed this way, which is why they seem so true to life. For example, your Sim won't enjoy a movie if she's hungry. Aesthetic appreciation of a movie is a higher-order pleasure—and she can't do it if her stomach is growling.

That means that you, the player, must learn and obey the rules that govern Sim life, many of which are hauntingly familiar. "You want to buy them a washer-dryer?" Wright asks. "OK, but you might not have enough money left over for a phone. So what's more important, communication with your friends, or saving time cleaning?" he laughs. "It lays bare all these ethics of everyday life. What you shop for implies these moral choices."

The game also incorporates the ideas of physicist-turned-economist David Friedman. In his book *Hidden Order*, Friedman argued that our everyday lives are a series of quasi-economic choices. In the grocery store, for example, we pick which line to stand in based on a calculus of anticipated time and hassle: "If we decide to move over to a line that seems to be moving faster," Wright notes, "we have to give up our spot in our current line. So it's a sacrifice hoping to get something out of it." To replicate these little mental trade-offs, Wright gave a Sim the ability to decide between, say, sleeping late (which will make him feel more rested) or cleaning up (which might make him feel happier about his house).

In Wright's hands, theories like Friedman's have fashioned a game that allows you to play out your fantasies, relive your life or rejigger your identity. Ever wonder what would happen if you had seven kids? Or if you were living in a huge frat house? Try it out— set up a Sim with that lifestyle and turn it loose. In one sense, The Sims is a private laboratory to experiment with the forbidden "what-ifs" of your existence. It may be the first form of high-tech self-gnosis: mass therapy disguised as a computer game.

The first thing most people do when playing the game is re-create themselves, says Wright, and they often learn something in the process. He once got a letter from the parents of an adopted Romanian boy, orphaned at age 9 or 10. The child seemed depressed—even traumatized—and wouldn't talk about his background. "Then they got him The Sims," recalls Wright. "And he ended up replaying his childhood in the game for them. He created a version of his [biological] family and showed them what had happened. [The game] became a tool for self-expression."

"It gives you a model for a realistic environment," agrees Henry Jenkins, a professor of comparative media studies at the Massachusetts Institute of Technology and an expert in video gaming. "You can program your Sim to look and sound like your last girlfriend and figure out why your last relationship fell flat." Some psychologists say their patients actually discuss their Sims games on the couch, an updated version of the classic therapeutic technique of playing with dolls. "When The Sims works well, it's kind of like a projective test. You can really see a lot of their psyche spilling out into their games," says John Suler, a psychology professor at Rider University in Lawrenceville, New Jersey who specializes in cyberculture. "I spoke to one teenager who created a version of herself and her boyfriend. Then she created another version of herself—an evil version—to try to steal her boyfriend. She wanted to see what it's like to be evil."

In fact, nefarious behavior may be the best part of the game. In real life, you wouldn't dream of doing nasty things to your friends and family. But in The Sims, the lid blows off your id. In hundreds of fan Web sites devoted to the game, players gleefully describe the wicked ways they've killed their Sims—such as putting them in the pool, then removing all the ladders and waiting to see how long it takes them to drown. As in fiction and art, of course, tragedy can be powerfully cathartic. "People really love to explore 'failure states,'" Wright says. "In fact, the failure states are really much more interesting than the success states."

The strongest draw of The Sims, though, may be the way it allows you to indulge your acquisitive streak. Wright knew that buying stuff for your Sim household—designer clothes or wide-screen plasma TVs—would be a major part of self-expression, just as it is in real life. But possessions also suck up time, as documented by sociologist John Robinson, a scholar of "time studies"—how much time the average American spends on routine activities. Robinson discovered strange truths about our lives, like the fact that we might spend half an hour in total each day getting from place to place in the house; he also found that we spend 154 minutes watching television and 20 minutes on child care.

As players build increasingly lavish homes, they find that the high life can be more of a hassle than it's worth. "Your Sim winds up spending all his time just navigating the place," Wright says, laughing. "Sure, you've got the pool table in the west wing—but you've got to get there." Players buy their Sims more and more gadgets and toys, but reality bites back. "They want the dishwasher because they think it'll save them time. But if a player loads their house down too much, soon they find the stuff breaks and needs maintenance," Wright says. "Suddenly, these things you wanted so much all became time bombs, when you originally bought them as time-savers."

Nonetheless, most long-term players say designing Sim households is the chief delight of the game. "I don't really even play with the families anymore. I just focus on the design. I spent a couple of days setting up a Moroccan-style house, complete with a courtyard and a market," says Andrea Grimison, a woman in Germany who spends a few hours a day playing the game. "Now, this is a place I'd like to live!" She set up a Web site to share her work, and now thousands of fans download her concepts every month.

By putting interior design at the heart of his game, Wright took a page from influential architect Christopher Alexander. The psychologically astute Alexander argues that ordinary people innately grasp how environments and urban planning affect us; it's why young couples often argue heatedly about what neighborhood or city to live in. "We intuitively understand the need for privacy or our affinity for light," Wright notes. "[Alexander] was always saying that you don't need a professional—you can do this yourself. He became kind of the anti-architect."

While reading Alexander, Wright discovered a curious fact: Home-design software sells millions of copies a year. Wright figured it was hardly likely that so many people were actually embarking on massive remodeling projects; in reality, they probably just wanted to play with architecture. The Sims, Wright deduced, could be a laboratory for understanding not only our personalities, but also our personal spaces.

In the process of designing the ultimate split-level, players sometimes learn a few things about their own lives. Grimison tried creating a virtual replica of her own house. When she finished it, something weird happened: Her Sims didn't like it. "It was because my bathroom doesn't have windows since it's in the middle of the house. And my Sims always want light in all the rooms or they won't be happy." Lisa Anne Craig had a similar epiphany, but in reverse. "I actually used The Sims when I was painting the house. I couldn't decide what color to paint it, so I made a model of our house and I tried out various colors. Unfortunately, we picked a periwinkle. It's very Florida," she jokes, "but now I kind of hate it."

The Sims is still nothing like real life in some very important ways: there are no taxes, children never grow into adults and there aren't any tightly packed cities such as Chicago or New York. But the virtual citizens will soon be taking another great leap toward real life. Electronic Arts, Maxis' parent company, plans to launch The Sims 2. This sequel has the same basic plot but with a few intriguing refinements: In the new game, Sims will age and die. What's more, the events of their youth will leave them with psychological baggage as they get older. "If your Sims have particularly happy childhoods—or unhappy ones—you'll be able to see the way that's going to impact them later in life. You can see how they kind of ricochet on into the future," Wright says. He suspects it'll turn the game into an even more precise emulation of our existence—a spreadsheet for life." He's probably right. We'll play it, millions more of us, poking and prodding our virtual selves to see what happens.

Discussion and Writing Questions

1. How does Thompson describe The Sims in a way that makes it both interesting and exactly like the most mundane and (possibly) boring aspects of everyday life? Which of his descriptions of The Sims is most/least engaging for you, as a reader? Why?

2. If one of the attractions of The Sims is the freedom it allows gamers to behave badly, then is this largely nonviolent game as bad (or worse) than much-maligned violent video games, from Doom to Grand Theft Auto IV, from Postal to Resident Evil: Nemesis? In an essay, describe both your own experiences with video games and the effects that you believe violent and nonviolent video games can have on those who play them to excess.

Intertextual Question

3. Modern technology allows a gamer to play The Sims on his/her home PC with various updates and bits of bonus content available for download over the Internet—including advertising, as Steve Tilley argues in Chapter 5. Should real-world products and politicians run advertisements in virtual worlds? Why/why not?

Tiger Woods
ROGER O. CROCKETT

Roger Crockett, Business Week *Chicago deputy bureau manager since 2006, reports on telecommunications and technology, the Internet and e-commerce, and race and cultural issues in business. He has worked at the* The Oregonian, The Battle Creek Enquirer, *and* Newsweek. *He is a graduate of UCLA and the Columbia Graduate School of Journalism. In the following article about Tiger Woods, Crockett examines Woods's influence on sports business.*

Prereading Question

Have you ever been influenced to purchase a product because of the endorsement of a super star athlete? Are there certain brands that you choose based on who represents the company? How do celebrity endorsements affect your spending habits, or do they?

✦

SIDELINED FROM GOLF, HE'S TEEING UP
BIG BUSINESS, SUCH AS A NEW COURSE IN DUBAI

Tiger Woods strolls into our interview room in New York's W Hotel. He's wearing jeans, Nike gym shoes, a white T-shirt, and wraparound sunglasses. While recovering from knee surgery, Woods is sidelined from golf tournaments and spending more time on his business dealings. But even at his desk in his Orlando office, he is the plain-clothes type. "My dad used to say," Tiger tells me, "'Just because you dress up in a coat and tie, it doesn't influence your intelligence.'"

I'm tempted to yank the tie from around my neck. But then I stop, resisting the pull of his celebrity, which has mesmerized so many. Woods' fashionable on-course golf wear has made Nike the No. 1 seller of golf apparel worldwide, with more than $300 million in revenue. While he's rehabbing his knee—fans will recall how he winced his way to victory at the U.S. Open in June—sports valuation experts estimate Nike could be out more than $70 million in swoosh exposure. Buick executives are sweating, as well. Since Woods showed up in its car ads in 2000, sales have climbed steadily among the under-40 crowd. His connection with fans is the reason earnings for PGA Tour players have surged 200% since 1998, to an estimated $374.5 million.

So it's little wonder that this year, a panel of sports experts voted him No. 1 in *Business Week's* second annual Power 100 list of the most influential people in the sports business. "Tiger is such a powerful international presence," says Sean McManus, president of CBS News and Sports. "There aren't two or three people in the world that are more famous than Tiger."

For all his fist-pumping bravado on the course, Woods, 32, comes across as a humble guy in person. This is a man who will make some $90 million from sponsors this year and has earned more than $750 million in endorsements throughout his 12-year career—plus more than $82 million from his 65 PGA Tour titles. Of course, he owns a yacht and a gargantuan estate. Yet except for his wedding ring and watch, he doesn't do bling. Advertisers say he's easy to work with, and he doesn't push for preferential treatment on the PGA Tour. "He has never said, 'I absolutely think such-and-such has to be this way,'" says PGA Tour Commissioner Timothy W. Finchem.

But make no mistake: Woods is hands on. A self-described "gamer" since the days of Atari's Pong, Woods has spent hours with programmers at Electronic Arts explaining how putts roll on the courses the pros play, so virtual greens in the Tiger Woods PGA Tour game series are contoured like actual ones. "He is a stickler for perfection," says EA Sports President Peter Moore.

These days, Woods is throwing himself into a new endeavor. He arrived in New York fresh from a tour of Al Ruwaya, a 7,800-yard, par 72 course in Dubai, the first he's designed. In the three hours Woods spent walking the course, he offered lots of approval, says Bryon C. Bell, president of Tiger Woods Design, but occasionally requested changes, such as a sand bunker on the fourth hole that he wanted moved from the left side of the fairway to the right for better balance.

After Woods and I have talked for close to 30 minutes, I get a nod from his agent that our time is nearly up. Tiger has other engagements, including a taping of Late Night with Conan O'Brien, meetings with EA Sports executives, and that night, hanging out with Olympic swimmer Michael Phelps. Woods has no time to go back to the W Hotel's presidential suite to change. No matter. He swaps his jeans and T-shirt for a black suit—no tie, of course—right on the spot. As he changes, I ask about his injured knee. "Getting better," he says. "I'm busting my ass to try and get back."

Discussion and Writing Questions

1. How does Crockett's description of Tiger Woods's appearance affect your perception of him as a super star athlete? Why would the author include these details in this article?

2. Do you think the large salaries, bonuses, and sponsorships Tiger Woods and other super star athletes receive correspond to the amount of business they generate for the organizations they represent? Should there be any regulations of these salaries, bonuses, and sponsorships? Who would be responsible for such regulations? In a brief essay, present your conclusions. Use one other example of sponsorship, in addition to Tiger Woods.

Intertextual Question

3. How do the salaries of professional athletes compare to those of teachers? What is the justification for millions of dollars for a single player, for a professional athlete, and salaries of teachers as described in Hess's "Teacher Quality, Teacher Pay?"

The Adult Film Industry: Time to Regulate?

CORITA R. GRUDZEN AND PETER R. KERNDT

Corita R. Grudzen, MD, specializes in emergency medicine and frequently writes on topics at the intersection of public policy and public health, including the spread of HIV and the impact of condom use on the spread of STDs.

Peter R. Kerndt, MD, specializes in public health and internal medicine. Like Grudzen, his research often focuses upon STDs, including, a 2002 study on the spread of syphilis among incarcerated men and its potential dangers beyond prison walls.

In the following article, Drs. Grudzen and Kerndt consider the pornographic film industry in America and its role in the spread of HIV.

Prereading Question

Is it right, in your opinion, for major television networks, hotel chains, and other mainstream businesses to quietly make billions of dollars annually through the production of pornographic films? Does it matter if a company that crafts its image as "family friendly" on one hand also supports the production and distribution of pornography? Why?

—————————— ✦ ——————————

The United States adult film industry produces 4,000–11,000 films and earns an estimated $9–$13 billion in gross revenues annually [1]. An estimated 200 production companies employ 1,200–1,500 performers [2]. Performers typically earn $400–$1,000 per shoot and are not compensated based on distribution or sales.

Los Angeles County is the largest center for adult film production worldwide. In 1988 the California Supreme Court, in *People v. Freeman*, found adult film production to be protected as free speech under the First Amendment, since such films were not considered obscene based on prevailing community standards. Unlike other legal but highly regulated activities such as gambling and commercial sex work in Nevada, the adult film industry was legalized in California through case law, not by statute, and has for the most part escaped governmental oversight. Regulation of the industry has been limited to prevention of child pornography. Title18, Section 2257 of the United States Code of Regulations explicitly prohibits performers under age 18 and provides for civil and criminal prosecutions for any violation [3]. Adult film production companies are required to have a Custodian of Records to document and retain records of the age of all performers, to enforce the age entry restriction.

Adult film performers engage in prolonged and repeated sexual acts with multiple sexual partners over short periods of time, creating ideal conditions for transmission of HIV and other sexually transmitted diseases (STDs). All the more concerning, high-risk practices are on the rise [4]. These practices include sex acts that involve simultaneous double penetration (double-anal and vaginal–anal intercourse) and repeated facial ejaculations. At the same time, condom use is reportedly low in heterosexual adult films—approximately 17% for adult performers [5]. In 2004, only two of the 200 adult film companies required the use of condoms for all penile–anal and penile–vaginal penetration [2]. Performers report that they are required to work without condoms to maintain employment.

These practices lead to high transmission rates of STDs and occasionally HIV among performers. After four performers contracted HIV in 1998, Sharon Mitchell, a former adult film performer, founded Adult Industry Medical (http://www.aim-med.org), a clinic to counsel and screen performers monthly for HIV using a PCR test. It was expanded later to include other STD testing. The testing program began as an effort to reduce transmission of infections through early diagnosis, treatment, and "quarantine" should a performer test positive for HIV. Performers are required in most cases to pay for all screening tests, and to sign a consent form that permits disclosure of their test results to other performers and producers before filming. Both of these practices are explicitly prohibited under California Occupational Safety and Health Administration (Cal/OSHA) regulations. HIV-positive female performers are permanently excluded from participating in adult films.

WORKER SAFETY AND PUBLIC HEALTH

The current practice of periodic HIV and STD testing may detect some disease early, but often fails to prevent transmission. The most-recent HIV outbreak occurred when three performers who had been compliant with monthly screening contracted HIV in April of 2004 [6]. At that time, a male performer who had tested HIV negative only three days earlier infected three of 14 female performers.

Other STDs are also highly prevalent in the industry. Among 825 performers screened in 2000-2001, 7.7% of females and 5.5% of males had chlamydia, and 2% overall had gonorrhea [7]. These rates are much higher than in patients visiting family planning clinics, where chlamydia and gonorrhea rates were 4.0% and 0.7%, respectively [8]. Some might argue that this program of STD testing keeps rates of HIV and other STDs lower than in other sex-related industries, and in fact, a recent study of prostitutes in San Francisco found 6.8% and 12.4% positivity rates for chlamydia and gonorrhea, higher than rates in the adult film industry [9].

Between January 2003 and March 2005, approximately 976 performers were reported with 1,153 positive STD test results. Of the 1,153 positive test results, 722 (62.6 %) were chlamydia, 355 (30.8%) were gonorrhea, and 126 (10.9%) were coinfections with chlamydia and gonorrhea [10]. Less is known about the prevalence and risk of transmission of other STDs such as syphilis, herpes simplex virus, human papillomavirus, hepatitis B or C, trichomonal infection, or diseases transmitted through the fecal–oral route.

Efforts to reduce the risk of HIV and other STD transmission must include the use of condoms. Even with the PCR testing currently used within the industry, a recently infected performer can test negative during the window in which they are highly infectious and go on to transmit the virus to others. A meta-analysis suggests that condoms are 90%–95% effective in preventing HIV transmission [11]. Condoms are especially important given the high-risk sex acts increasingly being performed in the industry. When looking at HIV exposure risks by site, receptive anal sex has the highest risk at 80 instances of transmission per 10,000 exposures [12], higher than needle stick injuries (10–50 per 10,000) [13] or receptive vaginal penetration (10 per 10,000) [14]. Preexisting infection with other STDs also increases tile risk of HIV transmission. One study showed that the relative risk of HIV acquisition in a vaginal receptive partner increases 2- to 4-fold when the receptive partner is infected with herpes simplex type 2 [15].

Performers may also be exposed to HIV and other STDs outside the workplace. Performers may be engaged in commercial sex work through escort services or use intravenous drugs, risking HIV and hepatitis C infection. The use of condoms would prevent performers who had acquired HIV and STDs outside the workplace from transmitting these infections to other performers in the workplace. Additionally, condoms would help prevent unwanted pregnancy and the complications of STDs, which include ectopic pregnancy, pelvic inflammatory disease, and infertility. Little is currently known about the prevalence of these diseases in performers.

The portrayal of unsafe sex in adult films may also influence viewer behavior. In the same way that images of smoking in films romanticize tobacco use, viewers of these adult films may idealize unprotected sex [16]. The increasingly high-risk sexual behavior viewed by large audiences on television and the Internet could decrease condom use. Requiring condoms may influence viewers to see them as normative or even sexually appealing, and devalue unsafe sex. With the growing accessibility of adult film to mainstream America, portrayals of condom use onscreen could increase condom use among viewers, thereby promoting public health.

In contrast to heterosexual adult films, homosexual-targeted productions more consistently require condoms. Due to the large number of HIV-positive performers, there is no requirement for HIV testing and condom use is the norm. Despite the ubiquitous use of condoms, homosexual adult movies are popular and profitable for production companies. In fact, there is some evidence that homosexual male audiences would not tolerate movies with unsafe sex, likely due to their proximity to many with HIV in the homosexual community. Some homosexual audiences regard watching sex without condoms as "watching death on the screen" [16].

REGULATION OF SEX-RELATED INDUSTRIES

Legislators can look to Nevada for a model for the successful regulation of a legal sex-related industry. Since the institution of mandatory condoms in Nevada's brothels in 1988, not a single sex worker has contracted HIV [17]. Workers must be repeatedly tested for HIV, syphilis, gonorrhea, and chlamydia to maintain a state health and work card. There are numerous other international models for condom enforcement in sex work, from Mexico City to Amsterdam. While there is no clear model for mandatory condom use in adult film, Brazil boasts an 80% condom usage rate in their adult films [18], while still maintaining a large share of the international market as the world's second largest adult film industry [18]. This suggests that condom use in adult films does not have to erode profitability. It is also possible to use filming techniques to reduce the visual effect of condoms, by using flesh tone–colored condoms or by digitally removing them post-production. Facial ejaculations could be simulated through the use of inert materials such as liquid antacids combined with filming techniques, which would eliminate any health risk to the performer.

Vivid Entertainment Group, one of the largest producers of Adult film in the US, temporarily implemented a condom-only policy after the HIV outbreak in 2004 but has since reversed this company policy. Although some companies may voluntarily decide to be condom-only, it is unlikely that this industry will establish safer working conditions for employees without external regulation. A state or national mandate would level the playing field for all companies and not give an unfair advantage to those who decide to produce films without condoms.

OCCUPATIONAL HEALTH AND SAFETY

In California, every employer is required to ensure that employees have a safe working environment. In 1973, the California Occupational Safety and Health Act was enacted to assure "safe and healthful working conditions for all California working men and women by authorizing the enforcement of effective standards, assisting and encouraging employers to maintain safe and healthful working conditions, and by providing for research information, education, training, and enforcement in the field of occupational safety and health" [19]. Each employer must establish, implement, and maintain a written Injury and Illness Prevention Program according to Title 8 of the State Code of Regulations [20]. This includes components for training programs and disciplinary actions. Employers must protect employees from blood-borne pathogens and not discriminate against employees that complain about safety and health conditions. Companies are required to prevent workers from coming into contact with blood or other potentially infectious material, including semen and vaginal fluid, and to provide post-exposure prophylaxis. Universal precautions, which assume all material is potentially infectious, are part of the blood-borne pathogens standard.

In the health care setting, it is hard to imagine a clinic or hospital not providing and requiring its employees to wear gloves or other personal protective equipment. If a health care worker has a needle stick or other potentially infectious fluid exposure on the job, systems are in place to rapidly and effectively treat the employee to prevent transmission of HIV and other infectious diseases. Although a legal industry, adult film has allowed consistent exposure of its employees to HIV, hepatitis, human papillomavirus, herpes simplex virus, chlamydia, gonorrhea, and other diseases without liability or worker recourse.

Cal/OSHA has recently made recommendations specific to adult film to protect performers from acquiring sexually transmitted infections [21]. This includes the use of personal protective equipment (condoms and dental dams) as barriers, simulation of sex acts post-production, and ejaculation outside the partner's body. In addition, post-exposure prophylaxis after possible exposure to pathogens such as hepatitis B and HIV would be required. This would greatly reduce transmission of HIV and other STDs and would likely prevent transmission in cases where a screening test does not detect an infected performer. Cal/ OSHA also requires a procedure for exposure incidents when an employee has contact with potentially infectious material. The employer must provide a medical evaluation and follow-up at no cost to the employee. The final component is a requirement that each employee receive training about blood-borne pathogens, including how they can protect themselves against infections and what to do if they are exposed.

ATTEMPTS AT EXTERNAL REGULATION

Mandatory reporting in California is required for chlamydia, gonorrhea, HIV, syphilis, chancroid, non-chlamydial non-gonorrheal urethritis, and pelvic inflammatory disease. The Los Angeles County Department of Public Health has monitored the industry to assure that performers receive adequate treatment and follow-up for STDs and has endorsed external regulation of the industry that would require condom use, STD screening, and education to prevent STD transmission.

Recognizing that local regulations would have limited impact and seeking to establish existing standards for work health and safety in the industry, officials from the Los Angeles Department of Public Health requested an investigation of the April 2004 HIV outbreak. In September of 2004, Cal/OSHA fined the two production companies in the outbreak $30,560 each for failure to comply with blood-borne pathogen standards [22]. Having established that regulation does apply to the industry, enforcement of the workplace standards is now the issue. OSHA is limited by the number of enforcement officials and therefore will only act in response to a complaint. Workers may be unaware of their rights or reluctant to file a complaint for fear of loss of employment or employer retaliation.

Response from California legislators has been limited. In June of 2004, Assemblyman Paul Koretz, Chair of the Assembly Committee on Labor and Employment, organized an informational hearing in the San Fernando Valley to consider the feasibility and potential impact of mandating HIV/STD screening and condom use. The hearing, entitled, "Worker Health and Safety in the Adult Film Industry," drew together officials from Cal/OSHA, the Los Angeles Department of Public Health, the California Department of Health Services, the American Civil Liberties Union, and the industry trade organization, Free Speech Coalition [23]. In response to the hearing, Assemblyman Koretz sent a letter to 185 adult film production companies urging them to adopt condoms or face legislative action [24].

Two years later, this letter has had little to no effect and the adult film industry continues to produce the great majority of films without condoms. In October of this year, a multistakeholder meeting was convened at the University of California to readdress the issue of worker safety. A group of 65 participants including performers, industry executives, state and local health officials, and legal representatives spent the day debating the controversies and difficulties of mandated STD screening and condom regulation. Concerns were raised about the industry going underground or moving out of state should there be a state but no national requirement. Many present felt it would be difficult to regulate small production companies that distribute their films primarily via the Internet. There was an emphasis on the need for a multi-faceted solution that involves the extension of existing worker protection to this industry with better enforcement, the organization and potential unionization of performers, increased public awareness, and thoughtful legislation.

THE FUTURE

Lacking the will or ability to regulate itself, the adult film industry needs state and federal legislation to enforce health and safety standards for adult film performers. Local officials lack the authority to impose fines and Cal/ OSHA's monitoring and enforcement capability is limited. Short of legislation mandating performer protection, restricting distribution of adult movies to condom-only films may be the one way to have an impact on the industry. If there were organized and truly effective advocacy for performers, then large hotel chains, video retailers, and cable networks could be pressured to purchase adult films under a condom-only "seal of approval." Alternatively and more effectively, legislation could require that the Custodian of Records (already required under Federal law) maintain documentation of screening tests and condom usage in a film's production. Distribution could be restricted to those films produced pursuant to the standard prior to any sale to cable companies or hotel chains, over the Internet, or in other markets.

While some argue that adult film will go underground if condoms become mandatory, it is hard to imagine that a legal multi-billion dollar industry would disappear. Distributors and production companies have become so entrenched in Southern California that it seems unlikely that they would move to another location or go clandestine. Adult film is now so accepted and widespread that it cannot easily escape regulation, especially now that is so readily accessible on the Internet, cable networks, and in most major hotels. Unfortunately, the growing popularity of adult film has not translated into safer working conditions for performers. It is unethical for industry executives, legislators, and consumers to continue to enjoy the profits, tax revenues, and gratification of adult film without ensuring the safety of performers.

ACKNOWLEDGMENTS

We would like let thank Paula Tavrow, Director of the Bixby Program in Population and Reproductive Health al the University of California, Los Angeles, for reviewing and providing comments on the manuscript.

References

1. Schlosser E (2003) *Reefer madness: Sex, drugs, and cheap labor in the American Black Market*. New York: Houghton Mifflin. 320 p.
2. Kaiser Daily HIV/AIDS Report (2004 April 23) Group says HIV "outbreak" contained among adult film actors; L.A. health officials obtain workers' medical records. Kaiser Family Foundation. Available: http://www.kaisernetwork.org/daily_reports/rep_hiv_recent_rep.cfm?dr_cat=1&show=yes&dr_DateTime=23-apr-04. Accessed 17 May 2007.

3. Office of Law Revision Counsel, United States House of Representatives (2005) Sexual exploitation and other abuse of children. 18 USC Chapter 110. Available: http://uscode.house.gov/uscode-cgi/fastweb.exe?getdoc+uscview+t17t20+994+0++()%20%20AN. Accessed 17 May 2007.
4. Liu C, Richardson L (2004 June 10) Health Officials concerned about extreme sex acts in porn. Los Angeles Times; Sect B4. Available:http://www.caitlinliu.com/articles/extreme_sex_movies.html. Accessed 17 May 2007.
5. Mitchell S (2004 May 2) How to put condoms in the picture. *The New York Times.* Available: http://query.nytimes.com/gst/fullpage.html?res=9C04E6DF153DF931A35756C0A9629C8B63. Accessed 17 May 2007.
6. Centers for Disease Control and Prevention (2005) HIV transmission in the adult film industry—Los Angeles. California, 2004.
7. Kodagoda D, Boudov M. Mitchell S, Smietana G, Kerndt PR (2002) STD Screening of actors in the adult film industry: Alternative testing opportunities to detect and treat STD's [poster]. National STD Prevention Conference; 4–7 2002; San Diego. United States of America. Available: http://www.lapublichealth.org/std/STD%20screening%20of%20actors.pdf. Accessed 17 May 2007.
8. Einwalter LA. Ritchie JM. Ault KA. Smith EM (2005) Gonorrhea and chlamydia infection among women visiting family planning clinics: Racial variation in prevalence and predictors. *Perspect Sex Reprod Health* 37: 135–140.
9. Cohan D. Lutnick A, Davidson P. Cloniger C, Herlyn A, et al. (2006) Sex worker health: San Francisco style. *Sex Transm Infect* 82: 418–422.
10. Aynalem M, Kerndt P. Rotblatt H, Montoya JA, Kim-Farley R, et al. (2006) Recurrent and multiple sexually transmitted infections among performers in the adult film industry: A need for a model industry exposure control plan [abstract]. International Society for Sexually Transmitted Disease Research; 2006; Amsterdam. The Netherlands. Available: http://www.parthen-impact.com/cgi-bin/pco/6_05STD/public/index.cgi?unit=pub_search_results&form_id=303&abstract_id=522&fsession=yes. Accessed 17 May 2007.
11. Pinkerton SD, Abramson PR (1997) Effectiveness of condoms in preventing HIV transmission. *Soc Sci Med* 44: 1303–1312.
12. Vittinghoff E, Douglas J. Judson F, McKirnan D, MacQueen K, et al. (1999) Per-contact risk of human immunodeficiency virus transmission between male sexual partners. *Am J Epidemiol* 150: 306–311.
13. Ippolito G., Puro V., De Garli G (1993) The risk of occupational human immunodeficiency virus infection in health care workers. Italian Multicenter Study. The Italian Study Group on Occupational Risk of HIV Infection. *Arch Intern Med* 153: 1451–1458.

14. Padian NS, Shiboski SC, Glass SO, Vittinghoff E (1997) Heterosexual transmission of human immunodeficiency virus (HIV) in northern California: Results from a ten-year study. *Am J Epidemiol* 146: 350–357.
15. Corey L, Wald A, Celum CL, Quinn TC (2004) The effects of herpes simplex virus-2 on HIV-1 acquisition and transmission: A review of two overlapping epidemics. *J Acquir Immune Defic Syndr* 35: 435–445.
16. Huffstuner PJ (2003 January 12) See no evil: In California's unregulated porn film industry, an alarming number of performers are infected with HIV and other sexually transmitted diseases. *Los Angeles Times Magazine.* Sect 12. Available: http://www.aegis.com/news/Lt/2003/LT030110.html. Accessed 17 May 2007
17. Reade R, Richwald G, Williams N (1990) The Nevada legal brothel system as a model for AIDS prevention among female sex industry workers [abstract]. International AIDS Conference; 20–24 June 1990; San Francisco, United States of America. Available: http://gateway.nlm.nih.gov/MeetingAbstracts/102196554.html. Accessed 17 May 2007.
18. Clendenning A (2004 April 27) Brazil has safe sex lessons for United States. Associated Press. Available: http://www.signonsandiego.com/news/world/20040427-0012-brazil-porndestination.html. Accessed 17 May 2007.
19. California Occupational Safety and Health Act (1973) Labor Code. Section 6300–6332. Available: http://caselaw.lp.findlaw.com/cacodes/lab/6300-6332.html. Accessed 17 May 2007.
20. California Code of Regulations, Title 8 (2007) Division of Occupational Safety and Health. Available: http://www.dir.ca.gov/samples/search/query.htm. Accessed 17 May 2007.
21. Division of Occupational Safety and Health (2006) Vital information for workers and employers in the adult film industry. Available: http://www.dir.ca.gov/DOSH/AdultFilmIndustry.html. Accessed 17 May 2007.
22. Division of Occupational Safety and Heath (2004) Cal/OSHA issues citations to adult film companies for failing to protect employees from health hazards. Available: http://www.dir.ca.gov/dirnews/2004/ir2004%2D10.html. Accessed 17 May 2007.
23. Committee on Labor and Employment (2004) Worker health and safety in the adult film industry. Available: http://www.nswp.org/pdf/CAL-ADULTFILM.PDF. Accessed 17 May 2007.
24. Madigan N (2004 August 24) Sex-film industry threatened with condom requirement. *The New York Times*. Available: http://query.nytimes.com/gst/fullpage.html?sec=health&res=9803E2DF153EF937A1575BC0A9629C8B63. Accessed 17 May 2007.

Discussion and Writing Questions

1. Consider the sections into which this article is broken. What is the main point made in each section? How does each section support the overall argument that the authors make about pornographic films and regulation?

2. How do Grudzen and Kerndt avoid—successfully or unsuccessfully—discussing pornographic films in moralistic, religious, or subjective ways? Why? In a short essay, consider how adding such subjective, value-driven analysis to the article would potentially change a reader's perception of the issue.

Intertextual Question

3. How would John Miller, author of "Call It Slavery" (Chapter 4), react to the argument made by Grudzen and Kerndt? Why?

And Now a Game from Our Sponsor
STEVE TILLEY

Frequently writing on issues of culture clashing with change— especially the changes wrought by video gaming—Steve Tilley wants everyone to acknowledge that games have already gone as (or more) mainstream than movies. Yet gaming still labors beneath a blanket of criticism and scorn, including frequent laments that video games are corrupting, in virtually every way possible, America's youth. This was the focus of a recent article he wrote for the Toronto Sun, *titled "Lazy, Cheap and Disappointingly One-Sided" and available online. In the following article, this from* Xbox *magazine, Tilley considers the new deployment of advertising in the new world of online gaming.*

Prereading Question

Advertising surrounds us, from traditional billboards and magazine inserts to less traditional placement inked on the physical backs of athletes, projected onto backdrops at sporting events, and linked to the names of stadiums and other large venues. Does this virtually constant and unavoidable bombardment by advertising messages matter? Does such advertising have an effect—direct or indirect— on you, on the choices you make, and the products you buy?

◆

Imagine: You, as Master Chief, are pinned down by a horde of Covenant forces. Your assault rifle is low on ammo, and you realize you're out of grenades as a pair of Brutes advances on your passion. Desperately, you blaze away but manage only to wound them before your gun runs dry. Your death is swift and violent.

Then, over the image of your motionless, armor-suited corpse, a message pops up: "Restarting at your last checkpoint. This second chance at life is brought to you by Prudential Insurance. Even cybernetic Spartan soldiers need a piece of the rock."

An unlikely worst-case scenario of advertising in a videogame, sure. But there's no denying that in-game advertising is enjoying an upsurge, as pitchmen look for new ways to reach ever more fragmented audiences. In the age of PVRs and podcasts, traditional commercials just don't cut it

"Alas!" wail these mega-corporations and their advertising agencies. "TV viewership among our most coveted demographic, the 18- to 34-year-old male, is in sharp decline! They don't read newspapers or listen to radio anymore, and their 'Net' surfing habits are fleeting and fickle! If only there was some entertainment medium that still attracted millions of young, hip, cash-flush consumers and held their rapt attention for hours on end every week! Think of what we could do if we could pimp our wares to that kind of eager and engaged audience!"

Then, the light bulb goes on. The cash register ka-chings. And suddenly, videogames have a big ol' bullseye painted on them. Except it's green, like so many bills stuffed in your wallet. The question that will directly affect the future of gaming is: What happens to your favorite pastime if advertisers score a direct hit?

FOLLOW THE MONEY

Advertising in videogames is hardly new. In Electronic Arts' 1994 FIFA international Soccer, billboards on the sidelines displayed logos for Panasonic and Adidas, marking one of the first times third-party advertisers staked out presence in a game environment.

Simple stuff, that. But pixelated sideline logos begat realistic roadside billboards in racing games, and branded skateboard gear in the Tony Hawk series has evolved into entire in-game stores centered around a single designer, like the Ben Sherman outlet in Test Drive Unlimited.

In the last couple of years, in-game advertising has become serious business worth serious coin. Industry watchers predict advertising in videogames will rake in nearly $2 billion worldwide annually by the end of 2011, and the evolution of online services like Xbox Live makes it possible for companies to update ads within games on a monthly or weekly basis, like changing an in-game movie poster to reflect a flick that's hitting theaters that very weekend.

Remember when there used to be no commercials before the preview trailers at movies? Five years from now, we could well be asking, "Remember when there used to be no billboard ads and product placement in videogames?" Will we be nostalgic? Bitter? Resigned to the march of progress? Or—can you imagine?—actually thankful that our gaming experiences are being enriched artistically and financially through careful use of in-game marketing?

Not surprisingly, game publishers and companies that specialize in brokering in-game ads, like recent Microsoft acquisition Massive Incorporated, paint a rosy picture of the future in which the gamer is the ultimate winner. "Ads will appear in places where one would expect to see them in real life," says Alison Lange, marketing director for Massive. "The goal is to enhance realism and to never detract from gameplay. For example, in MLB 2K7, instead of seeing a made-up consumer product name, you'll see an ad for XM Satellite Radio—brands you might see in the stadium at a [real-world] ballgame."

SAM & AXE

Ubisoft, in particular, has been especially aggressive in chasing in-game advertising opportunities, from Sam Fisher's Sony Ericsson cellphones in Splinter Cell Pandora Tomorrow to the can of Axe body spray in Rainbow Six Vegas that triggers the Fremont Street light show and a "blooper reel" Easter egg when shot.

Rainbow Six Vegas producer Alex Parizeau argues that a strong case can be made for ads in certain game genres and settings. He says his team tried concocting fake posters and billboards for some of Vegas' neon-lit environments, and it just looked wrong. Why not use real ads for real products, have another company worry about futzing with the details, and put some extra cash in the budget, all at the same time? "The costs are increasing with next-gen games, so we need to find alternate ways of reducing development costs while not taking money out of players' pockets," Parizeau says

But Hal Halpin, founder of the non-profit gamer advocacy group Entertainment Consumer Association, says putting ads in games while still charging players premium prices isn't fair. "The problem is that gamers are paying more for less," Halpin claims. "Next-gen titles generally retail for $10 more than in the previous generation. And while I appreciate that development costs and cost of living have both increased, asking gamers to [pay more] smacks of opportunism without disclosure."

Disclosure is the key word, says Halpin, who feels game publishers should be forced to reveal that a game contains advertising upfront, on the box, so that we can decide whether we want to be exposed to marketing messages in our entertainment. "That way consumers make the purchase fully aware of the product's content."

He may be on to something, since Internet forums will often light up at the first whiff of commercial taint in a game, and many gamers find the mere notion of marketing messages being inserted into interactive entertainment distasteful. Do advertisers actually care about the wills and wishes of the gamer? And do they care enough to act on any feedback from the gaming public? "We definitely keep an eye on the forums: we definitely see what gamers are saying about our (ad) placements and what they're saying about our competitors' placements," notes Jeffrey Dickstein, Ubisoft's strategic sales and partnerships manager. "We are sensitive to this, but at the same time we realize everybody has an opinion. If it's unanimous or it's so predominant that we've done a bad integration, we definitely need to learn from that."

THE REAL THING

If in-game advertising is done perfectly, gamers might not even realize that what they're seeing is an advertisement at all. For example, players storming the casinos in Rainbow Six Vegas to trade fire with terrorists might not have been immediately aware that the cars they were taking cover behind were Dodge vehicles, or known that the vehicles' presence there stemmed from a deal struck between DaimlerChrysler and Ubisoft. If the vehicles were "inspired by" real models but not actually licensed, suddenly they stick out as fantasy clones. "We can use real cars, or we can create cars of our own," reasons Vegas producer Parizeau. "But we're not car designers so they're always going to look a little bit off. It's always a plus when you can use a real product and base the modeling in the game on real stuff."

But if gamers don't make the connection between the in-game vehicles and the Dodge brand, is the advertisement still a success? Game publishers and ad agencies are still experimenting with ways of accurately measuring how in-game ads are seen and absorbed—prospect much trickier than measuring, say, TV viewership For instance, how long did the player spend near the ad? Did he look directly at it? Was he viewing it head-on or at an angle? If the ad is in a later level of the game, what percentage of gamers will actually make it that far to see it? With Massive, for example, a gamer has to spend 10 cumulative seconds in reasonably close proximity to an advertisement during one gaming session before the company registers it as an "impression" of that ad. (Maybe the gamer spent those 10 seconds emptying a clip into a billboard, cursing the name of the advertiser and vowing to boycott the product. But hey, they looked at it.)

Because of this, advertisers and developers will often try to integrate products into the actual gameplay in an effort to forge a stronger link with gamers and goods. If using a Nike shoe in a basketball game gives your athlete avatar a stat boost, are you more likely to seek out the same kicks in the real world? If a game's hero drives a Ford, will you want to drive one?

Advertisers get supremely stoked about this kind of unprecedented flexibility and interaction with their target audiences—you can't get that with TV, print or radio, after all—but again, what about those of us who are actually playing the games? Detracting from gameplay seems to be the prime concern among gamers when it comes to advertising invading one of entertainment's last commercial-free bastions. No one wants an out-of-place poster or product disrupting the immersive illusion of a game world. And it's safe to say that absolutely no one wants a Lord of the Rings RPG in which Frodo and pals stop at a McDonald's to load up on Egg McMuffins for the trek to Mordor. Second breakfasts indeed.

Game publishers and marketing firms lay their hands over their hearts and swear that they will never intentionally disrupt a gaming experience with ads. "If done right, ads enhance the reality of the game, and keep [it] up-to-date," says Jonathan Epstein, CEO of in-game advertising agency Double Fusion. "Our No. 1 goal is to preserve the experience and immersion in the game world."

Still, the precedent of game-sullying advertising has certainly been set. And some of us may feel that having advertisers promise to protect gamers' interests is a little like asking the fox to guard the proverbial henhouse.

ADVERGAMES: THE DIRTY WORD

Then there are advertisers who skip the middleman altogether. Videogames built from the ground up as marketing tools might be the ultimate example of combining brand-pimping with joystick-jiggling, except for one small problem—these so-called advergames usually suck with such vigor that they're quickly forgotten by the very gamers they seek to sway. Remember Spot Goes to Hollywood on the 16-bit systems? Are you feelin' 7-Up?

Then came his royal highness, the Burger King. We may have initially scoffed at the notion of a fast-food outlet developing and selling $3.99 Xbox/Xbox 360 games starring the King, Sub-servient Chicken, and Brooke Burke, but more than 3.2 million copies of Sneak King, Pocketbike Racer, and Big Bumpin' were snapped up, along with the requisite value meal. "The BK Xbox promotion helped contribute to a 41% increase in profits over the same time period the previous year," says Martha Flynn, Burger King's senior director of national promotions and sponsorships. "We created all three games in less than a year, so timing was our biggest challenge."

While Burger King bristles at the term "advergame"—"The BK Xbox games extend much further in scope and user experi-ence," responds Flynn—there's no denying that the games did an ace job of pushing the BK brand deeper into the cultural con-sciousness, not to mention generating a whole lot of King ka-ching. Though Burger King says they don't have any plans to do a similar promotion any time soon, could their success mean we're about to be flooded with a new wave of next-gen advergames? Can an Unreal Engine 3–powered Chester Cheetah Goes to War be far off?

"Marketers who opt to create an advergame get all the cre-ative control and brand exposure they want, but at the risk of designing a dud that no one will want to play," explains Ilya Vedrashko, a Boston-based emerging-media strategist who wrote his MIT thesis on advertising in computer games. "Burger King had a unique combination of the right demographic and a power-ful distribution channel—their restaurants—working for them. Not every business has these advantages."

WE'LL BE RIGHT BACK

And maybe that's for the best. With the average North American city dweller already bombarded by anywhere from 3,000 to 5,000 marketing messages per day, according to advertising-watchdog magazine *Adbusters*, some argue that incorporating advertising into videogames simply pushes that number to greater mind-pol-luting heights.

Kalle Lasn, founder and editor-in-chief of *Adbusters*, fears that videogames could face the same hyper-commercialization that eventually overtook television, movies, the internet, and most other forms of art and media. But unlike product placement in films, which ultimately became accepted and even expected, he thinks our edgier, wiser, post-modern gaming selves might not sit quietly and take it.

"I think we may be reaching an era now where the people who are trying to put these ads into games won't get away with it as easily as those product-placement people who got away with it in movies," believes Lasn. "Our society has evolved into a much more wary [one]."

So whether advertisers and gamers find a symbiotic co-existence, or consumers end up drawing a time in the virtual sand to say "Keep your real products out of my imaginary worlds." It's going to be an interesting few years. Let the games begin . . . after a word from our sponsors.

Discussion and Writing Questions

1. Is Tilley's argument directed only at people who play video games, or does it have a broader target audience? What aspects of the text suggest an audi-ence of gamers and what aspects of the text suggest Tilley wants to reach nongamers?
2. If the average consumer spends as much time watching television as he/she spends playing video games, then why wouldn't companies want to find ways to reach into gaming with their ads? If the technology allows this sort of advertising to take place, if consumers don't raise an outcry, and if no laws are being broken, then why does this encroachment of real-world advertising into the virtual world matter, according to Tilley? Why should it

matter or not matter, in your estimation? In a brief essay, consider your position on this issue of online advertising, games, and the actual versus virtual worlds.

Intertextual Question

3. How would Morgan Spurlock, author of "Do You Want Lies with That?" (Chapter 3), be likely to respond to Tilley's arguments about advertising in video games? Why?

CHAPTER 2

Big Ideas Launching Bigger Businesses

In twenty-first century America, "big business" is virtually synonymous with Wal-Mart—a mega-corporation that, in 2007, planned to open more than 600 stores (that year alone) and employed nearly 2 million people. By 2009, this number of employees surged over 2 million, with annual profits rising to more than $400 billion (in a company with operating expenses of "only" circa $30 billion). Although it is criticized for its anti-union labor policies and low wages, Wal-Mart is also engaged in community building, donating more than $270 million across the United States in 2006, and in low-cost prescription drug sales—both areas where Wal-Mart's charitable giving has increased every year. While drug prices rose sharply for many seniors on Medicare, Wal-Mart began selling thousands of generic-drug equivalents for only $4. When the economic crisis that began late in 2008 caused school budgets to fall sharply, Wal-Mart increased its stores' local donations, particularly to elementary schools.

There are undeniable benefits associated with Wal-Mart and its business model—the same model used by such corporate giants as Home Depot, Target, and Lowe's (albeit less successfully, overall). There is a similar "big idea" behind each of these successful business practices, and the readings in Chapter 2 range across this landscape where big ideas become mega-corporations, a landscape on which Wal-Mart is only one of many corporate landmarks.

Chapter 2 includes both a consideration of Wal-Mart's "green" philosophy and the political ramifications of its business practices. Other topics covered within this section include the sprawling prison industry that, by 2009, was the largest single budget expenditure in many states, including California, and Starbucks, a straightforward coffee-selling franchise that dominated the market in the United States across the 1990s but, early in 2009, also posted a 77% loss in profit from the same period a year before. While the readings in Chapter 2 cover a wide range of "big" businesses in America, the discussion opens with an industry that strikes close to home for virtually every college student: the business of student loans.

In the end, the most central question you may ask yourself as you work through this chapter is a simple, rude-sounding one: So what? If Wal-Mart and Target sell products cheaper than do their competitors, including the locally owned clothing and hardware stores, then why would a consumer shop at those smaller stores? If student loans allow people to go to college when they otherwise would not be able to, then does it matter if those loans are also crippling to the economic lives of those same young people? There are small, personal consumer decisions behind all of these businesses, but their answers have repercussions both forward and backward along the chain of causation.

But there are no easy answers to complicated questions, yet we all must find answers of our own, regardless. Buying clothing and coffee and Disney products and McDonald's food—what's your little decision that echoes in a big way?

The Student Loan Scandal
WILLIAM BEAVER

William Beaver, PhD (1985) in applied sciences from Carnegie-Mellon University, is a professor of sociology at Robert Morris University. In June of 2005, Beaver published "Battling Wal-Mart: How Communities Can Respond," a departure from his frequent focus upon issues in education, which is reflected in the following article on the "scandal" of student loans in America—where societal costs and personal benefits are hard to disentangle.

Prereading Question

Think about your own experiences as a college student and those of your closest friends. How are you—and how are they—paying for the education being received? Ask one of your professors to describe how she/he paid for college— a daunting expense if it included a BA, MA, and PhD.

———————————— ✦ ————————————

Nearly two-thirds of all college students take out loans to help finance their education. Most assume that the process is above board with schools acting in the student's best interests to ensure they get the best deal possible. Unfortunately, such might not always be the case. The results of an investigation by Andrew W. Cuomo, New York's attorney general, revealed that many private lenders had offered improper inducements to colleges and their financial aid officers to secure greater loan volumes. Cuomo's initiative also sparked the interest of several other state attorney generals who opened their own investigations. Congress has also held hearings regarding the questionable relationships between lenders and colleges, which appear to be fairly widespread in what has become an $85 billion industry. Indeed, a recent Senate report on student loans concluded, "It is clear that the problem is systemic and cannot be isolated to a few problem lenders or schools."

The purpose of this article will be to explore more fully those systemic elements that facilitated the scandal. To do so, some historical background regarding student loans will be provided showing that however well intended, the guaranteed loan program has had a checkered past that spawned controversy and eventually momentum for change. The current scandal will then be described. A scandal that can be traced to increased competition for student loans, which ultimately produced much of the questionable behavior that became the subject of the investigations, and competition the Department of Education (DOE) failed to regulate. Finally, I will discuss the implications of the scandal, and the steps taken to change the environment that nurtured it.

GUARANTEED STUDENT LOANS

In 1965, Congress enacted the Guaranteed Student Loan Program, later called Stafford loans. The major aim of the legislation was to increase access to higher education. Lending institutions were asked to offer loans to prospective college students regardless of their financial status. In return, the government would subsidize the loans to secure a lower interest rate, pay the interest while the student attended college, and assume the debt if a student defaulted. At the time, Congress felt that such incentives were necessary, since it was unclear how many lenders would actually support the program. At first the loan industry was slow to respond. The concept was new and there was some uncertainty about administrative costs. However, the program gradually caught on. In reality, government incentives made for a very attractive business model. Unlike other types of loans, lenders faced no risk, since the legislation ensured that the loans would be repaid either by the student or the government. Moreover, interest rates were calculated to favor lenders. In a somewhat complicated formula, the interest rate students pay to lenders is derived once a year by the government. There is also a lender rate calculated quarterly and based upon the costs of commercial paper, which is guaranteed to the lender. If the student rate happens to be lower than the current lender rate, the federal government pays the difference to the lender. On the other hand, when the student rate is higher than the lender rate, the lender keeps the difference. All this to ensure that loan money would be available to prospective college students.

The program, now formally known as the Federal Family Education Loan Program (FFELP), clearly succeeded, helping millions of students to attend college. Nonetheless, the program has had its share of problems. By the early 1990s student default rates had risen dramatically, totaling more than $13 billion to the point that one-half the cost of the program went to repaying defaulted loans. The majority of the defaults occurred at for-profit institutions. These schools enroll more lower income students making defaults more likely. Plus the fact that many for-profits fraudulently obtained loans for students by falsifying data submitted to the federal government. Lenders were accused of making questionable and, in a few cases, fraudulent loans, while not making valid attempts to collect on defaulted loans, since there was little or no incentive to do so. After an extensive investigation, the General Accounting Office (GAO) labeled the student loan program as "high risk" for fraud and abuse and began to examine the possibility of having the DOE make Stafford loans directly to students, eliminating the need for private lenders. An initial GAO study concluded that direct lending would simplify the application process for students, while saving taxpayers approximately $1 billion a year.

The idea of direct lending was controversial. Congressional Democrats and the Clinton Administration favored direct loans, not only for their presumed efficiencies, but also because they believed that FFELP, with its generous lender subsidies, had become another form of corporate welfare. On the other hand, Republicans and the lending industry argued just as strongly that overall the program had performed well and were skeptical that any government program could be more efficient than the private sector. Concerns about the DOE's capabilities were not unfounded. Almost from its inception inadequate staffing and poor management had plagued the department. Republicans also disliked the idea that the government would have to borrow more money to finance direct lending. Nonetheless, after much Congressional debate and despite the intense lobbying efforts of the loan industry, the William D. Ford Direct Loan Program became law but only after Democrats, who still controlled Congress, were able to tuck it into the 1993 federal budget agreement.

Direct lending did not replace FFELP. Instead, schools choose one program or the other and many began to switch to direct loans. By 1997, the new program captured approximately one-third of the market and many assumed that a majority of schools would eventually opt for direct loans. (The law allowed for 60% of the colleges to do so.) What most attracted colleges to direct lending was the fact it did simplify the process. Besides requiring less paperwork, students usually knew within a few days if they had been granted a loan as opposed to weeks when dealing with private lenders. Direct lending also made life easier for financial aid officers who now dealt with only one entity as opposed to any number of lenders. It also appeared that direct loans were saving taxpayers money. For instance, one study concluded that direct lending costs taxpayers five times less per loan than those made by the lending industry. Another study found that for every $100 borrowed, direct loans brought in 22 cents, while the same amount costs the government $12.80 if the loans are made by a private lender. The reasons for the savings were tied to the fact that the federal government can procure loan capital at lower rates and that loans are repaid to the government and not a private lender.

The rapid rise in the popularity of direct loans posed a major threat to the lending industry. Not only would they have to compete with each other for loan volumes but also with the federal government. The potential losses were significant, and lenders responded in a fairly typical manner by attempting to make their product more attractive to potential customers.

INDUSTRY RESPONSES

The effects of competition first surfaced in the late 1990s, when private lenders began to pay some of the fees required by the government on all guaranteed loans. By doing so, the student's total loan balance could be reduced by 3% to 4%. The discounts offered by private lenders were aggressively marketed and some colleges did begin to drop out of the direct loan program. As one financial aid director put it, "The terms and conditions being offered were so generous, we felt that we would be doing our students and families a disservice if we ignored them." Thus, although saving borrowers money was never a primary aim of either program, at least initially, competition between private and direct lending did seem to be working to the benefit of students and parents.

The Clinton Administration feared that such discounts would severely weaken direct lending. Hence, in 1999, President Clinton gave the DOE the authority to essentially match the discounts made by private lenders. Soon thereafter, a lawsuit by nine lenders and two lobbying groups was filed claiming that the DOE had no legal right to lower fees. Although the lawsuit was eventually withdrawn, it highlighted the ongoing conflict over direct lending with Democrats generally in support and Republicans and the loan industry opposed. Indeed, soon after gaining control of Congress in 1994, Republicans attempted to end direct lending but were unsuccessful.

Once the Clinton administration allowed the DOE to match the discounts being offered by private lenders, new incentives were devised to ensure that the loan industry would regain market share. One of the more intriguing strategies involved revising the "school as lender" program. Federal law had long allowed colleges and universities to offer loans to graduate students but few did so, not wanting to get directly involved in the lending business. By the mid-1990s, only 22 schools used the program. All this began to change when Sallie Mae, the nation's largest student lender, introduced a strategy that urged colleges to establish a line of credit with a lending institution and then make loans to graduate and professional students. Schools would hold the loans for 2 or 3 months collecting interest. The loans would then be sold to a private lender at a guaranteed premium of between 2% and 6% of the total loan volume. Annual profits to colleges ranged between several hundred thousand to a few million dollars depending on the number of loans made. College officials maintained that most of the profits were rolled back into student-aid programs, and the loans actually saved graduate students money, since they were not charged for certain fees.

The strategy did attract a number of colleges. By 2005, 157 schools were participating. Yet, despite the apparent benefits, critics charged that the revamped "school as lender" was problematic. First, colleges might encourage students to increase their indebtedness to boost revenues. Second, profits incurred from the sale of loans could be used for any number of activities and not necessarily financial aid, since colleges were under no legal obligation to do so. "Basically what we have are storefronts being set up so schools can make money," charged one university official. The fact that colleges were receiving funds from the loan industry for seemingly doing very little did raise suspicions that something more was involved. As a result, Congress placed a moratorium on new schools entering the program in 2006.

Another innovative program created by the loan industry was so-called "opportunity loans." In this scenario, lenders give colleges funds to be distributed to students with poor credit histories. The loans have higher interest rates, making them profitable, although the risk involved was also higher, since they were not guaranteed. One example of how the program worked occurred at Indiana University where Sallie Mae offered the school $3 million to form an opportunity pool. In return, the school left the direct lending program and Sallie Mae became the exclusive lender for the university. University officials justified "opportunity loans" on the grounds that they allowed more students to attend college and that the terms offered to undergraduates by private lenders were cheaper than direct loans. Nonetheless, such agreements also raised suspicions, since federal law prohibited any quid pro quo between lenders and colleges.

In other scenarios, colleges simply received a percentage of the principal on each student loan. Schools including Drexel and the University of Pennsylvania had entered into such agreements. For instance, Penn had received over $1.6 million from Citibank as part of their revenue sharing accord. Other schools encouraged students to consolidate loans with a private lender and in return the school would share part of the revenue. In addition, lenders also sponsored various school events, made donations to alumni associations or helped to staff financial aid offices. It should also be pointed out that wrongdoing occurred at the individual level. The Cuomo investigation uncovered a number of instances where something of value was offered or demanded by college officials to ensure that a lender would receive preferential treatment. For instance, six officials at Columbia, Johns Hopkins, and the University of Texas received stock options from Student Loan Express. In another instance, a Johns Hopkins official asked for and received $65,000 from Student Loan Express for consulting fees and money to cover her tuition expenses, while the former financial aid director at the University of Texas demanded certain favors from Citibank and when the bank refused, they were removed from the University's preferred lender list.

As it turns out, the driving force behind many of these arrangements was for a private lender to be placed on a college's preferred list, which simply consists of the names of lenders that a school recommends to students and parents. Ostensibly, the major criteria for an institution to prefer one lender to another was that they offered the best service and value for students. In addition, a preferred list simplified the process for borrowers considering that there are approximately 3,500 private lenders in the student loan business. For lenders being on a preferred list can be crucial, since those making the list often receive 90% of a school's loan volume. Thus, it is easy to understand why lenders were willing to offer schools such lucrative arrangements. More recently, the DOE revealed that at more than 900 colleges, 80% of the loan volume was held by a single lender, suggesting that if inducements are attractive enough preferred lists can be very short.

Nine hundred schools is not an insignificant number and reinforces the notion that the scandal is widespread. Nevertheless, it is difficult to tell exactly how common these agreements were. It should be remembered that the Cuomo initial investigation only focused on 60 schools. Hence, the investigations, more than anything, are meant to send a message. In this regard, the attorney general's office has notified more than 400 colleges around the country, including all those in New York state, that they should end agreements with lenders that compromise their ability to act in the best interests of students. To help spread that message, Cuomo has reached agreements with 13 private lenders and several colleges totaling $13.7 million to create a fund that would go toward educating students and parents about loans.

THE DEPARTMENT OF EDUCATION

The current scandal should not have come as a surprise to the DOE. The department had received a number of warnings concerning questionable ties between lenders and colleges. In 2003 the department's assistant inspector general recommended that rules concerning improper inducements needed to be updated. The GAO warned in 2005 that colleges were being drawn by the quest for revenue and were not insuring broad access to student loans. In 2006, the DOE's inspector general reported that the department had not provided adequate oversight or enforcement of the lending industry. More recently, a GAO investigation discovered that out of 26 complaints made between 2001 and 2006 concerning improper inducements, the DOE had taken action on only two. This, despite the fact that Congress passed legislation in 1995 that banned incentives from private lenders to colleges in order to increase loan volumes.

Part of the problem was that there was always some uncertainty about what exactly constituted an improper inducement. It is one thing for a lender to distribute pens to incoming freshman and quite another to offer substantial sums of money to colleges. Near the end of the Clinton administration, the DOE did put together a proposal with more specific guidelines. For instance, one proposal would have made it illegal for a lender to offer "something of value" to a school at which it had at least 20% of a school's loan volume. However, when the Bush Administration entered office, the move toward more specific regulations ended. The DOE argued it could not offer guidelines, since it had no authority over certain types of private loans, even though several lenders requested clarification concerning improper inducements. Instead, the loan industry was urged to develop their own standards. Two attempts at some form of self-regulation were made (the last in 2006) but both failed to bring any meaningful results.

A more industry friendly attitude was also reflected in personnel changes at the Bush DOE. The most notable case was Matteo Fontana, a senior official in charge of the national student loan database. Before joining the department Fontana had worked for Sallie Mae. While at the DOE, Fontana continued to hold $100,000 in stock from Student Loan Express. Moreover, it appears that department officials were aware, or should have been aware, of Fontana's stock holdings, since he listed them on disclosure forms. It was also revealed that lenders had gotten access to the student loan database, although they were not permitted to do so. When all this became public knowledge, Fontana was placed on administrative leave pending the outcome of an investigation by the department's inspector general. The DOE then announced they were taking steps to safeguard the student database. In all, more than a dozen officials had either worked for the loan industry or obtained jobs within the industry when they left the department. The DOE maintained that such private sector connections improves efficiency and provides "better services to students and families," while one critic claimed that "the Department of Education has been run as a wholly owned subsidiary of the loan industry . . ."

Critics of the department's policies were particularly outraged when Nelnet, a Nebraska based loan company, was allowed to keep $278 million in subsidies to which they were not entitled. An audit by the department's inspector general concluded that Nelnet had improperly exploited a 1985 law, passed when interest rates were high, that guaranteed a 9.5% rate on loans. Nevertheless, the DOE made no attempt to recover the money on the grounds that a precedent might be set requiring the department to pursue other loan companies, which would drive some smaller firms out of business, reducing borrowing options. "We were trying to make the best decision for the taxpayer and the student," stated a DOE official.

Not surprisingly, the Bush DOE favored private lending over direct loans. DOE-sponsored workshops that were used to inform college administrators about direct lending were cancelled early on in the Bush administration. In 2002, one DOE official claimed that private loans were actually cheaper for taxpayers than direct loans when government administrative costs were taken into account. Such beliefs combined with a lack of oversight appear to have had some of the desired effect. By 2006, direct loans

accounted for 25% of the student loan volume, down from
roughly one-third in 1997.

More recently, however, there has been an abrupt turnaround
at the DOE in regard to direct lending and to regulation. In 2006,
the department, to the surprise of many, decided to retain incentives that make direct lending more competitive with private
loans. The unexpected support for direct loans can be traced to
larger political concerns. In an attempt to bring down federal
spending and make the Bush tax cuts permanent, administration
officials had discovered that direct lending did save money due to
"significant cost inefficiencies" in the FFELP program. The Office
of Management and Budget concluded that if all student loans
were direct loans, $4.6 billion a year could be saved. As for regu-
lation, once the loan scandal became front-page news DOE secretary Margaret Spellings told a Congressional subcommittee that
"Federal student aid is crying out for reform." Shortly thereafter
the DOE proposed new rules that specifically governed relationships between private lenders and colleges.

IMPLICATIONS

There are a number of implications to be drawn from the current
scandal. Most obvious is the impact of competition between
direct and private lending. On the positive side, research suggests
that competition between the two programs did bring about
increased efficiencies that benefited borrowers and lowered government costs. On the other hand, it was an imperfect competition fueled in part by government subsidies that enabled the loan
industry to offer improper financial inducements to higher education. The fact that the two programs competed side by side is
more a testament to divided government than anything else.
FFELP, the established program, had built a strong constituency
in Congress over the years, particularly within the Republican
Party bolstered by the loan industry. Only when it became apparent that there were serious inefficiencies and abuses were coun-
tervailing forces within the Democratic Party able to push
through direct lending.

In retrospect, the potential negative effects of competition
were not unanticipated by Congress. As mentioned, inducements
by private lenders to increase loan volume were banned in 1995.
What it could not have foreseen was the DOE's response to it. It
now seems obvious that much of the scandal could have been

avoided had the DOE provided sufficient oversight as its own inspector general had urged, and which it had the Congressional authority to do and should have done with such substantial amounts of government funds involved. From any balanced perspective, it is difficult to comprehend the DOE's behavior other than the fact that policing a system involving thousands of lenders and schools can be extremely difficult. Beyond this, the department's hands-off approach can only be understood from an ideological perspective that supported the goals of the loan industry regardless of the methods used to obtain them, while assuming that the continued well being of private enterprise has only positive consequences.

The behavior of the loan industry was not surprising. We have come to expect that Corporate America will pursue profits to their logical extreme until prevented from doing so. Of course, private lenders did not act alone; higher education was an integral part of the scandal. In some instances, schools were simply victimized by their own officials who could not resist the opportunity for easy financial gain. More problematic, however, is the fact that any number of colleges and universities entered into questionable arrangements with the loan industry, which in some respects should not be surprising. Over the last three decades, higher education has become increasingly entrepreneurial. Numerous activities have been pursued to generate revenues including investment of endowment funds, industry/university research partnerships, real estate ventures, along with the outsourcing of such things as bookstores and food services. Thus, arrangements with private lenders to boost income fits a long-term trend to the point that many schools undoubtedly saw it as business as usual and business that was beneficial to their institutions.

Yet there is something unsettling about the entrepreneurial approach to student loans. As tax-exempt non-profits, society expects higher education to serve the public good, part of which involves dealing with students in an upfront and open manner. When this does not occur some sense of trust is lost and the image of higher education tarnished as the Cuomo investigation has emphasized. On a more practical level, it is difficult to know exactly how many students have been penalized, since very little data has been presented. Conversely, any number of university officials maintain that their agreements with private lenders benefited students. On balance, research indicates there is no significant financial advantage to having either private or direct loans.

Consequently, although the major theme of the various investigations has been framed in terms of the victimization of students and parents, this portrayal seems more political than actual. In the end, it appears that the big losers are taxpayers who subsidize the system.

Perhaps more troubling is the fact that colleges obviously knew that federal regulations made financial inducements by private lenders to secure higher loan volumes illegal. The knowledge that such behavior was unlikely to be investigated or punished undoubtedly facilitated these agreements. All of which does nothing to bolster public confidence in those who manage our institutions of higher learning. Although it would be naïve to think that the commercialization of higher education will subside, the current scandal will hopefully cause college administrators to reexamine the lengths to which it should extend.

One point that became salient during the various investigations is that a government program can be more efficient than one involving the private sector, which goes against many of the assumptions that have dominated policy formation over the last 25 years. While it is true that direct lending is more efficient, when one takes into account the subsidies involved with FFELP, it would not be that difficult for an alternative program to be more economical. Nonetheless, the simple fact that the federal government can procure funds at lower interest rates does provide an inherent advantage. Moreover, if there is a societal consensus that a program should be universal, as is the case with student loans, a government-directed program makes sense if the program can be adequately funded and managed.

Notwithstanding, private lending will continue. New regulations recently passed by a Democratically controlled Congress never contemplated ending FFELP. With 75% of the loan volume, the system is highly dependent upon private lenders, to say nothing of the expectations and needs of the investment community. Instead, various measures will attempt to curb its excesses. Most important, subsidies to the loan industry will be reduced by $21 billion over 5 years, cutting student interest rates from 6.8% to approximately 3.4%. With fewer funds available, it is assumed that the loan industry will be less able to offer financial inducements to higher education. This, combined with new DOE regulations that specifically ban the type of incentives that produced the current scandal, along with requiring colleges to list at least three preferred lenders and explain why they were chosen, should do much to mitigate the environment that facilitated the scandal. As a result, the use of direct loans will undoubtedly increase, while private lenders face a time of uncertainty. The loan industry has already warned that lowered interest rates could mean less loan money for students, jeopardizing their future and an outcome that Congress has always wanted to avoid. However, this scenario is far less likely to occur with direct lending in place. In this regard, it will be interesting to see if a major shift in the student loan program now occurs as a result of the scandal and becomes part of a larger movement toward more direct government involvement and less dependence on the private sector to meet social needs.

Discussion and Writing Questions

1. How effectively does each section of this article argue a single point? How well does each individual section help to support an overall argument about student loans and scandal?

2. How would the inclusion of one or more personal stories change the way you react to this article? Would the argument be stronger or weaker if it profiled one or more college students who exemplify the issue being discussed? Why? In a profile of your own, describe a college student you know well. How does she/he fit into the economic picture that Beaver paints?

Intertextual Question

3. Consider Beaver's attitude toward student loans. How might he respond to the argument made by Tim Struby in "A Fist Full of Dollars" (Chapter 1)? Why?

Starbucks Cutting More Jobs, Closing Stores
BRUCE HOROVITZ

Bruce Horovitz is a marketing reporter in USA Today's *Money section. He joined the newspaper in 1994. Prior to joining* USA Today, *Horovitz worked as a marketing columnist for the* Los Angeles Times *for nearly ten years. In 1993, the* Journalist and Financial Reporter *named him the nation's top ad/marketing writer. In the following article, Horovitz describes the changes that Starbucks is making in response to the slowing economy.*

Prereading Question

What is the "Starbucks experience" as you understand it? Is there a value to the "Starbucks experience"?

———————— ✦ ————————

TURNAROUND EFFORT TAKES ON MCDONALD'S, ADDING VALUE BREAKFAST MEALS

Starbucks, hammered by the contracting global economy, is taking the ax to its once unstoppable coffee empire.

Equally unthinkable: Breakfast value meals are on tap.

An unusually subdued CEO Howard Schultz on Wednesday announced painful plans to cut jobs, close stores and slow growth around the world after reporting 2009 first-quarter results that showed U.S. same-store sales down a stunning 10%.

Taking a cue from fast-food rivals such as highflying McDonald's, Schultz even announced vague plans to roll out value breakfast deals in March that, for the first time, will bundle drinks and food at a discounted price. "We've heard those of you calling for more action," said Schultz, in reference to the value meals.

"We will be moving to correct misperceptions," he said, about Starbucks being slow to react to consumers who are facing serious economic challenges.

He also announced these planned cutbacks at Starbucks in 2009:

- Store closings. Starbucks will close 300 underperforming company-operated stores worldwide—about 200 in the U.S. These closings are in addition to the 600 U.S. stores and 61 in Australia announced last year. Overall, that's nearly 1,000 announced store closings in less than two years.
- Fewer store openings. In the U.S. market in 2009, Starbucks will open 140 stores—60 fewer than its previous target of 200. And internationally, it will open 170 stores—100 fewer than its previous target of 270.
- Job cuts. Store closings and fewer openings in 2009 could result in up to 6,000 store positions being eliminated—the bulk of which will be in the U.S. Starbucks also plans to cut 700 corporate and non-retail positions globally—about half of them at the company's support center in Seattle.

Perhaps the most surprising move, however, was Schultz's announcement that Starbucks soon will enter the value-meal race. Schultz has long belittled such a move and said that customers were willing to pay a premium for the Starbucks "experience."

But value-leader McDonald's has been on a tear. Its same-store sales grew 7.2% in the fourth quarter, and its new McCafe coffee bars—slowly spreading nationally—have stolen business from Starbucks with lower-priced premium coffees, lattes and cappuccinos.

Now, Schultz says, "There is an acute understanding of the situation. We're taking courageous steps to make sure Starbucks not only weathers the storm, but comes out stronger."

Greg Schroeder, Wisco Research analyst, says Starbucks is doing what it has to do. "Starbucks will always be a good coffee company, but the competitive environment has changed permanently."

Discussion and Writing Questions

1. Horovitz describes Starbucks' cuts and changes to remain competitive in a contracting economy. Do you think Starbucks' plans to offer value meals to compete with McDonald's will be effective? Why do you think McDonald's has been able to effectively enter the premium coffee market?

2. Starbucks CEO Howard Schultz said that Starbucks will make changes to "correct misconceptions" of Starbucks' response to economic challenges that their consumers are facing. How can companies like Starbucks effectively respond to economic pressures consumers face during a recession? Review the current products offered by a company and propose changes that would be acceptable to consumers and keep them purchasing products and/or services.

Intertextual Question

3. Jeffrey Goldberg in his article "Selling Wal-Mart" and Horovitz address how companies are trying to create specific images for consumers. How does Starbucks' decision to offer value meals compare to Wal-Mart's plans to appeal to a more "liberal" demographic? Are Starbucks and Wal-Mart acting responsibly toward consumers? Toward their companies?

The Green Machine
MARC GUNTHER

Marc Gunther is a senior writer at Fortune *magazine and a columnist at CnnMoney.com. He is the author of* Faith and Fortune: How Compassionate Capitalism Is Transforming American Business *(Crown Business, 2004). Gunther has contributed to the* New York Times, *the* Washington Post, *and other publications, and he has appeared on NBC, ABC, PBS, CNN, and NPR. In the following article, Gunther writes about Wal-Mart's plans to "go green" and the criticisms of the plan.*

Prereading Question

Some of the criticisms of Wal-Mart's decision to "go green" include Wal-Mart using green strategies as a marketing ploy to improve Wal-Mart's image. Can Wal-Mart change its image by using sustainable practices?

◆

The 800 Wal-Mart Stores employees gathered in the home office for an all-day meeting were used to this kind of rah-rah talk. Top executives from Fortune 500 companies regularly trek to Bentonville, Ark., to pay homage to one of the world's most powerful companies and to shout out the Wal-Mart cheer.

This time, though, the cheerleading was coming from an unlikely source: Al Gore.

Wal-Mart had invited America's most famous environmentalist to show his movie, "An Inconvenient Truth." "Having the former Democratic Vice President was a shock" to some people at the company, chief executive Lee Scott told the crowd. "At least based on a couple of my e-mails."

But as the credits rolled, Gore strutted onto the stage to a standing ovation. Dressed in a blue suit and cowboy boots, he joked with the audience, answered questions in his best Southern drawl, and coyly denied that he had any plans to run for President again. (This wasn't exactly his base: He took just 32% of the vote in Benton County in 2000.)

Before heading off to dinner with Wal-Mart chairman Rob Walton and Scott, Gore delivered a parting thought: As Wal-Mart embarks on a far-reaching plan to adopt business practices that are better for the environment, he said, the world will learn that "there need not be any conflict between the environment and the economy."

Wal-Mart, you see, has decided to help save the earth.

ENVIRONMENTAL VALUES

Just listen to Scott. "To me," he says, "there can't be anything good about putting all these chemicals in the air. There can't be anything good about the smog you see in cities. There can't be anything good about putting chemicals in these rivers in Third World countries so that somebody can buy an item for less money in a developed country. Those things are just inherently wrong, whether you are an environmentalist or not."

In a speech broadcast to all of Wal-Mart's facilities last November, Scott set several ambitious goals: Increase the efficiency of its vehicle fleet by 25% over the next three years, and double efficiency in ten years, Eliminate 30% of the energy used in stores. Reduce solid waste from U.S. stores by 25% in three years.

Wal-Mart says it will invest $500 million in sustainability projects, and the company has done a lot more than draw up targets. It has quickly become, for instance, the biggest seller of organic milk and the biggest buyer of organic cotton in the world. It is working with suppliers to figure out ways to cut down on packaging and energy costs. It has opened two "green" supercenters.

CREDIBILITY QUESTIONED

Plenty of people won't buy it—or anything else from Wal-Mart. To labor leaders, left-wing elites, and the small-is-beautiful crowd, the $312-billion-a-year retailer stands for everything that's wrong with big business.

They see the company in a race to pave the planet and turn it into a giant emporium of cheap goods built on the back of cheap labor. The union-funded website walmartwatch.com dismisses Wal-Mart's environmental push as a "high-priced green-washing campaign."

Wal-Mart, though, has a whole lot more to worry about than convincing a few ideological critics that its eco-intentions are pure. Its business, for starters.

Its same-store sales growth has slowed down, trailing Costco's and Target's. Its stock price is another big concern. After rising 1,205% during the 1990s, the stock has fallen by 30% since Scott took over as CEO in January 2000.

It's no wonder that inside Wal-Mart some veteran executives grouse that Scott's green crusade will be a costly distraction. Many remember the last time Wal-Mart set out an initiative this broad: founder Sam Walton's 1985 "Made in the U.S.A." campaign.

That move burnished Wal-Mart's red-white-and-blue image, but it wasn't long before critics noted that Wal-Mart continued to seek out goods from the absolute lowest-cost supplier- and typically that meant "Made Anywhere but America."

Indeed, Wal-Mart's single-minded desire to save its customers money has been its raison d'être for 44 years. Which raises two questions: Why is the world's largest retailer so determined to become the greenest? And how green can a company that operates 6,600 big-box stores really get?

Rob Walton, his son Ben, Pearl Jam guitarist Stone Gossard, and conservationist Peter Seligmann were scuba-diving off Coco Island, a lush, uninhabited Costa Rican national park populated by manta rays, dolphins, and sharks.

HIGH-LEVEL INFLUENCE

During a ten-day trip in February 2004, Seligmann, co-founder and CEO of Conservation International, a big Washington, D.C., environmental organization whose mission is to protect the world's biologically rich habitats, had been pointing out fleets of fishing boats that were destroying the delicate Costa Rican marine habitat. Toward the end of the trip, Seligmann looked Walton in the eye: "We need to change the way industry works. And you can have an influence."

Like all Sam Walton's children, S. Robson "Rob" Walton, 60, grew up in the Ozarks with a love of the outdoors. "All our family vacations were camping trips," he says in a rare interview. His younger brother John, who died last year in a private plane crash, was a conservationist. And his son Sam, who worked as a Colorado River guide, sits on the board of Environmental Defense, a nonprofit group.

About four years ago, after a trip to Africa, Rob Walton began to think about ways his family could help preserve wilderness areas through its foundation, which has assets of about $1 billion. (The Walton family's 40% stake in Wal-Mart is worth about $80 billion.)

A mutual friend then introduced Walton to Seligmann. Over the next two years the preppy ex-biologist guided Rob and his two sons on a series of adventures. They hiked in Madagascar. They took a boat trip through the world's largest freshwater wetland, in Brazil. They went diving in the Galápagos Islands. "We spent a lot of time diving and talking," says Seligmann. The family foundation eventually made a $21 million grant to CI for ocean-protection programs, and Walton joined the group's board.

But Seligmann had another agenda, one that he finally put on the table in Costa Rica. Whatever money the foundation could contribute would pale in comparison to what Wal-Mart the corporation could do. "I suggested to Rob that Wal-Mart could be a driver of tremendous change," Seligmann says.

HUGE FOOTPRINT

He wasn't exaggerating. The company is the biggest private user of electricity in the U.S.; each of its 2,074 supercenters uses an average of 1.5 million kilowatts annually, enough as a group to power all of Namibia.

Wal-Mart has the nation's second-largest fleet of trucks, and its vehicles travel a billion miles a year. If each customer who visited Wal-Mart in a week bought one long-lasting compact fluorescent (CF) light bulb, the company estimates, that would reduce electric bills by $3 billion, conserve 50 billion tons of coal, and keep one billion incandescent light bulbs out of landfills over the life of the bulb.

If Wal-Mart influenced the behavior of a fraction of its 1.8 million employees or the 176 million customers that shop there every week, the impact would be huge. And because of the extraordinary clout Wal-Mart wields with its 60,000 suppliers, it could make even more of a difference by influencing their practices.

Walton was intrigued, but he had taken himself out of an operational role at Wal-Mart years ago. He didn't want to overstep his bounds. "We are really, really careful about mixing personal interests and the business," he says. Still, he agreed to introduce Seligmann to Lee Scott.

PR PLAY

The timing was fortuitous. Scott had just undertaken a review of Wal-Mart's legal and PR woes—and it wasn't a short list. A lawsuit alleging that Wal-Mart discriminated against its female employees had been certified as a federal class action. Opponents blocked new stores in the suburbs of Los Angeles, San Francisco, and Chicago.

A study found that Wal-Mart's average spending on health benefits for its employees was 30% less than the average of its retail peers. The company's environmental record was nothing to boast about either: It had paid millions of dollars to state and federal regulators for violating air- and water-pollution laws.

For years Wal-Mart simply brushed off such criticism. "We would put up the sandbags and get out the machine guns," Scott recalls. After all, business was good. They were saving their customers billions, fighting for the little guy.

But as the upstart rural retailer grew into one of America's biggest companies and clashed with unionized competitors, it made powerful enemies. Expectations of business were rising, and Wal-Mart was failing to meet them.

A McKinsey & Co. study leaked to the press by walmartwatch.com found that up to 8% of shoppers had stopped patronizing the chain because of its reputation.

Scott wondered, "If we had known ten years ago what we know now, what would we have done differently that might have kept us out of some of these issues or would have enhanced our reputation? It seemed to me that ultimately many of the issues that had to do with the environment were going to wind up with people feeling like we had a greater responsibility than we were, at the time, accepting."

In a drab Bentonville conference room, Scott, Rob Walton, Seligmann and Glenn Prickett of Conservation International, and a friend of Seligmann's named Jib Ellison, a river-rafting guide turned management consultant, convened a pivotal meeting in June 2004. For a presentation to the man who is arguably the most powerful CEO in the world and the man who is inarguably one of the richest, the pitch was surprisingly informal.

The five men chatted about the environment and about ways Wal-Mart could improve its practices. Seligmann and Prickett talked about their work with Starbucks, which developed coffee-buying methods to protect tropical regions, and about McDonald's, which was helping to promote sustainable agriculture and fishing.

Their argument was simple: Wal-Mart could improve its image, motivate employees, and save money by going green.

If there was any group that could deliver such a message to Scott, it was CI, whose board members include former Intel chairman Gordon Moore, BP chief executive John Browne, and former Starbucks CEO Orin Smith. CI works closely with corporations, and about $7 million of its $93 million in 2005 revenues came from such consulting arrangements.

ACCEPTING RESPONSIBILITY

Scott hired CI and Ellison's management consulting firm, called BluSkye, and asked them to measure Wal-Mart's environmental impact. The assessment would include not just Wal-Mart's operations, but the impact of growing or producing all the products it sells and shipping them to stores.

Wal-Mart was defining its responsibility broadly, in a way that would bring its vast supply chain—where its environmental impact is greatest—into the picture.

About a dozen people from BluSkye, CI, and Wal-Mart spent nearly a year measuring the company's impact. Fairly quickly, the environmentalists spotted waste that Wal-Mart's legendary cost cutters had overlooked.

On Kid Connection, its private-label line of toys, for instance, Wal-Mart found that by eliminating excessive packaging, it could save $2.4 million a year in shipping costs, 3,800 trees, and one million barrels of oil.

On its fleet of 7,200 trucks Wal-Mart determined it could save $26 million a year in fuel costs merely by installing auxiliary power units that enable the drivers to keep their cabs warm or cool during mandatory ten-hour breaks from the road. Before that, they'd let the truck engine idle all night, wasting fuel.

Yet another example: Wal-Mart installed machines called sandwich balers in its stores to recycle and sell plastic that it used to throw away. Companywide, the balers have added $28 million to the bottom line.

"Think about it," Scott said in his big speech to employees last fall. "If we throw it away, we had to buy it first. So we pay twice— once to get it, once to have it taken away. What if we reverse that? What if our suppliers send us less, and everything they send us has value as a recycled product? No waste, and we get paid instead."

That was talk any Wal-Mart executive could understand, even if few knew it came straight from the pages of *Natural Capitalism*, an influential book by Paul Hawken, Amory Lovins, and Hunter Lovins that lays out a blueprint for a new green economy in which nothing goes to waste.

Not coincidentally, Lovins and his Rocky Mountain Institute were also hired as consultants by Wal-Mart to study a radical revamp of its trucking fleet.

CASTING A WIDE NET

Wal-Mart was pulling ideas from everywhere—consultants, NGOs, suppliers, and eco-friendly competitors such as Patagonia and Whole Foods. This open-source approach worked so well that the company decided to form "sustainable value networks" made up of Wal-Mart executives, suppliers, environmental groups, and regulators; they would meet every few months to share ideas, set goals, and monitor progress.

Today there are 14 networks, each with a focus: facilities, internal operations, logistics, alternative fuels, packaging, chemicals, food and agriculture, electronics, textiles, forest products, jewelry, seafood, climate change, and China.

Experts from the World Wildlife Federation, the Natural Resources Defense Council, and even Greenpeace have made the pilgrimage to Bentonville. "I can honestly say I never expected to be at Wal-Mart's headquarters watching people do the Wal-Mart cheer," says John Hocevar, a Greenpeace campaigner. Environmental Defense announced plans to open a satellite office in Bentonville.

Though hundreds of people are in the networks, only five Wal-Mart employees, led by corporate strategist Andy Ruben, work full-time on the initiative. Key decisions are decentralized. "If you are a buyer, sustainability is going to be your business," says Scott.

Some environmentalists who are part of the networks worry the initiative is understaffed. They say that the Wal-Mart people responsible for keeping the networks going, all of whom already had full-time jobs like running truck fleets or buying jewelry, are stretched thin.

Still, getting tree-huggers and Wal-Mart lifers in the same room led to some unexpected benefits. "Sustainability helped us develop the skills to listen to people who criticize us and to change where it's appropriate," Scott says.

His managers are learning "not to be so afraid of venturing out there, thinking that if people see our warts, they're just going to castigate us." It also gives them another reason to feel good about Wal-Mart, a sense of working for a "higher purpose," he says.

Scott, too, was filled with the zeal of the newly converted. "I had an intellectual interest when we started," he says. "I have a passion today." As a lifelong angler from Baxter Springs, Kan., Scott, who is 57, was particularly worried about pollution in the world's rivers and oceans.

He visited Mount Washington in New Hampshire, where he chatted with a maple-sugar producer about the impact of global warming. And he traded in his Volkswagen Beetle for a hybrid Lexus SUV.

Hurricane Katrina, after which Wal-Mart employees mobilized to deliver vital supplies to victims, deepened Scott's resolve. "We stepped back from that and asked one simple question: How can Wal-Mart be that company—the one we were during Katrina—all the time?"

The environmental campaign that Scott admits started out as a "defensive strategy" was, in his view, "turning out to be precisely the opposite." His people were feeling better about the company. They were saving their customers money. That was one of Wal-Mart's strengths. Another was twisting the arms of suppliers— who would soon learn all about Wal-Mart's new crusade.

SUSTAINABLE AGRIBUSINESS

In the cold waters off Kodiak Island, Alaska, where the sockeye salmon are running in early June, a 45-year-old third-generation fishing-boat captain named Mitch Keplinger is having a disappointing day.

Operating under Alaska's strict regulatory regime, Keplinger and his crew labor for more than 12 hours to haul in about 1,000 pounds of sockeye, which they sell for 70 cents a pound to Ocean Beauty, a Seattle-based processor and Wal-Mart supplier. They catch another 500 pounds of pink salmon, which sells for 35 cents a pound. That's $1,050 before expenses, to be shared by the four of them—barely worth the effort.

What does that have to do with Wal-Mart? Keplinger—and fishermen like him who play by the rules—are getting killed by competition from unregulated fisheries and farmed salmon. In February, Wal-Mart announced that over the next three to five years it would purchase all its wild-caught seafood from fisheries that, like Alaska's salmon fishery, have been certified as sustainable by an independent nonprofit called the Marine Stewardship Council (MSC).

The company is working on a similar certification system for farmed fish, and it hopes consumers will come to value "brands" like MSC-certified as they do the organic label. Says Rupert Howes, chief executive of the MSC: "It's supply-chain pressure of the best kind."

Keplinger and his buyers at Ocean Beauty are watching Wal-Mart closely. Says Tom Sutherland, Ocean Beauty's vice president of marketing: "When Wal-Mart hiccups, it's all we can talk about." It's not just Alaskan fishermen who are talking. So are corn farmers in Iowa (who want to sell more ethanol through Wal-Mart), coffee growers in Brazil (who are being promised higher prices for their beans), and factory bosses in China (who are being told to cut their energy and fuel costs).

ORGANIC CLOTHES, TOO

Wal-Mart's campaign has already turned the small world of organic cotton upside down, thanks in part to Coral Rose, a ladies' apparel buyer for Sam's Club. In spring 2004—just before Wal-Mart held its first meeting with CI—Rose ordered a yoga outfit made of organic cotton for Sam's Club; the tops sold for about $14, the loose-fitting pants for $10. The 190,000 units sold out in ten weeks.

That got Scott's attention. Sales of organic food had grown at Wal-Mart; he wondered if organic cotton could do as well. With Scott's encouragement, Wal-Mart's buyers visited organic cotton farms. They learned about the environmental risks posed by conventional cotton farming, which uses more chemical pesticides and synthetic fertilizer than any other crop.

Wal-Mart's purchases of organic cotton have eliminated millions of tons of chemicals. Scott says. Today, Wal-Mart and Sam's Club stock a range of organic-cotton products—baby clothes under the Baby George brand, teenage fashion, and a line of bed sheets and towels.

The organic-cotton industry had found its best customer. Five years ago global production of organic cotton amounted to 6,400 metric tons, and some farmers who converted to organic methods, which can cost more, could not find buyers willing to pay a premium.

In 2006, Wal-Mart and Sam's Club alone will use 6,800 metric tons, and they've made a verbal commitment to buy organic cotton for five years, giving farmers an assurance that there will be a market for their crops.

Wal-Mart is also increasing the amount of organic food it sells, but some even find fault with this, assuming that it buys only from massive corporate organic farms. Not true. Wal-Mart buys locally in two dozen states, striving to reduce "food miles" to save shipping costs and increase freshness.

PEER PRESSURE

Scott, meanwhile, is personally pushing his cause with Fortune 500 CEOs. He has talked with Jeff Immelt at GE about LED lighting for Wal-Mart's buildings. He's talked with Tom Faulk, the CEO of Kimberly-Clark, about "compressed toilet paper," which squeezes three rolls into one. Steve Reinemund, PepsiCo's CEO, just sold Wal-Mart on a massive recycling contest involving Aquafina water.

Wait a minute. Recycling's great. But why consume Aquafina in the first place? Bottled water is bad for the environment, period. But neither PepsiCo nor Wal-Mart will stop selling it as long as consumers want to buy it. This is one place where tensions arise between what's good for business and what's good for the planet.

Packaging is another thorny issue. On my grocer's shelf are a bulky, 100-fluid-ounce, orange plastic jug of Procter & Gamble's bestselling Tide and a slim 32-ounce aqua plastic bottle of Unilever's "small and mighty" All.

Both contain enough detergent for 32 loads of wash, but the smaller package, made possible by condensing All, saves energy, shipping costs, and shelf space—a big win all around, right?

Not quite. Bigger packages command more shelf space, provide more surface area for advertising, and suggest to consumers that they're getting more for their money. Unilever executives voiced all those worries when they went to see Scott. He agreed to make "small and mighty" All a VPI (that's Wal-Mart code for "volume-producing item," and it means that Wal-Mart will promote it heavily). "That helps to increase their confidence," he says. You can now find "small and mighty" All in supermarkets everywhere.

And guess what? This fall Procter & Gamble will replace the bulky plastic jugs with condensed, slimmed-down versions of all its liquid laundry detergents—Tide, Cheer, Gain, Era, and Draft—in a test in Cedar Rapids, Iowa, to prepare for a likely national rollout.

We wondered if Wal-Mart had anything to do with that. "We've been doing sustainability for quite some time," replied a P&G spokeswoman. "And we're pleased to work with all our distributors, including Wal-Mart." You figure it out.

This is why Wal-Mart's eco-initiative is potentially more world-changing than, say, GE's. GE sells fuel-efficient aircraft engines and billion-dollar power plants to a few customers.

Wal-Mart sells organic cotton, laundry soap, and light bulbs to millions. When shoppers see a display promoting "the bulb that pays for itself, again and again and again," they'll be reminded of their own environmental impact.

By buying CF bulbs they'll also save money on their utility bills, leaving them more money to spend at, you guessed it, Wal-Mart. The bigger idea here is that poor and middle-income Americans are every bit as interested in buying green products as are the well-to-do, so long as they are affordable.

Plenty of places sell fair-trade coffee, for example. Only Wal-Mart sells it for $4.71 a pound. "The potential here is to democratize the whole sustainability idea—not make it something that just the elites on the coasts do but something that small-town and middle America also embrace," says CI's Glenn Prickett. "It's a Nixon-to-China moment."

ECO-STORES

Several weeks ago a dozen Japanese supermarket industry executives flew halfway around the world to visit a store in a suburb of Denver that is unlike any they had ever seen. They snapped pictures of wind turbines and solar cells and listened as a tour guide explained how dirty cooking oil from the deli and used motor oil from the lube department are recycled to heat the store.

They ran their fingers across jewelry cases built of renewable bamboo and peered into the dairy case at the superefficient light-emitting diodes that illuminate rows of organic milk.

The visitors wandered among shelves stocked with tuna certified by the Marine Stewardship Council and coffee endorsed by the Rainforest Alliance. They learned that spoiled food was composted into fertilizer and resold. They walked on sidewalks that are—no joke—made of recycled airport runways.

This is Wal-Mart Store No. 5334, which opened last winter. It's one of two experimental stores the company built to test ways to cut energy and reduce waste.

It sounds terribly futuristic, but this isn't totally new ground. In 1993 the company debuted a Bill McDonough–designed eco-store in Lawrence, Kan., with great fanfare. Two more stores followed, but the concept quietly died.

Wal-Mart's more serious now, but skeptics remain. Jeffrey Hollender is president of Seventh Generation, a Burlington, Vt., maker of nontoxic household products. Though Scott met with

Hollender in Bentonville and offered to carry some of his line, Hollender declined. "We might sell a lot more products in giant mass-market outlets, but we're not living up to our own values and helping the world get to a better place if we sell our soul to do it," he says.

Scott understands there are some critics he will never win over. He knows that not everyone at Wal-Mart shares his vision. But he's quite certain that one person would.

Midway through the daylong sustainability summit, the one where Al Gore showed his movie, Scott did what Wal-Mart executives always do when they want to get people's attention: He invoked the name of Sam Walton.

"Some people say this is foreign to what Sam Walton believed, that Sam Walton focused solely on the customers, driving prices down so the average person can have a higher standard of value," Scott said.

"What people forget is that there was nobody more willing to change. Sam Walton did what was right for his time. Sam loved the outdoors. And he loved the idea of building a company that would endure. I think Sam Walton would, in fact, embrace Wal-Mart's efforts to improve the quality of life for our customers and our associates by doing what we need to do in sustainability."

Then he posed a challenge to the audience: "What other company in the world could do this? This company is uniquely positioned. But we will not be measured by our aspirations. We will be measured by our actions." Of that there's no doubt. This is Wal-Mart, after all. The whole world will be watching.

Discussion and Writing Questions

1. Do you agree with Jeffrey Hollender, president of Seventh Generation, the manufacturer of nontoxic household products, that he would be selling out and not "living up to our own values" by contracting with Wal-Mart to sell its products? Does it make a difference in your opinion to know that Seventh Generation products are sold at Target?

2. Chief executive Lee Scott spoke about Wal-Mart's responsibility and influence regarding sustainable practices. Do large, influential companies such as Wal-Mart have a greater responsibility to promote sustainability practices than smaller companies? Who is ultimately responsible? In an essay based on your own experiences and reading of this essay, explain your conclusions about responsibility and Wal-Mart.

Intertextual Question

3. One of the criticisms of Wal-Mart's green policy is that it is not in-line with the business practices set out by Sam Walton. Do you think that Sam Walton would encourage the "green practices" that Lee Scott is suggesting for Wal-Mart? How do the sustainability policies support or deviate from the business practices that Walton outlined in "Rolling Out the Formula"?

Selling Wal-Mart
JEFFREY GOLDBERG

Jeffrey Goldberg is an Israeli-American journalist and writer. He has written for the Washington Post, *the* Jerusalem Post, *and the* New York Times Magazine, *among others. He was a writer for the* New Yorker *and more recently for* Atlantic Monthly. *He has received several awards, including Overseas Press Club's Joe & Laurie Dine Award for international human rights reporting and the National Magazine Award for reporting. He has also written* Prisoners: A Muslim and a Jew Across the Middle East Divide *(2006). In the following article, Goldberg discusses the public relations strategies Wal-Mart is utilizing to reshape its image.*

Prereading Question

What is your general impression of Wal-Mart? What helped to shape your impression of Wal-Mart (e.g., shopping experiences, employment by Wal-Mart, stories you have read about the company, discussions you have had with friends and family)? Do you think you have an accurate understanding of Wal-Mart's role in the American economy based on that impression? Why or why not?

———————— ✦ ————————

CAN THE COMPANY CO-OPT LIBERALS?

On the second floor of Wal-Mart's headquarters, in Bentonville, Arkansas, is a windowless room called Action Alley. In the Wal-Mart idiom, the term "Action Alley" usually refers to the main aisle of the company's two thousand Supercenters—the stores that have upended the retail business by selling enormous quantities of groceries and imported goods at prices that competitors find difficult or impossible to match. At the "home office," as Bentonville is known, Action Alley is the company's war room, a communications center that was set up and is staffed by Washington-based operatives from Edelman, a public-relations firm that advises companies on issues of "reputation management." Wal-Mart corporate culture is parsimonious except in the matter of executive compensation, but, according to a source, the company has been paying Edelman roughly ten million dollars annually to renovate its reputation.

Twenty years ago, Wal-Mart was widely viewed as a scrappy regional retailer, and its founder, Sam Walton, an Ozarks eccentric with a vision of super-discounting, was praised for intuiting the needs of his customers, and for maintaining high morale among his workers. When Walton retired, in 1988 (he died in 1992), the company had revenues of sixteen billion dollars. Today, Wal-Mart is the second-largest company in the world in terms of revenue—only ExxonMobil is bigger. Its revenues last year came to more than three hundred and fifteen billion dollars, with profits of more than eleven billion, and it has developed a reputation as a worldwide colossus that provides poor pay and miserly benefits to its 1.8 million employees. The image of the company is not helped by the immoderation of Sam Walton's widow and children, who together control forty per cent of Wal-Mart's outstanding shares, and who are worth roughly eighty billion dollars; they are, by a striking margin, the richest family in America. (They are worth more than Warren Buffett and Bill Gates combined.)

Wal-Mart is traditionally a Republican-leaning company (during the past fifteen years, more than seventy-five per cent of its political donations have gone to Republicans) and has become a favorite target of Democratic politicians. Hillary Clinton, who once served on Wal-Mart's board, recently returned a five-thousand-dollar donation because of what a campaign spokeswoman said were "serious differences with current company practices." Barack Obama and John Edwards have joined union-led campaigns to denounce the company for its wage-and-benefit policies. Wal-Mart is notably unfriendly to unions; in 2000, when meat-cutters at a single Wal-Mart in Texas organized into a collective-bargaining unit, Wal-Mart responded by shutting down its meat counters across Texas and in five neighboring states. It closed an entire store in Quebec, rather than see workers unionize.

The company has also been criticized for driving American jobs overseas, by demanding immense discounts from its suppliers. Senator Byron Dorgan, a North Dakota Democrat who is one of Wal-Mart's main foes in Congress, says that the company, by forcing its suppliers to manufacture goods in China, shows that it "doesn't stand for American values." Wal-Mart has been the subject of numerous unflattering documentaries and books. Even Ron Galloway, the maker of a recent pro-Wal-Mart documentary, "Why Wal-Mart Works and Why That Makes Some People Crazy," has turned against the company. Galloway told me that he now considers Wal-Mart to be a "heartless" employer. "They just instituted a wage cap for long-term employees—people making between thirteen and eighteen dollars an hour. It's a form of accelerated attrition. They can't expect me to defend that," Galloway said.

Two unions—the Service Employees International Union and the United Food and Commercial Workers—fund anti-Wal-Mart lobbying groups that catalogue what they see as the company's diverse sins. Each month seems to bring a new, self-inflicted embarrassment. Most recently, Wal-Mart announced that it had fired a technician from its Threat Research and Analysis division (which combats industrial espionage) for eavesdropping on telephone calls made by the *Times'* Wal-Mart beat reporter, Michael Barbaro. Wal-Mart claims that the technician acted alone; the U.S. Attorney in Arkansas is investigating.

In 2005, Barbaro and another *Times* reporter, Steven Greenhouse, cited an internal memo written by the company's chief human-resources executive, M. Susan Chambers, in which she suggested that the company could control personnel costs by not hiring unhealthy people. (To keep the sick and the lame off the payroll, Chambers suggested that all jobs should include "some physical activity; e.g., all cashiers do some cart-gathering.") In the same memo, Chambers noted that forty-six per cent of the children of Wal-Mart's million-plus American employees were uninsured or on Medicaid.

More recently, the company experienced a run of bad publicity when it announced new scheduling policies for its store workers (known as "associates"). Under what critics call the "open availability" policy, workers must make themselves available for different shifts from month to month or risk losing hours. Kathleen MacDonald, a cosmetics-counter manager at a Wal-Mart in Aiken, South Carolina, explained to me, "It's simple. They say you have to be there when the computer says the customers will be there. So if you have kids at home you can't show up, but then your hours are being cut."

The company is facing more consequential challenges over its treatment of women. A class-action lawsuit filed in San Francisco in 2001 by six female Wal-Mart employees, alleging that the company has denied promotions and equal pay to women, is proceeding steadily to trial; by some estimates, the suit could cost the company as much as five billion dollars. Wal-Mart has denied that it discriminates against women. Kathleen MacDonald joined the suit after she learned that a male counterpart, who, like her, was stocking shelves, earned more than she did. When she raised the issue, she told me, "my immediate supervisor said, 'Well, God made Adam first, and Eve came from him.' I was, like, what? That's when I decided enough was enough."

Full-time hourly workers at Wal-Mart stores make an average of $10.51 an hour, according to the company. Wal-Mart's most energetic adversary, a group called Wake Up Wal-Mart, which is sponsored by the food workers' union, notes that $10.51 may be the average full-time wage, but the company won't disclose the average hourly wage of part-timers. "We think the true average is probably less than nine dollars," Chris Kofinis, the Wake Up Wal-Mart spokesman, said.

The company has had its bright moments, most notably in the immediate aftermath of Hurricane Katrina, when Wal-Mart mobilized its truck fleet to deliver goods to the storm zone. But that was a rare instance of good public relations. Owing in part to its status as a retail behemoth, Wal-Mart has met with resistance in numerous communities (including New York City) when it has tried to open stores. And its recent business performance has been less than stellar; sales have slowed, and the stock price is stagnant. Problems like these have concentrated the minds of Lee Scott, Wal-Mart's C.E.O., and his top executives. "We used to be the David and now we're seen as the Goliath," John Fleming, the company's chief merchandising officer, told me.

The job of the Edelman people—there are about twenty, along with more than three dozen in-house public-relations specialists—is to help Wal-Mart scrub its muddied image. Edelman specializes in helping industries with image problems; another important client is the American Petroleum Institute, a Washington lobbying group that seeks to convince Americans that oil companies care about the environment and that their profits are reasonable. Edelman does its work by cultivating contacts among the country's opinion élites, with whom it emphasizes the good news and spins the bad; by such tactics as establishing "Astroturf" groups, seemingly grass-roots organizations that are actually fronts for industry; and, as I deduced from my own visit to Bentonville, by advising corporate executives on how to speak like risk-averse politicians.

It became clear to me in Bentonville that Wal-Mart's senior executives had been tightly scripted. When I talked with John Menzer, a company vice-chairman, a spokeswoman named Sarah Clark, my official escort there, told me that the conversation would be limited to the company's new Jobs and Opportunity Zones concept, which is designed to help smooth the arrival of new stores in urban areas. (A company source told me that the Zones idea was intended by Edelman as a public-relations maneuver to soften Wal-Mart's image among minority communities; the entire budget for the program is five hundred thousand dollars over two years.) Menzer, a slender man with a thin smile, explained the company's attraction to underemployed inner-city residents, saying, "One of the biggest opportunities a person has at Wal-Mart is to be part of this growth company. There are always opportunities for promotion, learning, and education, and people know they can build a career here."

When I asked about the "open availability" policy, Clark interrupted, while Menzer stared at me. "I can certainly take that one," Clark said. "I'll make a note of that. We'll talk about that later. We don't have 'open availability.'" Menzer continued as if the question had not been asked. "Now we're expanding outside our four walls to invest in the community, so let me add that in as another step we're taking," he said. (Sometime later, Clark suggested that I interview an employee about flexible scheduling, and she provided the name and number of one who would talk to me: Latoya Machato, a cashier at a Texas Supercenter. I called the store and asked for Machato, but was told that "cashiers can't come to the phone during work." I called later and was told that Machato could speak to me on her break, but would not be allowed to call long-distance from a company phone. I asked Clark if Machato could talk to me after her shift, but Clark said that that would be impossible, because the store would have to put her "on the clock," and thus file the paperwork to get her paid an extra hour's wage.)

The Edelman team assigned to Wal-Mart, I learned, is divided into three groups: "promote," "response," and "pressure." The Jobs and Opportunity Zones notion came from the promotions team.

The response-team members—veterans of political campaigns—
are supposed to quickly counter criticism in the press or on the
Web. The pressure group works on opposition research, focussing
on the unions and the press.

There is great mistrust of the press at Wal-Mart headquarters.
The chief spokeswoman for the company, a former AT&T executive named Mona Williams, keeps on a shelf a framed cover of a
2003 issue of *Business Week* featuring a story titled "Is Wal-Mart
Too Powerful?" The story asked tough questions about Wal-Mart's
influence on the American economy. "I keep that there to remind
me never to trust reporters," she said, without smiling. Sarah
Clark was friendlier, but similarly suspicious. It was Clark who,
without enthusiasm, brought me to Action Alley for a brief
glimpse inside.

Before opening the door, she instructed me not to write
down anything I saw—the third time that this particular direc-
tive had been issued. In some ways, the home office is not unlike
the headquarters of the National Security Agency—both contain
a large number of windowless rooms and both are staffed by
people who are preoccupied by the movement of strangers in
their midst. The N.S.A.'s headquarters, though, seemed to me
more aesthetically appealing; the Wal-Mart home office resem-
bles a poorly funded elementary school. Wal-Mart executives
take pride in their ostentatiously shabby surroundings. "When I
was working internationally, I got to be friends with Henry
Kissinger, and so I invited Henry to have lunch with us," Menzer
told me. "We had lunch in the Quail Room, and it's got pictures
of Sam Walton and all his bird hunting, and we handed out Subway sandwiches and said, 'Well, you're very special, so we threw
in a bag of chips,' and I daresay I don't know if he ever saw a
Subway sandwich before, but he was actually so impressed that
we live our culture."

I pointed out to Menzer that his salary would allow him to
purchase something more elegant. His face clouded over. "I'm just
not going to talk about that," he said. In 2005, Menzer earned six
and a half million dollars in salary, bonuses, and options.

Clark opened the door of Action Alley to reveal a dark, thread-
bare room, its walls, like most of Wal-Mart's walls, painted battle-
ship gray. Six desks were clustered at the center of the room, and
at these desks sat five Edelman executives.

When the presence of a reporter was announced, three
of the executives looked away and two stood up to greet me.

One was Greg St. Claire, at the moment the senior Edelman employee there. St. Claire, who is about forty and is a former Republican congressional staff member, got Wal-Mart in some trouble last year, because of a group called Working Families for Wal-Mart, which advertised itself as a "grass-roots" organization. St. Claire was one of the forces behind Working Families for Wal-Mart, which paid for his sister, Laura St. Claire, to travel across America in a recreational vehicle and keep a blog about visits with Wal-Mart employees. Everyone she talked to was delighted with Wal-Mart. At about the time that the trip came to an end, *Business Week* revealed that Wal-Mart had financed the journey. When I asked Richard Edelman, the company's chairman, about this rather blatant example of Astroturfing, he said, of Working Families for Wal-Mart, "I do believe that it is a real group of real people, as far as I know." Working Families for Wal-Mart is housed in Edelman's Washington office; its steering-committee members, some of whom have business ties to the company, were recruited by Edelman. They include the singer Pat Boone, who told me by e-mail that he volunteered his public-relations services to Wal-Mart several years ago, and Wal-Mart passed his name on to the group.

Greg St. Claire was not interested in talking to me, but the other Edelman executive stood up and said hello. He was a man of about thirty named Fred Baldassaro. I was surprised to see him. We had last crossed paths more than a year earlier, in a union hall in Albuquerque, New Mexico. At the time, Baldassaro was working for the Democratic National Committee chairman, Howard Dean, as his top travelling aide. Dean had spoken about democratic values at a rally, and said, "When you see that you're putting in as many hours as the C.E.O. of your company, and he's making five hundred and thirty-eight times what you're making, do you think capitalism works for you?"

Down some stairs from Action Alley is the office of Lee Scott, Wal-Mart's president and C.E.O., who last year earned $15.7 million in salary and bonuses. Early this month, the company announced that it was granting him an additional twenty-two million dollars in stock. In the past year, Scott earned roughly two thousand times the salary of the average Wal-Mart worker.

Sarah Clark was eager to move along, but I asked Baldassaro why he went from Dean's Democratic National Committee to Scott's Wal-Mart.

"Well, it's interesting here," he said. "I'm getting married soon, anyway, and, you know . . ." He trailed off, as Clark invited me to leave.

Later that day, I drove to a Wal-Mart Supercenter in the nearby town of Rogers with one of Clark's deputies, a young New Yorker named David Tovar, who, before joining Wal-Mart, spent nine years as a spokesman and lobbyist for Philip Morris, including a stint arguing against government regulation of cigarettes. He explained his position: "It's a legal product that adults can choose to use, or not use, as they see fit. I learned a lot by doing that sort of work." As we drove out of Bentonville, I asked Tovar if he thought it odd to find ostensibly pro-labor Democrats at the headquarters of Wal-Mart. In fact, he said, it would be quite normal for Democrats to join Wal-Mart's "cause," because Wal-Mart's customers are the Party's natural constituency.

Wal-Mart's executives are angry about Democratic attacks on the company. Tovar's boss, Mona Williams, told me, "Wal-Mart is taking care of the people the Democratic Party says it represents—the poor, the middle class. The Democrats are not taking care of them. We're like Lyndon Johnson's Great Society."

Tovar offered a more self-interested explanation for his service in the public-relations industry: "Why did I go work for Philip Morris? Because I wanted to get out of my parents' house. Why do people take jobs? It's like in 'Thank You for Smoking'"— Christopher Buckley's satire of the Washington public-relations industry. "What do they all say in that book? 'I've got to pay the mortgage.' You know, everybody's got to pay the mortgage."

In another novel, Buckley devoted a chapter to the exploits of a fictional White House advance man named Leslie R. Dach. "His motto was 'Get the fuck out of my way,'" Buckley writes of Dach, "Leslie was serene in his contempt for fools, a category which in his view included most of humanity."

Buckley borrowed Dach's name from an actual Leslie Dach, who was his roommate at Yale, and who, thirty years later, remains a close friend. The real Dach also worked in Presidential politics— first as an advance man for Senator Edward Kennedy in his failed run for the nomination in 1980, and, later, as communications director for Michael Dukakis's campaign in 1988 (a campaign that is still recalled for the moment when Dukakis was photographed, and ridiculed for, wearing a helmet as he rode in a tank). Today, Dach is Wal-Mart's executive vice-president for corporate affairs and government relations. Last year, Lee Scott hired Dach away from Edelman, where, among other duties, he was vice-chairman, and where he managed the Wal-Mart account. "Fresh from his triumph in staging Michael Dukakis's tank ride, it's on to Bentonville," Buckley said to me earlier this month. When I mentioned Buckley's comment to Dach, he demurred: "I was thousands of miles away in my office at that famous moment."

Dach, who is fifty-two, is the son of Holocaust survivors and grew up in Queens. He is wiry, with wavy graying hair and a pointed sense of humor—an improbable addition to the ranks of Wal-Mart's senior managers. He is not as impolitic as his fictional counterpart, although Buckley told me that Dach's friends are "bemused that he ended up in public relations, because, roughly speaking, he was the least tactful person on the planet.'"

Upon graduating from Yale, Dach worked for a time for the National Audubon Society, and then for the Environmental Defense Fund, and he became involved in Democratic politics. (He has worked in seven Presidential campaigns.) After the 1988 race, the public-relations expert John Scanlon, who was volunteering on the Dukakis campaign, recommended Dach to Edelman. He went to work there and stayed for seventeen years, interrupted quadrennially for campaigns. In 2000, he managed the program at the Democratic National Convention for the Gore campaign. At Edelman, he did public relations for a range of corporate interests, along with Michael Deaver, Ronald Reagan's former image-maker, who also works for Edelman in Washington.

One of Dach's first big clients was Starkist, a division of Heinz, which was being accused by environmentalists of slaughtering dolphins during tuna harvests. Richard Edelman told me that Dach worked to bring the two sides together, and helped create the dolphin-safe tuna campaign. Dach maintained his ties with the environmental movement throughout his career at Edelman. In 1995, he helped to plan a seminar for petroleum-industry executives on ways to counter the bad publicity that comes with oil spills, while at the same time serving on the board of the National Audubon Society.

Ethical ambidexterity is no barrier to success in the public-relations field, particularly in Washington. Many prominent Democrats spend the years between national elections representing corporate clients: the political consultant Carter Eskew, who has worked for such Democratic politicians as Al Gore and Christopher Dodd, also worked for the tobacco industry; Mike McCurry, the former Clinton White House press secretary, represents the telecommunications industry in its fight against, among others, Democratic bloggers on issues of Internet access. Democrats and Republicans frequently come together to build bipartisan lobbying firms that seek corporate clients; Clinton's onetime counsel Jack Quinn, who had as a client the international fugitive Marc Rich, for whom he helped arrange a Presidential pardon, built a successful firm with Ed Gillespie, the former Republican National Committee chairman.

Dach and Edelman have been innovators in their field. A press release issued in 2000 outlines a strategy that Dach has used repeatedly to good effect. "You've got an environmental disaster on your hands," the document reads. "Have you consulted with Greenpeace in developing your crisis response plan? Co-opting your would-be attackers may seem counterintuitive, but it makes sense when you consider that N.G.O.s (non-governmental organizations) are trusted by the public nearly two to one to 'do what's right' compared with government bodies, media organizations and corporations." The document goes on to describe Amnesty International, the Sierra Club, and the World Wildlife Fund as "brands" that the public believes "do what's right."

Edelman's co-option policy may already be on display at Wal-Mart. Greenpeace has talked with the company about the issue of environmentally sound product packaging, and earlier this year Lee Scott joined Andy Stern, the leader of the Service Employees International Union, in a coalition of businesses and unions calling for quality health care to be made available to all Americans by 2012. Stern, whose union pays for the activities of a group called Wal-Mart Watch, which regularly criticizes the company, told me he did not believe that he had been co-opted by Wal-Mart, but his allies in the labor movement weren't so sure. "Anyone who wants to take health-care lessons from Wal-Mart," Chris Kofinis, of Wake Up Wal-Mart, said, "needs to have a serious reality check." Government-sponsored universal health coverage would, of course, free Wal-Mart and other companies of the burden of providing health insurance for their employees.

Dach declined to take credit for Wal-Mart's foray into the health-care-policy debate, but Richard Edelman suggested that he is seeing Dach's influence on the company. Edelman called Dach an "idealist" who has carried to Wal-Mart his fervor for such traditional Democratic causes as universal health care and environmentalism. "I feel very strongly that Leslie Dach is making a very real contribution to Wal-Mart," he said. "When he left, I didn't get weepy, but I said, 'Go and make a great contribution.'"

Wal-Mart, in turn, is making a great contribution to Dach: he was given three million dollars in stock and a hundred and sixty-eight thousand stock options, in addition to an undisclosed base salary. He and his wife, a nutritionist, recently bought a $2.7-million house in the Cleveland Park neighborhood of Washington. He commutes to Bentonville during the week, to an apartment furnished out of a Wal-Mart store.

Dach's decision to join Wal-Mart has brought him, by his own admission, some mockery, most recently at a seventy-fifth birthday party for his former boss Edward Kennedy. (Dach said that, for each person who teased him, "two others asked if they could do business with us.") It has also strained relations with some friends. Joseph Sellers, a prominent civil-rights lawyer who is one of the lead attorneys in the Wal-Mart sex-discrimination lawsuit, said that his relationship with Dach has become awkward. "There's no question that his profession views reality as malleable," Sellers said. "I'm in the reality business."

Even Andy Stern, the president of the service-employees' union, who maintains a diplomatic relationship with Lee Scott, suggested that Dach is a turncoat. Lee Scott, he said, pursues harsh labor policies but is not a hypocrite about it, while Dach, an ostensible progressive, has, by declaring his allegiance to Bentonville, abandoned core principles of Democratic activism. "I would respect him if he said, 'Listen, I'm just trying to get rich,'" Stern told me. "If that was your goal, you did really well. If your goal is to say you're a progressive, then you're full of it."

In a recent conversation, Dach wanted to emphasize that he was not doing this for the money. He added, "I think I've been a person who has cared about issues over my entire professional career, and through seven Presidential campaigns I've tried to make a difference in my own limited way, and I firmly believe Wal-Mart's core proposition of saving people money so they live better, working on sustainability, being part of the solution, moving these policies forward."

Dach knows how to divert an unfriendly question with a flood of words, few of which address the subject at hand. I asked him whether it was moral for a self-styled progressive Democrat to work for a company that, among other things, maintains a mobile squad of union busters who can be dispatched by corporate jet to any store that gives off the faintest rumblings of union activity.

"I think that, first of all, morality is not the right language," he said. "I think the more than one hundred and thirty million people who shop at Wal-Mart each week, who are saving money so they can live a better life, who save money there, they'd be insulted by that frame. Some of these issues are complex, and the debates are complex."

Like the best P.R. men, Dach seems to find joy in spin. One day, while we were having lunch in the Wal-Mart cafeteria, I asked him why all the televisions in the building seemed to be tuned to Fox News. The television in the main lobby was on Fox, as were the televisions in the P.R. wing of the building and in the cafeteria, including one that was ten feet from his head.

"Is that true?" he said. After I assured him that it was, he said, "What about in the mornings? Do you know if they're on Fox in the mornings?"

Such matters, he said, are sideshows. The important thing, he told me, is that Wal-Mart is making changes that even the most loyal Democrat would have to acknowledge are beneficial to the working poor and to the environment. Dach mentioned Wal-Mart's newly instituted plan to provide its customers with generic drugs for four dollars a prescription. The program has been a success, even though, so far, a relatively small number of drugs—about three hundred—are on the four-dollar list. The program is being marketed as a way for Wal-Mart to "give back to the community," as Dach put it. It, too, has its critics. Charlie Sewell, a senior vice-president of the National Community Pharmacists Association, a lobbying group, called the Wal-Mart plan a "classic bait-and-switch," adding that most of the drugs on the list are older, less prescribed drugs.

Wal-Mart's executive vice-president responsible for pharmacies, Bill Simon, told me that the company is making large profits on the program. "It's not like these are twenty-dollar items that we're selling for four dollars as a loss leader," he said. By applying the Wal-Mart model to the generic-drug industry—pressuring manufacturers to sell to Wal-Mart for less—Simon said, the company has been able to make "more money" in pharmaceuticals "than we made last year." Wal-Mart's cost for some generics, he said, is as low as thirty-two cents. Not far from Simon's office is a wall covered with exhortations to the company's workers. One reads, "If you aren't working on sales or the things that enhance the profitability of this company, then you are working on the wrong things."

The generic-drug program has taken some public pressure off the company on the subject of its medical benefits. According to one study, Wal-Mart spends an average of thirty-five hundred dollars per employee per year on health benefits; the average for the retail industry over all is forty-eight hundred dollars. Recently, the company offered employees a "value plan" for health insurance, at a monthly premium as low as eleven dollars in some areas. But a family on the plan would have a three-thousand-dollar deductible, which would make it functionally unaffordable to a worker making seventeen thousand dollars a year. When I asked Linda Dillman, the company's vice-president for benefits, about this potential financial strain, she said, "Well, that's the problem we all have." Dillman was a strong defender of Wal-Mart's benefits plan, and said that the Susan Chambers memo that called for Wal-Mart to cease hiring unhealthy people had been misinterpreted. "The fact that we have to apologize because we want our associates to be healthier is absurd to me," she said.

At the core of Dach's campaign to prove that Wal-Mart is changing is the new "green" campaign—the company's efforts to cut fuel and electricity consumption and make its stores eco-friendly. The green campaign has won some important allies. John Flicker, the president of the National Audubon Society, told me that he is pleased to see Dach at Wal-Mart: "He truly believes in the cause, and at a company the size of Wal-Mart he can truly make a difference." Dach gives credit to Wal-Mart. "All of this began way before I got here," he told me. "The passion for change is widespread throughout the company. I'm just a helper."

As part of the green campaign, Wal-Mart has committed itself to cutting the fuel consumption of its truck fleet, the second-largest in America, and to reducing its electricity bill—Wal-Mart is one of the largest private consumers of electricity in the world—by twenty per cent in the next five years. Dach arranged for me to visit a recently opened Supercenter near Bentonville that was built to conserve energy.

For any number of reasons, this Wal-Mart seemed different from other Wal-Marts I'd been to. The prices were still low, but the workers appeared to be more enthusiastic, and I was impressed, in particular, by the store's environmental innovations. Skylights allowed so much natural illumination that the fluorescent lights were switched off. The lights in the vast freezers were controlled by motion sensors, so they switched on only if someone walked nearby. "In this store alone, we'll save more than a hundred thousand dollars in electricity this year," Charles Zimmerman, a Wal-Mart vice-president who showed me around, said. "What we're trying to do is make sustainability sustainable," Dach said.

Even doubters in the environmental movement acknowledge that Wal-Mart is attempting to lower its energy consumption. "The energy-efficiency piece of this is real," Carl Pope, the executive director of the Sierra Club, told me. "They will deliver on it. But it's a straight-out business call." Pope, who worked with Dach while he was at Audubon—"He was very good at what he did," he said— is now a member of the coalition that makes up Wal-Mart Watch. "The third and by far the most intriguing initiative is that they're going to green their supply chain"—to press their more than sixty thousand suppliers to embrace conservation as well. "They, and perhaps only they, have the market power to do it," Pope said. "It will be phenomenally important if they actually did it."

Pope acknowledged that Wal-Mart's liberalizing environmental strategy will win it new supporters, but he is skeptical of the company's motives. "You can't be a good progressive and support Wal-Mart because Wal-Mart is saving money on energy—that's all they've done so far," he said. On Dach, he was acerbic: "One of the remarkable things about the environmental movement is how rarely people from our side end up on the other side, and Leslie is on the other side."

Environmentalists, he said, should not be swayed by cost savings alone. "You can't say that they have a good business model. Their model is efficient. Henry Ford used efficiency to raise standards, to bring his workers into the middle class. Wal-Mart has that choice. Their game is to say that there's no other way to be efficient. But they've driven down wages across the retail industry, and they don't have to, in order to be profitable." Pope cited Costco, the chief rival to Sam's Club, Wal-Mart's membership warehouse. "Costco pays their workers well"—the average wage at Costco is $17.46 an hour—"and we know they're profitable."

Mona Williams, the chief spokeswoman for Wal-Mart, disagreed. When she was asked why the company could not simply give two-dollar-per-hour across-the-board raises to its store employees, her reply was free of obfuscation. "Wal-Mart's profit per associate is six thousand four hundred dollars," she said. "If we were to pay two dollars more an hour to associates, that would cut four thousand dollars out of our per-employee profit. If anybody ever stopped to do the math, they'd see this. It would take two-thirds of the profit if we gave everyone two dollars more." She added, "You could raise prices, but what about the woman who is shopping for Easter shoes for her kids? We can't raise prices on her."

Dach told me, "Wal-Mart pays competitive wages everywhere we have a store or club. We're one of the only companies to support an increase in the federal minimum wage. We have many more applicants than we have jobs, and we have more than one million people on our health care."

Dach, whose 1988 candidate for President, Michael Dukakis, called for "good jobs at good wages," said that "it's too early to tell" if he will work on the 2008 campaign. (He would not say which candidate he favored, or whether he would remain on the Wal-Mart payroll.) The company, Dach said, is handing out political donations in a more "evenhanded" manner now than it did before his arrival.

"It was very smart of Wal-Mart to appoint him to this job," Kenneth Adelman, the former Reagan Administration arms-control official and one of Dach's former colleagues at Edelman, said. "He's brilliant at what he does. He's a great advocate for Democratic causes." Each election year, Adelman recalled, he and Dach would stage a mock debate before employees in the Edelman office. "It would always start out seriously, and then get funny," he said. "I would argue the Republican line, and Leslie played the part of the Democrat."

Discussion and Writing Questions

1. Goldberg provides many examples of criticisms of Wal-Mart's public relations, specifically by Democrats. How does the article present the political agenda(s) of Wal-Mart? Is Wal-Mart's political agenda aligned with only one political party?

2. Goldberg provides several instances in his article where the motivations of Wal-Mart are questioned. However, the sustainability projects of Wal-Mart are presented as valid changes in Wal-Mart's business practices. Mona Williams claims both of these agendas help the lower and middle classes. Do they? Explain your thoughts on this complex issue of class and corporate agenda in an informal essay.

Intertextual Question

3. Goldberg provides readers with the salaries and bonuses of several key Wal-Mart executives. In comparison, he discusses the wages and benefits of Wal-Mart associates. What connections can you make between Goldberg's discussion and Ehrenreich's discussion in "Maid to Order" about the wages and benefits paid to Wal-Mart associates and maids?

CHAPTER 3

Business Practices

Virtually every human society develops, early on, some form of the Golden Rule: Treat others as you wish to be treated. It's not a bad rule to live by, really, but it isn't necessarily a good formula for successful operation in a capitalist society. In the competitive marketplace of capitalism, someone must always win—make more money, own more goods, open more stores, sell more software, and so on. But *winning*, by definition, can happen only if someone else loses—makes less money, owns fewer goods, opens fewer stores, sells less software. And the loser in capitalism faces tough realities: Go out of business or learn to live with less success than someone else.

Competition in the capitalist world is an example of that proverbial dog-eat-dog world, an economic manifestation of Darwinism at its best or worst. By its very nature, the situations of capitalist competition, of winners and losers, lead to difficult ethical decisions. The readings in Chapter 3 map out the boundaries of ethical and unethical business practices in America—or moral, immoral, and amoral business practices.

When Morgan Spurlock showed, in *Super Size Me*, that eating too much too often from McDonald's restaurants caused everything from lethargy to liver failure, Americans were shocked but not particularly surprised. The percentage of meals eaten at home versus the percentage of meals eaten at restaurants has steadily skewed in the favor of restaurants for fifty years—a skewing accelerated only as fast-food restaurants became both more common and less costly than non-chain competitors. But the franchise model works for businesses other than eateries, including such economic ventures as check cashing and payday advance "stores"—private businesses offering freakishly high interest rates on small loans (in the sort of usury that brought down Shakespeare's Shylock).

While the readings in Chapter 3 consider both fast food and fast finance, they stretch to include a range of business practices, ethical and otherwise. These practices include the constant "branding" of American culture, where advertisements now grace everything from the backs of city busses to the backs of professional wrestlers. Two especially common and overlooked business practices are interrogated within this mix: the use (and abuse) of automated phone systems and the use (and abuse) of the term-of-service (TOS) agreements that accompany computer games and online interactive venues such as Facebook. Few gamers or Facebookers read a word of the TOS before clicking "I Agree" . . . and they might be surprised to learn what they're agreeing to.

Readers familiar with Chapters 1 and 2 will recognize some familiar topics: the Internet and fast food, mega-corporations, and marketing. Questions raised in relation to earlier readings—questions you may feel you've answered satisfactorily—may now become uncomfortable again. Does it matter that fast-food companies market their products in ways that gloss over their nutritionally questionable (or nutritionally negligible) nature? Does anyone have the right to expect the marketing of a product to say honestly how bad it might be for most consumers?

The answer matters.

Brand Stake Ownership

MICHAEL WHITE

Michael White is the managing director of ITCH, a company created to unite events, production, and design. ITCH has helped clients like Virgin Media and the NFL. This article was published in the Experimental Essays section of Marketing, *a marketing Web site based out of the United Kingdom. "Brand Stake Ownership" was part of a series of essays contributed by leaders at experiential marketing agencies. In the following essay, White describes the impact he believes experiential marketing is able to create for his clients.*

Prereading Question

What comes to mind when you think of the word *experiential*? What associations do you have with this word? How would you define it?

───────────── ◆ ─────────────

Where do you begin with a word like experiential? The trick used to be for companies to submerge their brand into a consumer experience. Brands were almost apologetic about the events and activities they were bank-rolling, as if to say 'we shouldn't really be here so we're not going to intrude on your free time or your experience, and we're certainly not going to try to sell you anything'.

This nervous attitude may, in part, have stemmed from the approach of 'badging' an existing event and having little control over the consumer's experience, or not wanting to invade with an overtly commercial platform as part of their activity.

The consumer 'experiential' campaign box was one that needed to be ticked but couldn't be measured or evaluated, apart from the perception that it was cool and somehow added to the brand DNA. It usually delivered low numbers and made little impact.

However, as the rest of the below-the-line marketing world moves further toward advertiser-funded content, with digital downloads, mobile applications and online content, so an overtly branded presence at an event has also become acceptable, particularly if it adds value. Consumers now seem to actively embrace brands as part of their entertainment experience. Indeed, some look for the endorsement and assurance that a brand with which they are comfortable provides.

Brands now have confidence in their own identity to replicate or replace the entertainment provider roles, be it music promoter, record label or broadcaster.

As a result, commercial opportunities have grown exponentially for brands with the confidence to communicate aggressively at their events. This brave new world is a model that companies are rapidly embracing as consumers have grown to accept that brands and events are now inextricably linked.

Companies now view their entertainment platforms as viable commercial sellers; Virgin was one of the first to recognise this with the overtly branded V Festival that communicates as much about the brand as any of the bands on stage.

ITCH works closely with Virgin's sponsorship team to create multiple touch points across site. There are Virgin 'Angels' to help campers carry their tents and we provide useful things such as recharge points for their phones.

We ensure we link everything back to the phones as well through 'Text the Fest', an interactive messaging service on the main stage. There's also an opportunity to download performance times. Finally, there is the chance to swap to a free Virgin SIM, and even buy a handset.

Once a company has embraced experiential as a commercial opportunity, it reviews these events with the same critical eye as all of its other retail and marketing activities. How can we maximise the marketing opportunity and create commercial opportunities?

Where once companies were limited to the people who turned up on the day, now media fragmentation and new media opportunities can deliver the kind of numbers that a promoter could previously only dream about.

Consumers happily download live music as well as watch heavily branded TV shows. Meanwhile Second Life, the virtual world, recently created a virtual festival as part of a campaign with *The Guardian*. In effect an extension of the newspaper's Glastonbury work, the activity delivered significant audience figures.

These opportunities have now elevated 'experiential' activity to marketing's top table. At ITCH, we are now being brought into planning meetings much earlier and being used to help develop client marketing strategies. Experiential now delivers the same kind of numbers and ROI as advertising, and is evaluated and quantified by similar criteria.

Indeed, brand tracking for one of our clients even showed that an event compared favourably against its TV campaign. Long live brand engagement.

Discussion and Writing Questions

1. White compares the way brands are using experiential marketing to how promoters sell music bands. Do you think this is an accurate comparison?
2. White describes experiential marketing as an immersion of the brand in the experience of an event, such as a concert. He contrasts this with "badging," which, he says, takes a less invasive approach to marketing. Do you think that experiential marketing is particularly suited to certain products or companies, such as Virgin marketing phones? Is badging better suited for other products? Explain your conclusions in a brief essay.

Intertextual Question

3. The branding that experiential marketing creates for a product can be powerful. How does this approach to selling a product compare to the approach of selling the image of Wal-Mart as discussed in Goldberg's essay, "Selling Wal-Mart"?

Do You Want Lies with That?
MORGAN SPURLOCK

Morgan Spurlock is best known for his documentary film, Super Size Me, *in which he reported the consequences of consuming McDonald's food for three meals a day for one month. Spurlock is an independent film director, TV producer, screenwriter, and playwright. He graduated with a BFA in film from New York University's Tisch School of the Arts in 1993. In the first chapter of his book,* Don't Eat This Book, *Spurlock examines the ways in which Americans are influenced by advertising and the personal and corporate responsibilities.*

Prereading Question

In his article, Spurlock describes how increases in advertising for the automobile industry have coincided with increases in the number of automobiles in the United States. Do you think your buying habits are influenced by advertising? Why or why not?

◆

DO YOU WANT LIES WITH THAT?

Don't do it. Please. I know this book looks delicious, with its light-weight pages sliced thin as prosciutto and swiss, stacked in a way that would make Dagwood salivate. The scent of freshly baked words wafting up with every turn of the page: *Mmmm*, page. But don't do it. Not yet. Don't eat this book.

We turn just about everything you can imagine into food. You can eat coins, toys, cigars, cigarettes, rings, necklaces, lips, cars, babies, teeth, cameras, film, even underwear (which come in a variety of scents, sizes, styles and flavors). Why not a book?

In fact, we put so many things in our mouths, we constantly have to be reminded what *not* to eat. Look at that little package of silicon gel that's inside your new pair of sneakers. It says DO NOT EAT for a reason. Somewhere, sometime, some genius bought a pair of sneakers and said, "Ooooh, look. They give you free mints with the shoes!"—soon followed, no doubt, by the lawsuit charging the manufacturer with negligence, something along the lines of, "Well, it didn't say *not* to eat those things."

And thus was born the "warning label." To avoid getting sued, corporate America now labels everything. Thank the genius who first decided to take a bath and blow-dry her hair at the same time. The Rhodes scholar who first reached down into a running garbage disposal. That one-armed guy down the street who felt around under his power mower while it was running.

Yes, thanks to them, blow-dryers now come with the label DO NOT SUBMERGE IN WATER WHILE PLUGGED IN. Power mowers warn KEEP HANDS AND FEET AWAY FROM MOVING BLADES. And curling irons bear tags that read FOR EXTERNAL USE ONLY.

And that's why I warn you—please!—do not eat this book. This book is FOR EXTERNAL USE ONLY. Except maybe as food for thought.

We live in a ridiculously litigious society. Opportunists know that a wet floor or a hot cup of coffee can put them on easy street. Like most of you, I find many of these lawsuits pointless and friv-olous. No wonder the big corporations and the politicians they own have been pushing so hard for tort reform.

Fifty years ago it was a different story. Fifty years ago, adult human beings were presumed to have enough sense not to stick their fingers in whirring blades of steel. And if they did, that was their own fault.

Take smoking. For most of us, the idea that "smoking kills" is a given. My mom and dad know smoking is bad, but they don't stop. My grandfather smoked all the way up until his death at a grand old age, and my folks are just following in his footsteps—despite the terrifying warning on every pack.

They're not alone, of course. It's estimated that over a billion people in the world are smokers. Worldwide, roughly 5 million people died from smoking in 2000. Smoking kills 440,000 Americans every year. All despite that surgeon general's warning on every single pack.

What is going on here? It's too easy to write off all billion-plus smokers as idiots with a death wish. My parents aren't idiots. I don't think they want to die. (When I was younger, there were times when I wanted to kill them, but that's different.) We all know that tobacco is extremely addictive. And that the tobacco companies used to add chemicals to make cigarettes even more addictive, until they got nailed for it. And that for several generations—again, until they got busted for it—the big tobacco companies aimed their marketing and advertising at kids and young people. Big Tobacco spent billions of dollars to get people hooked as early as they could, and to keep them as "brand-loyal" slaves for the rest of their unnaturally shortened lives. Cigarettes were cool, cigarettes were hip, cigarettes were sexy. Smoking made you look like a cowboy or a movie starlet.

And it worked. When my parents were young, everybody smoked. Doctors smoked. Athletes smoked. Pregnant women smoked. Their kids came out of the womb looking around the delivery room for an ashtray to ash their Lucky Strikes. Everyone smoked.

The change began in 1964, when the first surgeon general's warning about smoking and cancer scared the bejesus out of everybody. In 1971, cigarette ads were banned from TV, and much later they disappeared from billboards. Little by little, smoking was restricted in airplanes and airports, in public and private workplaces, in restaurants and bars. Tobacco sponsorship of sporting events decreased. Tighter controls were placed on selling cigarettes to minors. Everyone didn't quit overnight, but overall rates of smoking began to decrease—from 42 percent of adults in 1965 to 23 percent in 2000, and from 36 percent of high school kids in 1997 to 29 percent in 2001. The number of adults who have never smoked more than doubled from 1965 to 2000.

Big tobacco companies knew it was a war they couldn't win, but they didn't give up without a fight. They threw billions and billions of more dollars into making smoking look cool, hip, sexy—and safe. They targeted new markets, like women, who increased their rate of smoking 400 percent *after* the surgeon general's report. Yeah, you've come a long way, baby—all the way from the kitchen to the cancer ward. They expanded their markets in the Third World and undeveloped nations, getting hundreds of millions of people hooked; it's estimated that more than four out of five current smokers are in developing countries. As if people without a regular source of drinking water didn't have enough to worry about already. Big Tobacco denied the health risks of smoking, lied about what they were putting into cigarettes and lobbied like hell against every government agency or legislative act aimed at curbing their deadly impact.

Which brings me back to those "frivolous" lawsuits. Back when people were first suing the tobacco companies for giving them cancer, a lot of folks scoffed. (And coughed. But they still scoffed.) Smokers knew the dangers of smoking, everyone said. If they decided to keep smoking for thirty, forty years and then got lung cancer, they couldn't blame the tobacco companies.

Then a funny thing happened. As the lawsuits progressed, it became more and more apparent that smokers did *not* know all the dangers of smoking. They couldn't know, because Big Tobacco was hiding the truth from them—lying to them about the health risks, and lying about the additives they were putting in cigarettes to make them more addictive. Marketing cigarettes to children, to get them hooked early and keep them puffing away almost literally from the cradle to the early grave, among other nefarious dealings.

In the mid-1990s, shouldering the crushing burden of soaring Medicare costs due to smoking-related illnesses, individual states began to imitate those "ambulance-chasers," bringing their own class-action lawsuits against Big Tobacco. In 1998, without ever explicitly admitting to any wrongdoing, the big tobacco companies agreed to a massive $246 billion settlement, to be paid to forty-fix states and five territories over twenty-five years. (The other four states had already settled in individual cases.)

Two hundred and forty-six billion dollars is a whole lot of frivolous, man.

What these lawsuits drove home was the relationship between personal responsibility and corporate responsibility. Suddenly it was apparent that sticking a cigarette in your mouth was not *quite* the same thing as sticking those sneaker mints in your mouth. No one spent billions and billions of dollars in marketing, advertising and promotions telling that guy those sneaker mints would make him cool, hip and sexy. Big Tobacco did exactly that to smokers.

Still, a lot of people were skeptical about those lawsuits. Are the big bad corporations with all their big bad money and big bad mind-altering advertising really so powerful that we as individuals cannot think for ourselves anymore? Are we really so easily swayed by the simplest of pleasant images that we'll jump at the chance to share in some of that glorious, spring-scented, new and improved, because-you-deserve-it goodness, without a thought about what's best for us anymore?

You tell me. Every waking moment of our lives, we swim in an ocean of advertising, all of it telling us the same thing. Consume. Consume. And then consume some more.

In 2003, the auto industry spent $18.2 billion telling us we needed a new car, more cars, bigger cars. Over the last twenty-five years, the number of household vehicles in the United States has doubled. The rate of increase in the number of cars, vans and SUVs for personal travel has been six times the rate of population increase. In fact, according to the Department of Transportation, there are now, for the first time in history, *more cars than drivers* in America. That's ridiculous!

Did we suddenly *need* so many more vehicles? Or were we sold the idea?

We drive everywhere now. Almost nine-tenths of our daily travel takes place in a personal vehicle. Walking, actually using the legs and feet God gave us, accounts for appallingly little of our day-to-day getting around. Even on trips of under one mile, according to the Department of Transportation, we walked only 24 percent of the time in 2001 (and rode a bike under 2 percent). Walking declined by almost half in the two decades between 1980 and 2000. In Los Angeles, you can get arrested for walking. The cops figure if you're not in a car you can't be up to any good. If you're not in a car, you're a vagrant. Same goes for the suburbs, where so many of us now live.

And what do you put inside that SUV, minivan or pickup truck you're driving everywhere, other than your kids? Well, lots of *stuff*, that's what. In 2002, the retail industry in this country spent $13.5 billion telling us what to buy, and we must have been listening, because in 2003 we spent nearly $8 *trillion* on all kinds of crap. That's right, trillion. How insane is that? We are the biggest consuming culture on the planet. We buy almost twice as much crap as our nearest competitor, Japan. We spend more on ourselves than the entire gross national product of any nation in the world.

And all that shopping—whew, has it made us hungry. Every year, the food industry spends around $33 billion convincing us that we're famished. So we all climb back into our giant vehicle filled with all our stuff from Wal-Mart, and we cruise to the nearest fast-food joint. If not McDonald's or Burger King or Taco Bell, then a "fast casual" restaurant like Outback Steakhouse or TGI Friday's or the Olive Garden, where they serve us portions larger than our smallest kid, with the calories to match.

What does all that consumption do for us? Does it make us happy? You tell me. If we were all so happy, would we be on so many drugs? Antidepressant use in the U.S. nearly *tripled* in the past decade. We've got drugs in America we can take for anything: if we're feeling too bad, too good, too skinny, too fat, too sleepy, too wide awake, too unmanly. We've got drugs to counteract the disastrous health effects of all our overconsumption—diet drugs, heart drugs, liver drugs, drugs to make our hair grow back and our willies stiff. In 2003, we Americans spent $227 billion on medications. That's a whole lot of drugs!

This is the power of advertising at work, of billions of hooks that've been cast into our heads in the last thirty years, billions of messages telling us what we want, what we need and what we should do to feel happy. We all buy into it to some degree, because none of us is as young as we'd like to be, or as thin, or as strong.

Yet none of the stuff we consume—no matter how much bigger our SUV is than our neighbor's, no matter how many Whoppers we wolf down, no matter how many DVDs we own or how much Zoloft we take—makes us feel full, or satisfied or happy.

So we consume some more.

And the line between personal responsibility and corporate responsibility gets finer and more blurred. Yes, you're still responsible for your own life, your own health, your own happiness. But your *desires*, the things you *want*, the things you think you *need*—that's all manipulated by corporate advertising and marketing that now whisper and shout and wink at you from every corner of your life—at home, at work, at school, at play.

Consume. Consume. Still not happy? Then you obviously haven't consumed enough.

Like this book, the epidemic of overconsumption that's plaguing the nation begins with the things we put in our mouths. Since the 1960s, everyone has known that smoking kills, but it's only been in the last few years that we've become hip to a new killer, one that now rivals smoking as the leading cause of preventable deaths in America and, if current trends continue, will soon be the leading cause: overeating.

Americans are eating themselves to death.

Discussion and Writing Questions

1. Spurlock repeatedly brings up the question of who is responsible. He asks, what is the relationship between personal responsibility and corporate responsibility? How would you answer this question?
2. Spurlock opens his chapter with a sarcastic plea to the reader not to eat the book. He uses his sarcasm to introduce the ridiculous nature to which warning labels and advertising have gone. How do you think his sarcasm affects your response to his chapter? In an essay, describe a warning label that you have seen on a modern product—cup of coffee, cigarette pack, and so on. What purpose does such a warning serve, beyond the issue of legal responsibility?

Intertextual Question

3. Spurlock describes an increase in consumption bred by advertisers. How does the consumer mania that Spurlock describes fit into the sustainability practices that a corporation like Wal-Mart is trying to employ? Are consumption and sustainability inherently incompatible?

Facebook's Users Ask Who Owns Information

BRIAN STELTER

Brian Stelter, a 2007 graduate of Towson University, has worked in radio and on blogs, in addition to serving as editor-in-chief of the Towerlight, *a student newspaper. Currently, he is a media and technology reporter for the* New York Times. *In the following article, Stelter considers the legal issues virtually ignored by Facebook users who agree to the service's terms-of-service.*

Prereading Question

Studies show, again and again, that Web surfers rarely consider legal issues of privacy and ownership while surfing, creating their own pages, and so on, but such issues matter. In recent years teens who engage in "sexting," for example (the sending of pornographic images via cellular phone and/or sharing such images online), have found themselves targeted by police departments and prosecuting attorneys. When an individual under the age of 18 sends a pornographic image to another individual under 18 (or posts such an image online), this is, legally, the sharing of child pornography—and the punishment involves, by law, huge fines and/or years of imprisonment. This is true even when the teen takes a picture of himself/herself and sends it only to his/her girlfriend/boyfriend. But is this fair? And does the potential punishment fit the crime?

──────────────── ✦ ────────────────

Reacting to an online swell of suspicion about changes to Facebook's terms of service, the company's chief executive moved to reassure users on Monday that the users, not the Web site, "own and control their information."

The online exchanges reflected the uneasy and evolving balance between sharing information and retaining control over that information on the Internet. The subject arose when a consumer advocate's blog shined an unflattering light onto the pages of legal language that many users accept without reading when they use a Web site.

The pages, called terms of service, generally outline appropriate conduct and grant a license to companies to store users' data. Unknown to many users, the terms frequently give broad power to Web site operators.

This month, when Facebook updated its terms, it deleted a provision that said users could remove their content at any time, at which time the license would expire. Further, it added new language that said Facebook would retain users' content and licenses after an account was terminated.

Mark Zuckerberg, the chief executive of Facebook, said in a blog post on Monday that the philosophy "that people own their information and control who they share it with has remained constant." Despite the complaints, he did not indicate the language would be revised.

The changes in the terms of service had gone mostly unnoticed until Sunday, when the blog Consumerist cited them and interpreted them to mean that "anything you upload to Facebook can be used by Facebook in any way they deem fit, forever, no matter what you do later."

Given the widespread popularity of Facebook—by some measurements the most popular social network with 175 million active users worldwide—that claim attracted attention immediately.

The blog post by Consumerist, part of the advocacy group Consumers Union, received more than 300,000 views. Users created Facebook groups to oppose the changes. To some of the thousands who commented online, the changes meant: "Facebook owns you."

Facebook moved swiftly to say it was not claiming to own the material that users upload. It said the terms had been updated to better reflect user behavior—for instance, to acknowledge that when a user deletes an account, any comments the user had posted on a page remain visible.

"We certainly did not—and did not intend—to create any new right or interest for Facebook in users' data by issuing the new terms," said Barry Schnitt, a Facebook spokesman.

Greg Lastowka, an associate professor at the Rutgers School of Law who is writing a book on Internet law, said Facebook's language was not unusual. "Most Web sites today offer terms of service that are designed to protect and further the interests of the company writing the terms, and most people simply agree to terms without reading them."

For Facebook, the ability to store users' data and use their names and images for commercial purposes is important as it seeks to make more money from the virtual interactions of friends.

But balancing the desire for sharing with the need for control remains a challenge for Facebook as it turns five years old this month. "We're at an interesting point in the development of the open online world where these issues are being worked out," Mr. Zuckerberg wrote.

Amid the evolution, at least a few members are showing their uneasiness about the stance that Facebook is taking.

Some members, including Sasha Frere-Jones, the pop critic and staff writer for *The New Yorker*, said they had deleted their accounts to show their opposition to the new terms.

"Zuckerberg's response to the protest is just the modern version of 'Ignore the fine print, ma'am, just sign here,'" Mr. Frere-Jones wrote in an e-mail message. "Why would anyone trust a company with his/her personal information, especially when that company's explicit legal language claims eternal rights to exploit that information, and there is good reason to expect that they will?"

Discussion and Writing Questions

1. How effectively (for you) does Stelter explain the controversy over information and ownership on Facebook? How effectively does he describe this for someone with little knowledge of the Internet and perhaps no knowledge of Facebook?

2. In an essay where you draw both on your own experience and your responses to this article, consider the following: How much control of content must a company such as Facebook exert in order to protect itself from lawsuits? Is the situation the same for other online providers of social networking space (such as dating sites and auction sites)? Does the same need for control extend into gaming, into virtual spaces such as World of Warcraft?

Intertextual Question

3. In what ways does Stelter's argument about Facebook compare and contrast with John Markoff's arguments about the cellular phone in "The Cellphone, Navigating Our Lives"? How has the Internet and the cellular phone affected your life and that of your friends? Do your feelings about these technologies mirror those of Stelter and Markoff? Why?

"But Wait, You Promised . . . "
". . . And You Believed Us? Welcome to the Real World, Ma'am"

CHARLES FISHMAN

Charles Fishman is a poet and writer. He created the Visiting Writers Program at the State University of New York in 1979, cofounded the Long Island Poetry Collective, and was a founding editor of Xanadu magazine and Pleasure Dome Press. He has been a consultant to the U.S. Holocaust Memorial Museum in Washington, D.C. Fishman's poems, essays, reviews, and translations have appeared in more than three hundred journals. In the following essay, Fishman explores the customer service industry and the consequences of technology on the industry.

Prereading Question

Fishman explores how the customer service industry has been affected by changes in technology. How do you think increased access to technology (such as the Internet) has changed customer service? What have been your recent experiences with customer service?

———————— ✦ ————————

I am in the belly of the beast. I have risen early, traveled far, and overcome lines, rudeness, and indifference. Now, heedless of my chances of coming back without serious psychological or physical injury, I am journeying into a swamp that has become a source of boundless irritation, frustration, confusion—even fury—for tens of millions of Americans. I open the door and step into a customer-service call center. And not just any call center either—one that is exclusively devoted to handling problems with cell phones. It's cool inside and fairly well lit, for a swamp. I am carrying the very tool itself: a Sprint PCS cell phone. I love my Sprint PCS cell phone. But God help me when I have to call Sprint PCS. I have sometimes called this very building in Fort Worth, Texas. Often, I'm not even sure that the customer-care advocate I finally speak with after I've been waiting on hold for seventeen minutes even knows what a cell phone is.

I have come here at the beginning of a long journey—really, a quest of the sort that was common in antiquity—during which I will cross the continent several times and seek out both oracles and common folk. I am determined to unravel a central mystery of life in modern America: why is customer service so terrible?

At the Sprint PCS call center, I am soon teamed up with customer-care advocate Chad Ehrlich, a gracious twenty-nine-year-old with years of experience delivering service by phone. Chad takes a call from a businessman in Lubbock, Texas. The man is upset about his bill: It was running $60 to $100 a month. Suddenly, it has shot up to $1,600. "I'm not going to pay it!" the man declares.

Chad is reserved. "Let me take a look at that bill," he says. Chad whirls through screens of information. "Hold on a moment for me, sir; I'm going to get a representative from the fraud department on the line." Chad puts Lubbock on hold and dials Sprint PCS's fraud department, where he reaches a familiar recorded message and is put on hold. Lubbock is on hold for cus-tomer-service rep Chad, and customer-service rep Chad is on hold for more customer service.

A female fraud rep takes Chad's call. She can see from Lub-bock's history that he's complained about this problem before. The conversation between Chad and his colleague in fraud is frisky.

> Fraud: "He thought he was cloned, but he wasn't."
> Chad: "His bills did go from almost nothing to sky-high. . . ."
> Fraud: "We can send him to a cloning specialist and make it 'official' if you want. . . ."
> Chad: "He's denying that he made or received the calls."

The impatient woman from fraud dials the Sprint PCS cloning customer-care department and . . . is put on hold.

Do you ever wonder what's going on while you're waiting on hold for customer service? Really, you couldn't even imagine.

Chad, Lubbock's customer-care advocate, is talking to a woman who is Chad's customer-care advocate. She has called *her* customer-care advocate, who is busy on another call. So now we have two customer-care advocates on hold waiting for a third cus-tomer-care advocate. Meanwhile, a fuming customer from Lub-bock (who may or may not be trying to rip Sprint off for $1,600) waits. On hold.

That, right there, is customer service in the new economy. It has become a slow, dissatisfying tangle of telephones, computers, Web sites, e-mail, and people that wastes time at a prodigious rate, produces far more aggravation than service, and, most often, leaves you feeling impotent. What's even worse is that this situation is a kind of betrayal. It wasn't supposed to be this way. One of the promises of the new economy was that the customer would finally be in charge. We weren't supposed to need to call customer care—but if we did, then someone would take our call quickly. (Why not? No one else would be calling.) A customer-service rep would under-stand our problem practically before we mentioned it, and all would be made right. Everyone believes in delighting the customer.

Don't you spend most of your day delighted? Here's a puz-zler. Why do we hear this sentence so often: "We are experienc-ing higher-than-usual call volumes . . . ." If you're experiencing higher-than-usual call volumes, then why aren't you experienc-ing higher-than-usual *staffing* volumes? How hard is *that*? What the new economy has done to customer service is exactly the opposite of what everyone predicted would happen. And as chaotic a time as it has been to be a customer, it has been a truly weird time to be delivering customer service. Consider just one example: Five years ago, discount broker Charles Schwab had 1,450 customer-service reps in call centers, and 85 percent of those reps' time was spent providing real-time quotes and basic company information, and executing trades. Those 1,450 people, sensing the Internet roaring down on them, were worried about their jobs. Rightfully so. At the end of this past year, Charles Schwab's customers did 81 percent of all of those activities without human assistance. So you would imagine that Schwab could have trimmed its costly battalion of customer-service reps to 1,000, even to 500.

In fact, the number of Schwab reps has tripled to 4,800. But they're not doing what they used to do. Customers have demanded new vistas of service. No one was more surprised than Schwab.

In short, the new economy was supposed to make service better, quicker, and more effective for customers—and easier and cheaper for companies. None of that has come to pass. What happened? I went on a journey to find out.

BOLD PROMISES, BAD RESULTS

AT&T is running television commercials for its Worldnet Internet service. One ad features a series of stand-up comics who are making jokes about the bad customer service of their Internet providers ("My on-line service is like my husband: I stare at it for hours, hoping it will move").

Cisco is running a TV commercial that opens with a regular guy on a cordless phone who hears, "Your call will be answered by the next available operator." Halfway through the commercial, the man has fallen asleep, phone to his ear.

Mockery is a great cultural barometer. Bad customer service is one of the universal—and unifying—experiences of being an American in the twenty-first century. You get it at Wal-Mart. You get it at Lord & Taylor. But is customer service really worse than it used to be? A panel of customer-service experts that I assembled couldn't agree.

Don Peppers, fifty, of the Peppers and Rogers Group, proponent of "customer-relationship management" and coauthor of the famous *One to One Future*: "I don't think that customer service sucks. I think it's bad. But I think it's better than it was five years ago."

Len Schlesinger, forty-eight, an expert in customer service, previously senior associate dean and a professor at Harvard Business School, now executive vice president of The Limited Inc.: "Let's see, we've gone from 'meeting customer expectations,' to 'exceeding customer expectations,' to 'delighting customers,' to 'customer ecstasy.' I hate to see what comes next."

Patricia Seybold, fifty-one, CEO of an e-business consulting company and author of the optimistic book *The Customer Revolution: How to Thrive When Customers Are in Control*, which is due out this month: "I agree that customer service hasn't gotten better since the Internet came along. It has gotten worse. But companies are beginning to realize that we're very angry at them. Companies that don't wake up and pay attention to this are going to be out of business."

Well, we can only hope.

Customer service is a notoriously slippery concept—hard to define, apparently impossible to quantify. But there is one guy who knows for sure what's happening to customer service, because he measures it in 65,000 interviews a year with American customers.

Claes Fornell, fifty-three, is a professor at the University of Michigan Business School and an expert on "the economics of customer satisfaction." Fornell is creator and director of the American Customer Satisfaction Index. The ACSI measures how content Americans are with the goods and services that they consume—in the aggregate, and industry by industry, company by company.

Fornell names names! His on-line data is a carnival for cranky consumers: you can click through and take glee in the lame scores of all of the companies that you love to hate.

First Union, my bank, is down 10.5 percent in satisfaction ratings since the index started in 1994.

Wal-Mart, my source for diapers, paper towels, and Tide, is down 10 percent since the index started and down 4 percent in just the past year alone.

Fornell conceived this herculean undertaking—scores are measured quarterly—because he thought that the U.S. economy was being severely mismeasured. "Eighty percent of GDP is service now," he says. "We have to behave as though we live in a service economy."

The ACSI measures the perceived quality of U.S. economic output—the experience of being a consumer in the United States. In the past five years, the ACSI is down from 73.7 to 72.9. But that number includes everything from Whirlpool appliances to the experience of shopping on Amazon.com.

Here's the amazing thing: every measured company in the appliance, beer, car, clothing, food, personal-care, shoe, and soft-drink industries is above the national average. Even the cigarette companies have above-average customer-satisfaction ratings.

Not so for airlines, banks, department stores, fast-food outlets, hospitals, hotels, and phone companies.

It's the service that's bad.

"Oh, I think we can say that for sure," says Fornell.

THE HARD TRUTH(S) ABOUT CUSTOMER SERVICE

I didn't begin my journey through the service jungle at Sprint PCS by accident, or because I think that the company would be a good target for mockery. Sprint PCS is a pure New Economy company. It offers nothing but service—and it's digital wireless service to boot. The company's only product is moving voices through the air. The first time that you could have made a Sprint PCS call was December 1996. From a standing start, in four years the company has grown to 28,328 employees (10,000 in customer care), 9.8 million customers, and annual revenues of roughly $6 billion. Sprint PCS signs up 10,000 new customers each day.

The company has access to every conceivable technological helper: the Net, automated phone services, and the most-sophisticated call centers. And yet my own experience dealing with Sprint PCS has been consistently aggravating. In eight years of having BellSouth provide our home service, I've had occasion to talk to them only three or four times. I've talked to Sprint PCS more than that since Halloween—always with unhappy results.

Sprint PCS knows the right thing to do. It just can't do it. Faerie Kizzire, fifty-one, senior vice president for Sprint PCS, is in charge of customer service for the company. She's a veteran: she spent nine years at Sprint managing customer service for the long-distance business, then managed customer service for a health-insurance company, and was wooed back to Sprint to create customer care for wireless.

I tell her the story of a call I have just listened to with Chad: Marlene in Ohio has had to call three times just to get a credit for charges that shouldn't have been on her bill in the first place. Before Chad, two customer-care advocates dealt with Marlene by simply telling her that she was wrong. As Chad discovers, Marlene was in fact improperly charged. So why did that happen? Why did two customer-service reps argue with Marlene, rather than credit her? Why does Marlene know more about her calling plan than customer care does?

Kizzire is disappointed. "The complexity of the product and the variations in the product can make that kind of problem very difficult," she says. "We do see some of our people falling on the side of 'I'm right' versus 'I'm going to make it right.'"

Sprint PCS looks as if it's doing all of the right things. The company's training program for reps is six to ten weeks long. Across the call center are exhortations to good service: "Did you dazzle your customers today?" Says Kizzire: "It is true that people who have a little bit of knowledge can be dangerous. We always say, Don't try to dazzle the customer with what you know. These days, many customers have years of experience."

And therein lies a clue to what's really happening to customer service—and why. The secret about customer service in the new economy isn't that it's bad—everyone *knows* it's bad. The secret is that it's harder to deliver good customer service than ever before. Why? Technology, especially in its early days, is always hard. No surprise there. Why would we expect companies that can't figure out how to run a phone center—talking to real people about problems is their own business—to be really good at using advanced technology to automate the process of taking care of us?

And customers are more demanding. We want good service, quickly. We don't wait at gas pumps, we're antsy in ATM lines, and we pay to FedEx things to avoid standing in line at the post office. Companies have created, nursed, and benefited from this impatience. We are victims of it in our own lives. They are victims of it too. It makes providing customer service brutally unforgiving.

Technology has, in fact, made some things quicker and easier, and it has allowed us to take care of ourselves. I can plunge through the details of my on-line bank statement more thoroughly in fifty seconds than any automated voice-mail system could permit in fifty minutes, or than even the most patient phone operator would tolerate. This means that when we talk to someone in person, either things are really screwed up or we are really angry and want to share that anger with a person. Or both. Technology has made the actual person-to-person customer service of big companies much more complicated and demanding.

Despite all of the consultants, gurus, and outsource providers, customer service is hard to deliver in a mass economy. I wasn't on the phones at Sprint PCS for more than a couple of hours, and I can see that the real problem isn't customer service or even culture. No, the real problem is more fundamental: Sprint PCS offers a simple service that is really very complicated. Best tip-off? It takes someone fifteen minutes to sell me a phone and a calling plan in a Sprint PCS store. It takes Faerie Kizzire six weeks— 240 hours—to teach a phone rep to handle any problems that I might have with that phone.

SOME GOOD NEWS: WHAT'S THE 411?

My favorite example of New Economy meltdown is directory assistance. Directory assistance should be the perfect New Economy product: it's just information—and simple information at that. There is an existing way to bill customers, and, given the swift accumulation of databases, directory assistance should be getting better and better all the time.

"It's gotten so much worse," says customer-service expert Patricia Seybold. "Now you get the wrong number all the time."

I've kept track during the past two months. Over several dozen calls, directory assistance delivered the wrong number about half of the time. Of course, you get charged for the wrong numbers, just as you do for the right numbers. If it's a long-distance number and it's wrong, you pay for that phone call too. As if that weren't enough, here's a moment of customer delight: call directory assistance and try to get a credit for a wrong number.

"I'm sorry, sir," says the abrupt operator. "We don't give credits."

"I beg your pardon?"

"We don't give credits, sir. You have to call your local phone company. When your phone bill comes."

"At the end of the month?"

"Correct, sir. Is there a number you need?"

So now I've paid once for the wrong number and paid again to be told that I have to call some other company, some other time, to get my $2 back.

Yet one company gives delightful directory assistance—polite, accurate, helpful. It is none other than . . . Sprint PCS. The contrast between cellular directory and landline directory is as dramatic as the contrast between Sprint PCS directory and Sprint PCS customer care. Ask Sprint PCS for a restaurant's number and they offer to make a reservation. Ask for the number of a movie theater and they offer to read you not just the number but also the movies that are playing at that theater, when they are playing, and who is starring in each movie.

Seybold was able to guess exactly what was going on immediately. "It's outsourced," she said.

And so it is. Metro One Telecommunications, a small company based in Beaverton, Oregon, handles directory assistance for Sprint PCS—and also for Nextel and many regional cellular companies. The quality of Metro One's service is no accident. As Seybold predicted, that is exactly what it is selling to cellular companies: *good* directory assistance.

The economics are great for everyone: even at what feels like an unhurried pace, Metro One's operators take fifty calls an hour (including breaks, slow periods, and training), which brings in $50 an hour. Half of that goes to Metro One; half is gravy to Sprint PCS. Of the $25 an hour that Metro One gets, operators start at some centers at $9 an hour in straight salary—before incentive pay or benefits. Me, as a customer? I get the right number, for about what BellSouth's wrong numbers cost me.

Metro One has twenty-nine deliberately small call centers: 200 operators or fewer, with 100 or fewer working at any one time. The call center in Charlotte, North Carolina, is lean—spartan compared to Sprint PCS's Fort Worth center. But you can understand the entire place in a single glance. Directory assistance, of course, is child's play compared to helping people with their cell phones. But remember: standard directory assistance is abysmal.

Heather McCuen, twenty-three, started at Metro One in March 1999, and after nine months she makes $12 an hour. Calls cascade in on her like a waterfall. "Leith Mercedes." "Larry's Plant Farm." "Start-to-Finish Tattoo Shop." "Just What the Doctor Ordered Restaurant."

"I'm amazed at what people name their businesses," Heather says.

In eleven minutes, she takes seventeen calls—38.8 seconds a call. Heather's style is efficient but deliberate. She reads the number slowly to avoid having to repeat it.

What is striking is how little it takes to make people happy, how little it takes to get it right, and how long forty seconds really is. But what is also striking is how hard it would be to automate this process. To do it right doesn't require much, but it does require a spark of human intelligence on both ends of the transaction.

Even in these brief encounters, the full range of human character is on display. "I'm looking for Shanon Pickering," says a man over a characteristically crackly connection. The Charlotte center serves mainly North Carolina and South Carolina, so the operators are familiar with local geography, but Heather and her colleagues can provide numbers nationwide. Heather patiently searches a couple of the towns that the man mentions, without luck.

"I found someone's day planner in the middle of the road," the man says. "I'm just trying to return it to her." Heather ups her intensity a notch. She broadens her search to all of North Carolina, South Carolina, and Virginia. She tries a variety of spellings for the names. Heather tells the man what she is trying. She is regretful. The man is regretful. The call spills past two minutes. No luck.

Metro One's databases are updated with fresh numbers in real time, all the time. Operators can send along complaints about wrong numbers. All kinds of searches are available. I saw one operator find a particularly elusive residential number by reading through a list of every person who lived on a street.

The Baby Bells shoot for directory calls lasting seventeen to twenty seconds, total, compared to Metro One's thirty-three-second standard. That, of course, is the difference. And as trivial as it may sound—what's fifteen seconds?—companies know how to do the multiplication. At least, they know how to do it when it's their fifteen seconds.

Metro One's Charlotte center handles roughly 275,000 calls a week. The math is easy. If each call lasts thirty-three seconds, as it does at Metro One, then 275,000 calls require 2,520 hours of operator time. If each call lasts twenty seconds, as it does at Bell-South, then 275,000 calls require only 1,528 hours of operator time.

It takes 50 percent more people to do it the Metro One way. To do it right.

SECRETS OF THE AMAZON

Customer Service as R&D

For all its struggles—with its balance sheet, its stock, the union drive, and layoffs—Amazon.com has done one thing brilliantly: customer service. I placed my first order with Amazon in 1997 and have been a steady customer since. In four years of making purchases for myself and for others, I've found what I needed, ordered it, received a flurry of e-mails about my orders, and then gotten either thank-you notes or what I ordered. I've never had to contact Amazon about any matter. I have had, in essence, no customer service from Amazon. Put another way, I have had such perfect customer service, the service itself has been transparent. That is exactly what Amazon wants. The goal is perfect customer service through no customer service.

In a very short time, Amazon has set a new standard for customer service, and I went to Seattle to see how. What I discovered is a place that regards customer service as an R&D lab—a way not to help customers but to help the company.

"We want to make it easier and easier for our customers to do business with us," says Bill Price, fifty, vice president of global customer service for Amazon. "We want to have everything go so right, you never have to contact us. To do that, we have to stay tuned up. We have to keep asking, What are the problems?"

Of course, every customer-service VP in America, every customer-service VP in history, would agree with those sentiments. Two things make all the difference at Amazon: the view the company takes of customer service and customers, and the way the company is organized to drive home that view.

Amazon doesn't consider customer service to be the complaint department, or even the quality-control and customer-satisfaction department. Amazon considers Bill Price's outfit to be a research lab for discovering how to adjust and improve customer service. And Amazon considers customer service to be its core business. The company really offers nothing *but* customer service.

So every single encounter with a customer—by phone, by e-mail, even by clicking on Web pages—is considered to be the source of potentially vital information about the course of the entire company.

How does that work?

Well, to start with, the company tracks the reason for every customer contact. It keeps a list of the top ten reasons why customers contact the company—monitoring the list daily, weekly, monthly—and it is constantly working on ways to eliminate those reasons.

For years, the number one question that people asked Amazon was, Where's my stuff? Now, on every page, starting with the welcome page, there's a box labeled "Where's my stuff?"

Amazon's operations are so interwoven with customer-driven changes that employees are briefly baffled when you ask for examples.

"Two years ago," says Price, "one common problem was, 'I want to buy five books, and ship them to my five brothers, each at a separate address.' Our system was originally set up so that one order had to go to one address, forcing the customer, in a case like that, to place five separate orders. Now we have a 'ship-to-multiple-addresses' function. And you don't need to get in touch with us to figure it out."

Shortly after its consumer-electronics store debuted, Amazon was deluged with requests for a simple chart that would compare the features and prices of similar products, such as MP3 players and digital cameras. As a result, Amazon has developed a product: by-product "comparison engine" that does exactly that.

Just last year, a customer sent an e-mail pointing out something that had bugged him for years: on the main ordering page, customers are instructed to enter their e-mail address and their Amazon password. Next come two options: "Forgot your password? Click here" and "Sign in using our secure server."

Originally, the options were in that order. If someone simply tabbed from option to option, he would click "Forgot your password?"—even when what he wanted to do was sign in. Because of that single, irritated e-mail, the ordering page was changed.

Again, though, the head of customer service at any big company could tick off customer suggestions that have drifted up and changed products and operations.

But at Amazon, the notion of customer service as R&D isn't a slogan; it's a structure—an unavoidable force to be reckoned with. Price's division includes a group that does nothing but analyze and anticipate problems and cook up solutions. Indeed, representatives from customer-service project management sit on all launch teams as "the voice of the customer."

The ethic cuts deeper than it would first appear. "You can have a great overall culture," says Price, "with real empathy for the customer and passion for fixing the problems. You can have individual reps who say, 'This customer is *really* upset, and I have to deal with it.' I think we do that.

"What's missing almost everywhere else is, even if you have the empathy and the passion and you address the customer's problem, you haven't really given good customer service in total.

You haven't done that until you have eliminated the problem that caused her to call in the first place." Exactly.

It is, frankly, easy to be skeptical of all of this. For such a strategy to work, the entire company has to bend to it. One incident (of many that I encountered) shows how deeply ingrained the attitude is.

The problem materialized during the 1999 Christmas season, the first Christmas that Amazon sold toys. Almost as soon as the selling season began, the company received complaints that were notable more for the level of outrage than for the actual number of problems.

Some toys were big enough to be shipped in their original packing boxes. "They were arriving on people's doorsteps, and the people called and said, 'Hey, we weren't expecting this to look like a Big Wheel. My kid came home from school and found his present! Now I gotta buy another one!'" says Janet Savage, thirty-one, who was a customer-service manager that Christmas. This quickly became known as the Big Wheel problem, and it was Savage's job to resolve it.

It was an interesting moment. One possible response—a perfectly reasonable response—would be to start warning customers about items shipped in original cartons. After all, if you buy something at Toys "R" Us, you don't complain that it comes wrapped as what it is.

That response was never considered at Amazon. Savage simply started looking for durable, inexpensive wrapping material that would be available immediately and in large quantities. "Our customers were not happy," says Savage. "It was not acceptable to tell parents, Oh, well, too bad."

She found rolls of plastic material like the type used in big garbage bags, and Amazon started overwrapping every large toy and a selection of electronics items that were likely to be Christmas gifts. How urgent was it? "I bugged people about it on an hourly basis until we got it resolved," says Savage. "You're either Santa Claus or you're not."

GREAT SERVICE: BACK TO THE FUTURE

I have a running argument with customer-service experts that may be mostly an argument on my side. It is neatly summed up by *One to One* guru Don Peppers. He offers two key points about service. First, "Service is bad because it's hard to do." Second, "The secret to good service, really, is to treat your customer like you'd like to be treated yourself." Somewhere between point one and point two, I missed the hard part.

The hard part is not the service. The hard part is everything *but* the service. The hard part is how companies think about what they are doing and how they behave as a result. Why is the service of airlines so bad? Simple: Airlines don't think of themselves as service organizations. Airlines think of themselves as factories that manufacture revenue-seat miles. Airlines have been tuned in to the efficiency of their manufacturing operations, not to the quality of the journey that they provide.

When you spend weeks talking to people about customer service, when you visit people who do it as their livelihood, it is easy to become consumed with the challenges, the technology, and the measurements that obsess the world of customer service.

How much cheaper is it to deliver balances by automated phone menu than through a service rep? How much cheaper is it to deliver balances on the Web than over the telephone? What do people want to talk to a person about? What do they want to do themselves?

How do you create customer satisfaction, customer delight, and customer ecstasy? Most of these questions miss the larger point.

Dan Leemon, forty-seven, chief strategy officer for Charles Schwab, understands this dilemma clearly. Charles Schwab is a brokerage firm, of course. It keeps money for people, has custody of stock certificates, and functions as a bank in many ways. But like Sprint PCS or directory assistance, Schwab is really a pure customer-service organization. Its specialty is financial-services customer service—but it's service all the same. Everything else is record keeping.

"A lot of companies fall into the trap," says Leemon, "of believing that some new customer-service technology will take cost and management burden away and will eliminate the need to have very talented people on the phones and in their retail outlets.

"That has actually never been true," he says. Indeed, the complex demands of customers have increased the length of the typical call to Schwab by 75 percent during the past five years.

One Old Economy sector that is justifiably famous for service is the cruise industry. The high-end cruise lines achieve this by offering training, incentives, and quality facilities. One thing that they do particularly well is suck up customer feedback.

Royal Caribbean Cruise Lines (RCCL), for instance, has twenty-two ships. When a ship docks at home port at 7 A.M., before it clears customs, someone from RCCL has boarded to retrieve the customer-comment cards distributed to every cabin. The ratings are tabulated, the written comments are transcribed, and the results are returned to the ship's managers before the ship sails again at 5 P.M.

So before the next cruise begins, RCCL's captains, diningroom managers, housekeepers, and entertainers know how the previous cruise went—from praise to serious problems. Imagine what flying the big airlines would be like if you got a comment card at the end of each flight—and the company acted on what it learned.

Discussion and Writing Questions

1. Fishman claims that in modern America, bad customer service is a shared cultural experience. Why is customer service so terrible? Do you agree or disagree with the reasons proposed by Fishman?

2. Fishman provides the example of Amazon.com as a company that has an excellent customer service rating. Do you think customer service would improve if more companies followed the example of Amazon.com and used customer service as research and development? Do you think that eliminating the cause for customer service is a feasible option for most service companies? In a short essay, show one of your own experiences dealing with some aspect of corporate "customer service" providers. How does your experience reinforce or contradict the situations described by Fishman?

Intertextual Question

3. Sam Walton, the founder of Wal-Mart, prided himself that he was constantly thinking of the customer, but according to Fishman, Wal-Mart has a declining customer service rating. What do you think are the differences between keeping the customer as the focus and using customer service as research and development?

Check Cashing Outlets Financed by Large Banks, Study Finds . . .
ADRIAN RODRIGUEZ

Adrian Rodriguez is a staff reporter for the Business Journal, *a newspaper based in the Central San Joaquin Valley. In his article, Rodriguez examines pay-check cashing outlets, questioning who benefits from this industry and how it affects local communities.*

Prereading Question

Would you ever consider using a payday loan service? (Or have you?) What is your general impression of payday loan companies? Can you recall any commercials for these types of lending institutions?

—————————— ✦ ——————————

For the average worker in California, paying the bills can be a challenge in itself. Often those earning minimum wage scarcely can cover expenses from month to month, and if a costly emergency should occur, the next check can't come soon enough.

Now, workers have a place to get those funds soon enough at payday lending outlets—but it will cost them. With charges typically reaching $15 to $20 per $100 advanced for a two-week period, the ever-growing payday lending industry has found that many cash-strapped customers are willing to take on short-term loans, resulting in APRs that average more than 400 percent. In Fresno, some outlets reported, APRs at more than 1,000 percent.

Payday loan outlets offer loans by holding a consumer's post-dated check for the advance amount plus a fee. The check is held until payday, which is either deposited or the customer returns with cash to reclaim the check.

While the APR seems steep, many customers turn to the outlets because banks don't offer short-term loans and the fee itself is relatively small. The APR is a calculation that presumes the customer will use the service throughout the entire year.

But a new report released this month shows that payday lenders, which have increased nationally from 2,000 in 1996 to 22,000 in 2003, have been taking on loans themselves, often securing their finances through large banks. The study, conducted by San Francisco-based California Reinvestment Coalition, detailed extensive bank financing of payday lenders by California's largest banks, including Bank of America and Wells Fargo.

The report also found that the business of issuing short-term loans pulls more than $5.7 billion in fees from Californians each year.

Alan Fisher, the Coalition's executive director, researched the lenders' financing by reviewing publicly filed loan statements, including SEC filings. Fisher supplied *The Business Journal* with many of the documents for verification.

There are at least 70 payday lenders and check cashing outlets in Fresno County, with the vast majority located within the city of Fresno. More than a dozen line Shaw Avenue from Brawley to Fowler. A dozen or so lenders also can be found on Kings Canyon Road in central Fresno.

"Traditional mainstream banks have abandoned lower income communities and communities of color while they profit by financial predatory check cashers and payday lenders," Fisher said.

There are no bank branches west of Highway 99. The Fresno West Coalition for Economic Development estimates that the west Fresno community—which numbers more than 36,000—loses $2.5 million annually to payday lenders through fees.

In Fresno County, 60 percent of check cashers and payday lenders are supported by major financial institutions, the report found.

"Payday lenders and mainstream banks are in fact complementary faces of the current financial system," Fisher said.

The Community Reinvestment Act, which went into effect in 1977, requires banks to make public community development lending, with results evaluated every other year.

Officials from Wells Fargo could not be immediately reached for comment about payday financing.

In a written statement, Bank of America stated it does not engage in predatory or deceptive lending practices, and it supports efforts to "protect Americans from predatory lenders and their practices."

The statement continues, "Bank of America provides financial services to virtually every global and domestic industry, and this may include providing general working capital and other financial services to various lenders including subprime lenders."

Both banks received "outstanding" evaluations in the last report for Fresno County.

But Fisher said the problem is that certain banks are financing—and therefore profiting—from payday lenders, which do not fall under the Community Reinvestment Act.

"[Payday lenders] are not very seriously regulated," Fisher said. "They have been able to escape because they are saying they are not paying a loan, they are just charging a fee to get someone some money ahead by two weeks. But that's a loan."

While payday lenders serve the underserved, they are sometimes an annoyance to local banks, said Dan Doyle, president and CEO of Central Valley Community Bank.

"We're not fans of that kind of business," he said. "We think they should [be regulated] like the rest of us."

Doyle said that another problem is that legislators who seek to increase regulations for payday lenders often lump traditional banks with payday lenders, which are considered "fringe" financial institutions.

"That's the part that is difficult for us," Doyle said. "Like everything else, if it is a free market, you can't stop them, but it seems that Congress is looking at them as if they are banks."

Discussion and Writing Questions

1. Rodriguez says that customers turn to payday loan outlets because banks do not offer short-term loans. However, the payday loan outlets are actually financed by large banks like Wells Fargo and Bank of America. Do you think that banks should start offering short-term loans?

2. Should payday lenders be regulated in the same way as other lending institutions? What would be the potential consequences of regulating the payday lending industry? Drawing on your research and lived experience, draft an essay where you explain one way in which traditional lenders are regulated and argue that payday lenders should or should not be regulated in the same way.

Intertextual Question

3. Rodriguez claims that banks have abandoned lower-income communities and communities of color. How does the abandonment of these communities compare to the support that such communities received from the prison industry as described in Joelle Fraser's essay?

CHAPTER 4

Business Economies

Early in the twenty-first century, according to some reports (including those from the Justice Department), the U.S. prison population rose above 2 million for the first time—a number only slightly different from the number of employees who worked for Wal-Mart. By 2005, the number of incarcerated people—from those in local jails to those in federal prisons—rose by another 250,000. The vast majority of these convicted criminals are drug offenders—users, dealers, smugglers. These convicted criminals are primarily from the most impoverished sectors of the American economy. The cost of incarceration is spectacular, from the cost of prison construction to the cost of food for prisoners— as much as $60,000 per prisoner per year.

The state of California spends more annually on prisons than on any other budget item, including healthcare and education. Joelle Fraser begins Chapter 4 by describing this same industrial complex as it is manifested in one California town: Susanville (in an essay that inspired a documentary on PBS and continues to raise the issue—and readers' eyebrows—years after its initial publication). Prisoners grow a portion of the food they consume, launder the soiled bedding from the institution, and sew their own clothing. Prisoners also produce goods such as wooden furniture, canned food, and blue jeans. Additionally, prisoners also work as telemarketers and tech-support, all for as little as 50 cents an hour. The benefit to an employer is staggering— paying a prisoner 50 cents an hour to do the same work for which a non-incarcerated worker would be paid considerably more, even at minimum wage. Even better, from an employer's point of view, the incarcerated worker will never be late for work and never leave early, will have limited opportunities to steal from or otherwise defraud the company, and will enjoy no mechanism for negotiating a higher wage. In such a situation, employees can't even quit, as participation (or cooperation) is required, with solitary confinement and/or the threat of a loss of privileges as the consequence. The state or federal government even pays for the imprisoned employee's healthcare.

The readings in Chapter 4 explore the complex issues within both actual and virtual American economies, beginning with a consideration of prison labor and moving on to topics such as online play as real-world profit, the economics of slavery (literal and figurative), the threat to citizens' rights (including potentially the right to organize labor unions) from the U.S. government in a post-9/11 world, and the potential "triple play" to rescue the U.S. economy from itself. While some of the issues raised in Chapter 4 are new—such as the risky (legally and morally) practice of governmental spies infiltrating nonprofit organizations and other noncriminal groups—most have been raised before, in other ways, in other sections, by other authors. The issues are neither simple nor self-contained, and the connections between and among the subjects raised in this section and the three that precede it reflect this considerable complexity.

An American Seduction: Portrait of a Prison Town

JOELLE FRASER

Joelle Fraser is a graduate of the Nonfiction Writing Program from the University of Iowa and a recipient of many writing awards and fellowships. Her book, The Territory of Men: A Memoir, *was published by Random House in 2002. She lives in northeast California. In the following essay, Fraser describes the impact of a new prison on a small community.*

Prereading Question

The prison industry is among the fastest-growing sectors of the U.S. economy, especially in heavily populated states such as California. While it is reasonable to expect the number of people imprisoned in a nation to rise as the population of that nation rises, the percentage of U.S. citizens behind bars has risen dramatically in the last twenty-five years. America now imprisons more people than any other nation on Earth. Why? What in American society, large or small, consequential or inconsequential, could account for this?

———————— ✦ ————————

I've come home because the new High Desert State Prison needs teachers, and I need a job. At 8 A.M., I stop at the BP for the weekly paper: the first thing I notice is the place is full of prison guards. They're buying cigarettes and gas, stirring whitener into coffee. Each is decked out in full uniform, army green suit and parka with the California Department of Corrections gold patch, shiny black boots, belt hung with batons and pepper spray. Most are young and beefy; all have the soldier hairdo, trim mustache, crisp creases—these guys would pass any inspection.

Two more walk in. I should feel safe, but I don't. These uniforms are about keeping people in line. It feels more like a Central American border crossing than a gas station lobby in rural America. The young man with the ponytail apparently doesn't like the scene either; he walks in, then pivots coolly right back out.

Later, I learn this is shift change for Susanville's two prisons, when hundreds of correctional officers (COs) switch places and traffic triples in this town, population 7800. With 10,000 inmates already, a federal prison on the way, and talk of a women's prison and a sex offender jail still to come, this is Prison County USA, where everyone and his brother works in some way for the prison, where there are more people behind bars than outside of them.

Now, when I hear of other small towns campaigning for the panacea of a prison, I want to say, listen to this story first. I think: let me tell you about Susanville.

People told me the prison came to town just in time. The closing of two mines and an army depot, the shrinking logging industry and a general feeling that the town was collapsing in on itself—all led Susanville to open its arms for High Desert State Prison, a 4500-inmate, maximum-security facility to be built just eight miles from Main Street, where it would sit beside the California Correctional Center, a smaller prison built in 1963. With the new high-tech prison and plans for more, Susanville could one day quite possibly contain the largest penitentiary complex on the planet.

But such notoriety didn't concern the townspeople in 1992, when 57 percent of the voters said yes to the ballot proposal for another prison, mainly due to the public relations campaigns of the Chamber of Commerce and the Save Our Jobs Committee. A few months later, like a family preparing for the arrival of an important guest, the town readied itself for the prison.

And appropriately, this guest would bring gifts: a $57–70 million payroll, 1200 new jobs, and anywhere from 3500 to 4000 new residents, the families of inmates and prison personnel who would buy their groceries, their gas, their meals, who would pay their rent and mortgages in this town. Annexing the prison into the city limits would mean more grant dollars for the city as the population total, now including inmates, more than doubled to 16,000. The state Department of Corrections, eager to build another prison to stem the flow of a system already operating at 201 percent capacity, offered $2 million to compensate for impacts on schools, courts, and roads. It was the largest sum ever given to a community in which a prison was constructed, although it would be argued later that it was not nearly enough.

The people spread a banner across Main Street (WELCOME PRISON EMPLOYEES AND INMATES), builders drew up plans for new condominiums and homes, motels advertised special rates for prison employees and inmate families. Sierra Video offered coupons for one free rental with a prison employee ID card. Uptown Uniforms displayed khaki jumpers and shiny black boots in its windows—a smart move considering $200,000 would be spent annually on uniforms. People lined up at the karate school for self-defense classes. Susanville Supermarket hired four new people and structured work schedules around the state's first of the month paydays. Carpet cleaners, hired out by real estate firms and landlords of rental property, were swamped.

News of the prison found its way to companies like Wal-Mart, Taco Bell, Country Kitchen, Blockbuster Video, all of whom came and set up shop in advance. During prison construction in 1995, every motel in town put up "no vacancy" signs as new prison employees and construction workers camped in trailers and filled parking lots for weeks.

Three years later, as the strip lengthened and the stoplights multiplied and many small businesses, unable to compete with Wal-Mart, quietly boarded their doors, Susanville is reminiscent of so many towns that have outgrown themselves and lost something in the process. But it is also unlike many small towns—there is the overwhelming presence of men with military haircuts and trim mustaches, the constant talk of prison scandals and violence (eleven inmates have been killed or committed suicide since High Desert's opening), the clear division between locals and prison employees and inmate families. People complain about anonymity, about long lines at the bank, about traffic, about the rise in prices. The police department faces rising domestic violence, a 50 percent jump in juvenile delinquency and trade in hard core drugs like heroin from gang members associated with the prison. The real estate community holds a glut of property because the new prison employees are a transient lot, eager for promotion and transfer, and they're not settling in like they were supposed to.

It would be easy to apply literary allusions to this collision of frustrated expectations—the prison was a Trojan horse, a Faustian bargain, a Pyrrhic victory, but that would deny the fact that some of the promises have come true, to a certain extent. The town does have more money, and graduating seniors, with job opportunities at the new prison, no longer have to flee to Portland and Sacramento and other faraway cities. People can make fewer shopping trips to Reno and choose from six movies instead of two. There's a health food store, and at Safeway, people can buy goat cheese and focaccia bread. As one woman said, "Who knows, maybe we'll get a Mervyn's."

In a place where the economy is dying and the young people are leaving for places where it is not, the new prison was about money, about security and progress and hope for a better life.

But as Susanville has discovered, a new prison requires that the community adapt to a rapid leap in a specific kind of population—those drawn to and associated with the work of corrections, an industry for whom the raw material is the systematic incapacitation of hostile, despairing human beings, in this case over 10,000 of them.

In the end, this was a town in which everyone was seduced in one way or another, and because a seduction is ultimately a mutual act, there was no one to blame the morning after. In this town everyone held out for a promise that, when kept, turned out to be less—or more—than bargained for.

Bruce Springsteen never lived in Susanville, but if he had, he would have written a song about it, about the mills that closed, and the mines, the army depot, about how everything the town relied on had slipped away like a woman who'd seen something better on the other side of the road.

But damn, if the place had nothing else, it sure claimed gorgeous country—the high desert of northeast California, on the edge of the state that overlooks the arid sands of Nevada. Through this land of sage and scrub brush to the east, and dense forests to the west, the Diamond Mountains rise unevenly above the town and beyond until they join the Sierras 90 miles to the south, where the water of Lake Tahoe pools clear and still.

And the place had good people to work the land. For a century and a half folks have been coming to this town looking for gold or some form of it in timber or ranching, full of hope and grit and then the scratch to survive when the dream is gone, a search so definitively American that I began to see that Susanville was not just a small town but The American Small Town, and that it, like the Washo and Maidu Indians who lived here in the beginning, like the wolves who wandered this basin, is an endangered species.

As the biggest town in Lassen County, Susanville sits in the middle of prime ranching country, about 100 miles from any good-sized city—Reno, Chico, Redding and Red Bluff. Heading south towards Reno, drivers are treated to a comforting view of cattle scattered over ranchlands with high hills beyond like the warm backs of sleeping dogs. Here 4H is as important as church, and the Lassen County Cattlewomen hold an annual Mother's Day Beef Recipe Contest. Poems about beef are published in the local weekly paper, *Lassen Times* ("Yum Beef Yum! / Put it in the crock pot, place it on the grill / Invite some friends, give them a tasty

thrill!"). Youth compete in rodeos, experts in barrel racing, goat
tying and break away roping.

For these reasons it's often called cowboy country (or "redneck
country" by the less generous). The weather is harsh—with its
4500-foot elevation, in the summer it tops 105 degrees and in
the winter, snow can bury the town for weeks. It's a man's town,
where fishing and hunting are part of every good boy's education,
where the local community college offers more classes in auto
mechanics and welding than English or History. A place where
gunsmiths and well drillers receive the kind of recognition reserved
for professors and doctors in other parts of the country; where gun
racks are as ubiquitous as cowboy hats and at the gas station convenience store on Highway 395, you can buy bullet key chains. The
women, too, are tough, as adept at changing car parts or chopping
wood or rolling a cigarette as the men; this is not a delicate place,
and they grow old fast in the dry desert air, their faces lined and set.

But with the toughness of these people comes a respect for
life and an enormous capacity to love. Ten years ago, lured by the
gorgeous country and the promise of a small town life, my
mother fled the Bay Area with my little brother and bought
22 acres of land covered with waist-high rye and the tracks of
mule deer, coyotes and jackrabbits. Over those years I've spent
summers and holidays here; I've tutored at the vocational ed
office and taught at the community college. I've made good
friends and loved men and helped nurse my stepfather through a
summer of chemotherapy.

In this way I've come to know and admire the people of the
town, but it is also as an observer and visitor that I have seen the
changes. When I walk down Main Street, I am simply another
stranger, now. And I began to ask questions because in the space
of two years I had seen Susanville change into another kind of
place, and the change was one that was neither altogether good
nor altogether inevitable. These changes seemed important, and
though they were cropping up all over the country, no one was
talking about prison towns.

On my mother's dining room table lies a polished cedar bowl,
so smooth it seems lit from within, the kind of glow that requires
an attention both precise and time-consuming. On the bottom of
the bowl a typewritten note with a prison ID number is glued in
place: For Victims of Crime. She bought it from the annual Prison
Craft Fair, a charity event benefiting Lassen Family Services

Domestic Abuse program, where you can buy everything from an oak coffee table to an embroidered leather belt.

"That place sells out in an hour," she tells me. "The craftsmanship is amazing."

The inmates aren't there, of course, just their handiwork. For many of the townspeople, the fair is the closest they will get to the prison or its occupants. It is an example of the ways in which a town will ultimately co-exist with a prison, in partnerships that range from fundraisers to community work, where inmates groom baseball diamonds, plant trees on county property, paint governmental buildings—even dry-clean school band uniforms. As the California Department of Corrections boasts in a brochure, "While the inmates are paid only cents per hour, the benefit to the community is far greater."

Those benefits are the icing on the economic cake that is offered to isolated communities like Susanville, far from any major port or city, who often try in vain to attract new industry. The town then relies on logging, mining, ranching—and government. Here, with more than half the town working for a government agency, acronyms spill out easily in daily conversations: BLM (Bureau of Land Management), CDF (California Department of Forestry), USFS (United States Forestry Service), DFG (Department of Fish and Game) and of course, CDC (California Department of Corrections).

In 1963, the first prison, the 1,120-acre California Correction Center ("The Center"), was built to further conservation efforts. Inmates lived at the boarding school-style center, spending their time helping reduce fire hazard, managing forests and watersheds, clearing streams, and improving fish and game habitat. In the cyclical nature of prison policy, this was the rehabilitation era, the time of liberal reform. One local man told me it wasn't unusual to get a work crew of inmates to come out to help on someone's ranch. The Center, which began with only 1,200 inmates, more than doubled in 1987 to accommodate the more than 2,000 rapists, kidnapers and other violent offenders, who would be held behind razor wire in two-man cells with rifles trained on them 24 hours a day. It was a sign of the times—the "tough on crime" policies. Despite misgivings—there was no vote and hardly a public forum—the town adjusted to the expansion; after all, Susanville relied on CCC for 20 percent of its economy.

Over the past 10 years, as logging shrank and the mines and army depot downsized and then eventually closed, the idea of another prison seemed quite logical. After all, the state already owned the land, and it needed another prison to help with the dangerously overcrowded system. Even with High Desert, in mid 1998 the state's 33 facilities weren't enough to contain the state's criminals, whose number rises about 7 percent annually, the highest rate in the nation. (The state's punitive trends, the legacy of two tough-on-crime governors, included 1994's "three strikes" legislation which sentenced three-time losers to 25 years to life, doubled terms for many second-time felons and slashed time off for good behavior. The CDC's master plan predicts that inmate population will exceed maximum operating prison capacity of 178,432 by the year 2000—sites are under discussion or planned for California City, Delano, Sacramento, San Diego County and Taft.) But if CCC was a trickle that became a stream in Susanville, the $272 million High Desert State Prison was a river that became a flood.

Part of the problem was the state's bait-and-switch halfway through the process. Four months after voters approved a low to medium security facility, High Desert became a Level III and IV facility, housing the most violent offenders and those with 25-year to life terms. This required more staff, high security lights and other requirements. The implications of this newer security level were far-reaching but hard to nail down. It meant, for example, that more inmate families would move to Susanville to be near the incarcerated family member, stressing the social services more than anticipated.

County officials were furious, but there was little they could do. The state's mitigation money helped, and the city receives about $50 a year for each inmate, but it doesn't help enough with the cost of building roads, increasing law enforcement and expanding schools for an estimated 1,180 additional school children. The ranchers were against the prison from the start, claiming it exchanged open space and crop land for housing and infrastructure, and would siphon ground water now used for growing crops.

Perhaps the biggest problem with the prison is that unlike private industry, which generates as much as $600 per job in property taxes, a government industry produces no direct county taxes, the money counties need to supply health care and police protection. And about half of Lassen County's existing industry is local, state or federal government already.

When word of the new prison got out, former warden Bill Merkle saw 500 transfer requests for Susanville. "Lassen County is a good place to raise kids, has clean air and a nice environment," he said, a quote that began to take a kind of mantra-like status, as every correctional officer I talked to repeated it in turn. In all, nearly 1800 correctional officers (COs), some veterans but most new on the job, made their way to Susanville from Southern California and the nearby larger cities of Sacramento, Reno and Vacaville, a good number bringing families with them. For many of these men and their families, they might as well have crossed the border into another country.

Carol Jeldness, a licensed clinical social worker who contracted with the prison to provide counseling under the prison's Employee Assistance Plan, built her practice on CO relocation trauma. "A town like this, it doesn't welcome you much," she said.

The new COs needed to not only adjust to working in a brand new maximum security prison—with all of its start-up problems—but they had wives and children who'd come to a place with little to do, or at least it seemed so to many of them. There is no mall in Susanville, no factory outlet stores, no roller rink, no Boys & Girls Club—to find any of these requires a 160-mile round trip. The weather only exacerbates the isolation. It doesn't snow much in Orange or Sacramento counties, but in Susanville, for a good part of the winter people need chains to get down Main Street. Cabin fever quickly became a popular topic.

Compounding the adjustment problem was the financial one. To be a correctional officer, all you need (until recently it was only a high school diploma) is an AA degree and successful completion of a six-week training course. As a result, many of the COs at High Desert are, say, 22–30 years old, making $40,000 a year with overtime. A stroll down "CO Row," the neighborhoods of Howard Court, South Mesa and Fairfield Streets, offers a pretty good look at the lifestyle these new officers thought they could afford: fishing boats, ski jets, new American trucks and sport utility vehicles all sitting in front of brand new ranch style houses with two-car garages and manicured lawns.

The irony is that many of the younger COs are filing for bankruptcy, and those that aren't are struggling to make minimum payments on purchases that were bought too fast and in too many numbers. The Iron Horse Gym—a favorite of COs for its ample free weights—even has many delinquent CO accounts; the monthly payment is about $30.

"It's a mess, and it spills over onto the family," Jeldness said. "They start pulling double shifts, working 60, 70 hours a week out there. Even those without financial problems have to pull the bad shifts in order to get seniority."

To make matters worse, California leads the nation in inmate shooting deaths (12 since 1994, compared with six state prisoners shot across the entire nation during the same time period); High Desert accounts for three of those deaths over the past three years. Many of California's prisons, including High Desert, have recently been accused of scandalous activity on the part of the COs, everything from drug trafficking and torture (such as forcing inmates to play "barefoot handball" on scorching asphalt) to pitting inmates against one another like roosters in a cockfight, complete with spectators and wagering—and then shooting those who won't stop fighting. Two High Desert COs were charged early this year with filing a false crime report. Many of the COs I talked to were scornful of these activities, and some denied the existence of inmate abuse, claiming that the shooting of an inmate is an easy thing to twist in the media.

Regardless, the current spotlight on COs has made work even more difficult: for most of their waking hours, these men (and a few women) are immersed in one of the most oppressive, stressful environments imaginable. As one shop owner commented about High Desert, "That place rock n' rolls."

"What kind of husband and father do you think they can be after what they've been around for 14 hours?" asked Jeldness. "The issues are complicated, but all seem to stem from men not talking."

"The CO would say to me, 'my wife expects me to leave it at the door and be compassionate. It doesn't work like that.' It was awful," she said. "I had no authority to require time off. And the COs were always averse to that anyway. They're pressured to hide the counseling. It's all about being strong. And Lord, there's a lot of alcoholism. Many of my clients came home to a cleaned out house—the wife just couldn't take it."

Jerry Sandahl, a CO at High Desert with 14 years of experience, said it took him years to adjust.

"I spent 8 to 16 hours a day in solid bullshit," he said, looking out the window as logging truck passed by. On the street, I would have guessed him for a salesman, an accountant maybe. "You hear cursing all day, and you come home and that's all you think about. It did tragedy on my family. When you come in there, they tell you family values are the most important thing, but it's not true. The state was. We're like a store, a warehouse. You bring in the merchandise— when someone wants to parole it, we send it back out."

Sandahl chuckles as he talks about the new guys, whom he calls "hyper."

"I drive out towards the prison and 15 cars pass me, all new staff. I think, God's country will prevail. I keep telling them—look at the alfalfa growing in the fields. This thing will be here tomorrow. The problem is that they think they're cops 24 hours a day. I tell you what: if he doesn't have over eight years, the guy doesn't know anything. He's still in his mind glory days," he said.

Jeldness, who is also a mediator for Lassen County Family Court, saw her caseload—mainly child custody and divorce, jump from 167 to 320 in one year. During the two years after the prison opened, domestic violence as well skyrocketed in Susanville. Linda McAndrews, head of Lassen Family Services, said she got 3000 crisis calls from women in 1996. She went to the warden and told him "he had to do something." He did—the number of crisis calls has decreased during the past year—but many believe that's due to the new law that states if you've been convicted of domestic abuse, you're not allowed to carry a gun. If you can't carry a gun, you won't go far in the prison system. Consequently, women are much more reluctant to report abuse, fearing their husbands will lose their jobs, and then whatever problems they're facing will only spiral into something worse.

I thought about these interviews as I walked down Mesa Street, along the homes of the new CO families. I was struck by the emptiness—no children, on bikes, no dads tinkering in the garage; it was as if the sterility of the newness had not worn off, and wasn't about to any time soon.

Susanville, like most small towns, rests many of its hopes on its children, and so the jump in juvenile problems seems especially poignant. One afternoon, I met with Jason Jones, a juvenile probation officer, at Denny's, one of the most popular restaurants in town. While I waited for him, it struck me that many of the men in the restaurant, in particular the young ranchers and truckers, looked not unlike the inmates I have seen in prisons: jean-clad, sporting tattoos, talking easily with their companions. The comparison made me uneasy, and I was glad when Jones arrived.

Over the past three years, he's observed the changes in Susanville's youth, and the bottom line: juvenile delinquency has steadily increased, in both the number and scope of incidents, including truancy, petty theft, vandalism, fighting and problems associated with drugs and alcohol. There are gangs as well, especially the Hispanic North and South gangs; the Roman numerals XIV and XV are painted and scrawled on random walls, signifying affiliation with one group or the other. In one month alone, January 1998, juvenile gang violence was responsible for the beating of a student in the Safeway parking lot, the stoning of another, and the breaking of still another student's leg in three places in front of the high school. All three incidents led to hospitalizations. In December 1998, a 16-year-old honors student was severely beaten by a group of teens who call themselves the X-13s and wear gang colors. After weeks of terrorizing and death threats—the gang allegedly would park in front of the student's home and yell "we're gonna cap your ass"—the mother of the victim is leaving town with her family.

The town has responded. Recently, the juvenile hall more than tripled its capacity to 50 beds. Jones has had to take two guns, one a loaded .357, off kids in the past few months. He's seen the drugs get harder—from crank and the "blunt," a Philly cigar emptied and filled with pot, which is best, apparently, dipped in honey and microwaved for 3–5 seconds—to heroin, smuggled in and out of the prison.

None of this surprised Jones or his colleagues much. What surprised them was the origin of most of the problems.

"We expected trouble with the inmate families," he said. "But what we got were problems with the CO families."

Very often, a facility with so many Level III and IV inmates, many of them 25-year to lifers, will draw families who relocate to be near their husband, father, brother, son. The repercussions of this—several hundred people, many on welfare, many of them Hispanic and Black—could feasibly flood an insular, small town with social service problems, from juvenile delinquency to racial strife. The high school administration had these kids "red flagged" and were prepared for trouble, Jones said, but while he has handled only about five inmate family cases, he's dealt with more than 50 CO family cases.

"We weren't prepared," Jones said.

The CO kids, coming from urban centers, are more sophisticated, more impatient, and more noticeable in their urban-hip outfits, said Jones.

"These kids live in a para-military household," Jones said. "But really they don't have much supervision. They've got nothing to do."

At sunset, I walk down Riverside, the street that cuts through the mill district, where most of the inmate families live. It's a far cry from CO Row on the other side of town, where correctional officers live in brand new houses with driveways full of brand new American trucks and SUVs, boats and jet skis, courtesy of a job that pays over $40,000 in a town where the median income is about $27,500.

Not long ago, when my brother was still in high school, we had a house on Pardee Street, off Riverside, and we'd walk down to the river in the summer and spend our days swimming and sunning on the rocks. Back then, this was a town where you could recognize kids by the resemblance to their parents, where dogs would take naps in the middle of the road, where you never had to lock your doors.

Today the town's a modern version of the Wild West, only the cowboys are the guards and the Indians are the inmates and the inmate families. Here in the mill district, the asphalt's crumbling and a swath of dirt subs for a sidewalk; skinny cats slink through tall grass. Many of these residents have a father or son at one of the prisons, and sometimes it's not just the family that moves here, but the friends and "business acquaintances" from Fresno, Vacaville, L.A. High Desert is gang-infested, and it doesn't stay inside the walls.

Already used to the mill stink after a block, I notice a young Hispanic boy sitting on the steps in front of a small house. From inside, an Aerosmith song is blasting with a fist-like beat. The boy holds a blue water pistol on his knees. As I pass he looks at me with a cool intelligence, as if he knows all the trouble that could descend on me and is deciding whether to initiate it.

I risk a smile and he waves absently at me—it is unclear whether in greeting or dismissal.

One afternoon I meet with Misty, a pretty 17-year-old "inmate kid," who lives in a group home and attends a community school whose windows offer views of the county jail, the juvenile detention center, and the Susanville Cemetery. She says the community school exists for "fuck-ups," though it's clear that despite a mother addicted to crank and a father with an address at High Desert State Prison, she is most definitely not a fuck-up. In fact, she's active in dance (ballet), a responsible worker (part of the Taco Bell crew) and in the past three weeks she's tripled her credits and is now eligible to be a senior at Lassen High, from which she was expelled last fall for beating up a female CO student.

"We were friends, but then she started messing with the group home girls. A glass bottle was thrown and then I just went at it," says Misty, who looks young for her age and is probably the last person you'd expect to blacken a classmate's eye and, when the girl drops to the ground, knee her in the face.

"I'm not proud of it," she says, looking off to the west, where her father will serve 18 more months of a two-year sentence for parole violation. Her 36-year-old father, unable to kick the drug habit, has also lived in San Quentin and Vacaville prisons. Misty and he correspond through letters, and she is trying to work her schedule so that she can visit him. She admits she's nervous about going to High Desert.

"I've heard a lot about that place," she says. "It would be better to visit him at a drug treatment center. Isn't that where he belongs anyway?"

Misty hangs out with the "inmate and jail kids," a clique, along with the "CO kids," that one finds only in prison towns. The lines are clearly segregated, she explains.

"They're spoiled brats. The CO kids flaunt their parents' money and wear Tommy Hilfiger, DKNY, Calvin, cell phones and pagers. They party and spin out but they're also the ones who get straight A's. I don't know how they do it."

The CO kids aren't the only partiers; in fact, Misty informs me, only the band members are clean.

"There's nothing to do except party—that's why there are so many drugs," she said. Misty moved here two years ago from Vacaville, which she misses.

I ask her if she ever worries about following in her father's footsteps.

"I've seen him live and learn and fail. I don't want to be that person," she says.

Ironically, the increase in domestic abuse and juvenile strife didn't surprise many people. Susanville, like many country towns, is a place where violence is not just unknown but part of the natural order. Last summer I leaned on our fence and watched our neighbor brand and castrate his herd. Several times, he had to stop and bring back his weeping, frightened grandson; the boy, perhaps 4 or 5, clapped his hands over his ears as his grandfather sliced the testicles off the bellowing, rolled-eyed calves and then seared their flanks with his brand, the smoke rising like campfires. The lessons are learned early around here; toughness is bred into you.

Once my brother told me about an incident from his sophomore year in high school. He and a friend were playing cards in
his family's garage, and after a slight argument, the friend picked
up his father's nail gun and calmly aimed and shot nails at my
brother.

"You have to be hard in Susanville," he told me. As a new student he was given an unofficial initiation when a group of boys
took him four-wheeling out in the desert. Alone in the back of the
pick-up, he clung to whatever he could as they ran and skidded
over dips and bumps, the object being to bounce him out. For
days he couldn't walk for the bruises.

The acceptance of violence in a place like Lassen County,
where the living has always been hard and the soft rarely survive,
makes its own kind of sense. A certain comfort with violence is
necessary where the main sources of income come from the natural world—from felling timber, clearing land, digging for gold,
breeding and slaughtering cattle. But when the second prison
came in under the political wave of "get tough on crime," the col-
liding of the existing sense of violence—that it is one of necessity,
of survival—with that associated with a maximum-security
prison, mutated into a pervasive sense of antagonism.

"You can feel it in the air," Tony Esparza, who teaches land-
scaping skills at the prison, told me. "It's not just out at the prison,
it's right here."

In a town where high school football takes on a kind of religious fervor ("If you don't play football you ain't nothin,'" one
young boy remarked), the pitting of "us against them" is an easy
sell. There are the locals against the CO families, the COs against
the inmate families, the bitter and random battles of the gangs.
The most prevalent "them" is the inmates, and the feeling is manifested in random and curious ways. Take this example: on a wall
at the Iron Horse Gym hangs a large, color poster—a blown up
photograph actually. It depicts a group of about ten muscled,
stone-faced inmates, shirtless or wearing tank tops, all staring
defiantly into the camera. The text, in a form of Darwinian psychology, reads: "THEY WORKED OUT TODAY: DID YOU?"

For the prison tour, I dress carefully. No perfume, hair pulled
back, flat shoes—something you can run in. I've been to prisons
before, on tours, as a writing teacher, and this is my second to
High Desert. I forego breakfast; I'm too tense to eat. Spending
time at a prison is not something one gets used to, any more than
one might get used to a dangerous and unpredictable animal.

The tension in the air at a prison—and particularly in maximum security facilities—is one gesture away from violence, felt rather than understood, a tension that will stay with me long after I leave the gates behind.

Driving north on Johnstonville Road, I'm always struck by this shadowless land, bleached and empty save for the sage and wheat grass, dwarfing everything that has the nerve to make this place home: a juniper tree, a shack, the few houses, a horse. The land swallows up whatever's sat upon it. High Desert and CCC come into view on the right. Together, the prisons occupy nearly 1000 acres of desert, set on a terrain that rolls and spreads like an unnamed planet for the mad and the lonely. A flower here seems an alien and wondrous thing. The institutions not only confirm but seem to incorporate the surrounding desolation, blending into the distant desert hills, where on clear days the U.S. Army detonates bombs that explode in great flashes of orange seen long before heard.

At first glance, the scattered houses close to the prison seem abandoned. A rusted car lies belly up in the dirt, and everywhere boards, boxes, broken furniture. But then you see a small girl in green overalls, picking her way through a yard. If she had a ball, she would not have to walk far to throw it against the prison fence. You wonder what she thinks of her neighbors.

You might also wonder about her safety. CCC has had many escapes over the years (in a two-year period, from August 1995 to August 1997, 33 to be exact). But High Desert hasn't had any, and doesn't expect to. Everyone in town knows about the state-of-the-art measures, the elaborate alarm system, the electronic display screens with schematic maps, the constant ID checking, the 6-time a day head count, the 13 gun towers with a 360-degree overlook of every foot of prison yard. These measures were, in fact, part of the sales package for the town. Escape, as the townspeople were reassured, is nearly impossible—an inmate would have to be flown or smuggled out. No one can get by the 16-strand lethal voltage fence with enough electricity (85,000 kw) to kill a man eight times over. The "death fence" is, nevertheless, monitored 24 hours a day by a guard in a truck who circles it at a lazy 5 mph, gathering the charred ravens, rabbits, lizards and the occasional snake who get too close.

Like most prisons, High Desert spends more than half of its $81,533,000 budget on custody costs ($11,015 per inmate, per year). The bulk of the $59,665,000 payroll goes to the COs.

Lieutenant Paul Edwards escorts me through the series of gates and corridors that lead to one of the Level III yards. I show my driver's license and gate clearance form 10 times during the tour. Around us, COs are on their way to various areas, cell blocks, yards, the administrative offices. Most of the time they're quiet, but at other times there is the comradely feel of factory workers on their way to the line.

"Randy, you seen my new truck?" one CO asks another, who says no.

"You will!" and they both laugh, not as rare a sound in prison as one might think (in fact, as one CO told me, "I've heard inmates sing").

The staff oversee inmates' movements every minute, including when they sleep. During my tour, as I observed the "free hour" in the day room, in which the inmates shower, play cards, watch TV, or stare at the walls, I was embarrassed to see a man, not 15 feet away, slip out of his clothes and begin showering with only a glass wall between us. Another inmate shaved a friend's head with an electric razor. Others sat around in their underwear.

"This is their house," the CO remarked when he saw my surprise.

The lack of privacy is startling. Even the toilets are wide open to view via a picture window. Most unnerving are the halls with see-through ceilings, over which an armed guard strolls back and forth. The inmates eye me and saunter around and hang out at the tables. Racially and according to gang affiliation, they're segregated: blacks on the east end, Aryans and Southerns on the west. Day room feels very much like a recreation hall stripped of its foosball, pool tables and vending machines. But it is much more sterile than any rec room—no posters, no rugs, no cushions, no color—just bolted down steel tables, chairs and benches on gray cement floors. And then there is the smell, the smell of an institution: that unpleasant mix of metal and disinfectant which almost covers the human scents of sweat, breath and the faint trace of urine.

In another block we wait for yard time, when the second tier goes out to the yard to exercise and the first tier stays for day room, an arrangement that alternates daily. But something has happened, and so we wait. The men, locked in their cells during the delay, stare out the narrow slits of their cell windows. The frustration and confusion is almost palpable. Some pace by their windows—the passing is swift because of the tight space—they might as well be turning in circles. Three or four inmates are out of their cells, and a CO addresses one, a slight Latino.

"Jorge, get me that push broom."

The inmate says "okay" and heads for the broom. Such a simple exchange, holding within it the entire prison dynamic of authority, obedience and order. The lieutenant, who will be promoted soon to Sacramento, tells me the men are quieter because I'm here. Anytime I look around, at least two dozen pairs of eyes are pinned on me. He says they're not used to attractive young women, and the words are not a compliment but a statement of fact—and a warning.

As I drive away, it occurs to me not for the first time that it is only when I leave a prison that I most fully appreciate the meaning of the word "freedom," and I wonder what the prison employees think when they leave towards what is, for now, their home.

On my way to Rumors Sports Bar & Grill—I need a beer—I come to a stoplight next to a van full of prisoners, in glaring orange uniform. They look down at me from their windows like overgrown schoolchildren. They're smiling because this is fun for them. I flash a grin and drive on, only a little unnerved.

Rumors is empty except for a sad sack of a guy at the bar and two women downing shots of Jack Daniels at a corner table. Phantoms swirl in the smoke and dust-filled air, figures shaped from the late Sun slicing through the blinds. On the radio, John Cougar mourns his little pink houses.

I flip through my notes and think about a conversation with my friend—that you can't escape the prisons' presence. We had talked of souls, of whether souls have a voice. If so, what happens when 10,000 miserable souls are confined in one small place? What kind of voice do you hear then? Of course there is no measuring, but it provokes the underlying question: can any economy based on human punishment be good in the end? And the employees who spend 8, sometimes 16 hours a day in that environment—how much can a small town bear?

When I go home it's different now, and of course that's the paradox, you can't go home again because you've changed, but in this case, it's home that's changed. And I can no longer ignore a discomfiting idea: the profound truth of a prison town is that its future is sentenced as surely as the inmates'. Most of the inmates, though, can leave when their time is done, but the town will never leave the prison. Or more precisely: the prison will never leave this town.

No escape. The sad sack sidles over and sloshes over his words, "what are you writing?"

A letter.

"Is he in jail?"

It is ironic that the most concrete example of the change in Susanville—the prison itself—takes on its own abstract symbolism. During the day, no one could mistake the prison for anything but what it is, with its gray cement structures, high fencing with spiraling razor wire, guard towers with tinted glass—and silence.

But it is at night that the prison seems to take on a life of its own. At night, the proximity of the town to the prison is most evident because of the lights. Since more than half the inmates are Level III and IV, the prison is surrounded by 30-foot high poles topped with glaring amber lights. The resulting glow changes the night sky, affects the entire county—the yellow glow can be seen from 50 miles away, and even planes flying over Sacramento, 200 miles to the south, can see the prison. On overcast nights, the clouds reflect the prison's light, casting the sky into an eerie, hellish spectacle, like embers from a tremendous firestorm, fallout from a war.

The town was furious: the lights illuminated not just the irrevocable change to their environment, but their powerlessness as well. If the state had stuck with the original plan of a low-security prison, which voters approved, fewer lights would have been needed. The Committee to Restore the Night Skies formed to lobby to shield the lights or to reduce their number. But after three years of outcry and meetings and petitions, for security reasons, the lights remain.

Despite the problems with the prison—the gangs and domestic violence, the increasing prices and strip-mall growth, the transience of the prison employees, the vacant housing, the would-be developers who scorn penal towns—what most people complain about are the lights. They have come to represent the ultimate, and intangible, cost of High Desert State Prison.

"When I first came to Susanville about 10 years ago," my mother told me, "it was at night and your brother and I drove over Highway 36 and saw the town below us like a little constellation of stars. It was so dark all around and the town seemed to just hang there in mid-air, like some fairy village. Now you see this tremendous area rimmed with horrible yellow lights—and it's all you can see."

My brother, returning after a year at college, said he will never forget the change.

"I came around the Bass Hill corner and I couldn't believe it. There was the prison, bright as day. It looked futuristic, unnatural, something out of a science fiction movie. Like some giant alien mother ship had landed."

Discussion and Writing Questions

1. How does Fraser describe herself in this essay? How does she describe Susanville, California? How does her description of herself affect the way readers react to the essay? Why include herself in this argument at all?
2. According to Fraser what have been the positive and negative effects of the prison industry in and on Susanville, California? Which of her arguments about cause and effect are most persuasive and why? Which are least persuasive and why? Explain, in an informal essay, your own reactions to the persuasive/unpersuasive arguments about causation that Fraser makes.

Intertextual Question

3. While Fraser's analysis of the prison industry and its effects on people's lives is focused narrowly on one place, Douglas A. Blackmon, in "Hard Time," focuses much more broadly. Which of these arguments/analyses is most effective and why?

The New Spies
STEPHEN ARMSTRONG

Stephen Armstrong has written on topics ranging from reality television to the dangers of carrying certain nasal sprays while traveling to Japan to the inadvisability of wearing camouflage clothing in some Caribbean nations—the latter both hazards that frequently land British tourists in tropical or Oriental jails. He has written for GQ *and* Elle, Wallpaper *and the* Sunday Times. *In the following article, from the* New Statesman, *Armstrong explores the issue of governmental intrusion into legal, law-abiding protest groups.*

Prereading Question

In its early years, especially under the guidance of J. Edgar Hoover, the FBI frequently infiltrated protest organizations, including any group thought to represent communism in some way and such watchdog organizations as the American Civil Liberties Union. This was done even when there was neither evidence of a crime nor reason to suspect criminal behavior. Such practices were decried for decades but revived in the wake of the terrorist attacks of 9/11. Is it fair for nonviolent groups behaving in entirely legal ways to be infiltrated and investigated by "spies" for the government? Does fair matter in such a situation?

————————— ◆ —————————

A s you hunker down for the last few days of the Camp for Climate Action, discussing how to force your way into Kingsnorth power station in an attempt to prevent the construction of a new coal facility, cast your eyes around your fellow protesters. Do they look entirely bona fide to you? And don't look for the old-school special branch officers—Kent Police are a tiny force. It's the corporate spies hired by private companies you need to watch out for.

According to the private espionage industry itself, roughly one in four of your comrades is on a multinational's payroll.

Russell Corn, managing director of Diligence, one of a growing number of "corporate intelligence agencies," with offices high in the Canary Wharf glass tower, says private spies make up 25 per cent of every activist camp. "If you stuck an intercept up near one of those camps, you wouldn't believe the amount of outgoing calls after every meeting saying, 'Tomorrow we're going to cut the fence,'" he smiles. "Easily one in four of the people there are taking the corporate shilling."

In April this year, for instance, the anti-aviation campaign network Plane Stupid, one of the main organisers of the eco-camp built to protest against the expansion of Heathrow Airport, announced that one of its activists, Ken Tobias, was actually called Toby Kendall, was working for a corporate espionage firm called C2i, and had been leaking information about the group to paying clients and the media. He had been hired by an as yet unknown private company to provide information and disrupt the group's campaigning.

When Tobias first turned up at Plane Stupid's meetings in July 2007, he seemed a committed former Oxford student dedicated to reducing aircraft emissions. The group gradually became suspicious because he showed up early at meetings, constantly pushed for increasingly dramatic direct action and—the ultimate giveaway—dressed a little too well for an ecowarrior. When they showed his picture around Oxford they found an old college pal who identified him as Toby Kendall. A quick Google search revealed his Bebo page with a link to a corporate networking site, where his job as an "analyst" at C2i International, working in "security and investigations," was pasted in full public view.

Just a month earlier, a woman called Cara Schaffer had contacted the Student/Farmworker Alliance, an idealistic bunch of American college students who lobby fast-food companies to help migrant workers in Florida who harvest tomatoes. Like the cockle-pickers of Morecambe Bay, many of these workers are smuggled into the US by gangs, which then take their passports and force them to work without pay to clear often fictitious debts to regain their papers.

DIGGING UP DIRT

Again, Schaffer's excessive eagerness aroused suspicion, and again, the internet revealed her true identity. She owned Diplomatic Tactical Services, a private espionage firm which had previously hired as a subcontractor one Guillermo Zarabozo, today facing murder charges in Miami for his role in allegedly executing four crew members of a chartered fishing boat, an allegation he denies. Schaffer turned out to be working for Burger King—the home, perhaps appropriately, of the Whopper.

The cute thing about these two bozos is that they got caught pretty early on, but that was because they were young and had no background in espionage.

The real market is in proper, old-school spies who are suddenly entering the private sector. For professional spooks, the 1990s were no fun at all. The Cold War was over, defence spending was down and a detailed knowledge of cold-drop techniques in central Berlin was useless to governments looking for Arabic speakers who knew the Quran.

From New York and London to Moscow and Beijing, any decent-sized corporation can now hire former agents from the CIA, FBI, MI5, MI6 and the KGB. The ex-spooks are selling their old skills and contacts to multinationals, hedge funds and oligarchs, digging up dirt on competitors, uncovering the secrets of boardroom rivals and exposing investment targets. They are also keeping tabs on journalists, protesters and even potential employees.

"MI5 and MI6 in particular have always guided ex-employees into security companies," explains Annie Machon, the former

MI5 agent who helped David Shayler blow the whistle on the security services back in 1997. "It's always useful to them to have friends they can tap for info or recruit for a job that requires plausible deniability. The big change in recent years has been the huge growth in these companies. Where before it was a handful of private detective agencies, now there are hundreds of multinational security organisations, which operate with less regulation than the spooks themselves," she says.

Corn's company Diligence, for instance, was a set up in 2000 by Nick Day, a former MI5 spy, and an ex-CIA agent, Mike Baker. Before long, the duo had built up a roster of high-paying clients including Enron, oil and pharmaceutical companies, as well as law firms and hedge funds. In 2001, a small investment by the Washington lobbying company Barbour Griffith & Rogers propelled their growth. However, BGR and Baker sold their stakes in 2005, shortly before a scandal shook Diligence. KPMG, the global professional services firm, accused Diligence staff of impersonating British spies to gain information on a corporate takeover for a Russian telecoms client called Alfa Group. Diligence settled the lawsuit without admitting liability.

Since then, it has recruited the former Conservative Party leader Michael Howard as chairman of its European operations. And it is that sort of respectability and lobbying power that big players are after. In 2007, the parent company of the US private military firm Blackwater, which hit the headlines for gunning down Iraqi civilians in Baghdad last September, entered this market through Total Intelligence Solutions (TIS), a new CIA-type private operation, to provide intelligence services to commercial clients.

DISCREET INVESTIGATIONS

Blackwater's vice-chairman, J Cofer Black, who runs TIS, spent three decades in the CIA and the state department, becoming director of the Counterterrorist Centre and co-ordinator for counterterrorism, a job with ambassadorial rank. He describes the new company as bringing "the intelligence-gathering methodology and analytical skills traditionally honed by CIA operatives directly to the boardroom. With a service like this, CEOs and their security personnel will be able to respond to threats quickly and confidently—whether it's determining which city is safest to open a new plant in or working to keep employees out of harm's way after a terrorist attack."

Black also says TIS will operate a "24/7 intelligence fusion and warning centre" that will monitor civil unrest, terrorism, economic stability, environmental and health concerns, and information technology security around the world.

The established firms already operating in this area include Kroll, Aegis, Garda, Control Risks, GPW and Hakluyt & Co. More firms are opening every day and there is little regulation of the sector.

Hakluyt & Co was founded in 1995 by former British MI6 officers, with a reputation for discreet and effective investigations. The company butler, a former gurkha, greets visitors to its London HQ, a town house off Park Lane. In winter, meetings can be conducted beside the fire. Computers are rarely in sight. Hakluyt's advisory board has become an exit chamber for captains of industry and former government officials. Members have included Sir Rod Eddington, a former BA CEO, and Sir Christopher Gent, former chief executive of Vodafone.

"It is hard to work well for an oil company without knowing who all the key decision-makers in a government are and having the right contacts to reach them," explains Stéphane Gérardin, who runs the French private security company Géos. "We have an intelligence section where we employ some investigative journalists, people from the finance sector, from equity banks and some from security backgrounds.

"It is an important part of image protection for our clients as well. We have our own tracking and monitoring centre, with analysts doing risk mapping and preparing our clients for every potential problem. It could be about alerting them to local sensitivities. Or, in this globalised internet age, it can be a group of students in Cambridge who have launched a protest website, who may be sending out a petition.

"So we need to be able to understand and prepare our own propaganda to counter such attacks. This is work we do to protect our clients."

TRUSTED FRIEND

Like the state security services, which ended up running Class War in the 1990s after a hugely successful penetration, these spies work to become reliable members of any protest movement. In April 2007, the Campaign Against Arms Trade called in the police after court documents showed that the weapons manufacturer BAE Systems had paid a private agency to spy on the peace group.

BAE admitted that it had paid £2,500 a month to LigneDeux Associates, whose agent Paul Mercer—accepted as a trusted member of the campaign—passed information, including a legally privileged document, to BAE's director of security, Mike McGinty.

Unlike the security services, however, these services don't bother with penetrating the far left or anti-fascist groups. Their clients are only interested in the protest movements that threaten corporations. And as that is the nature of much protest in these times, it is a wide field, but with a particular impact on environmental groups.

At any of this summer's green protests the corporate spies will be there, out-of-work MI5 agents tapping green activists' mobile phones to sell the information on to interested companies.

Russell Corn knows of incidents where a spook at a meeting has suggested a high-street bank as a target, then left the meeting to phone the officers of said bank, telling them that he has penetrated an activist camp planning an attack and offering to sell the details. Corn has no time for such behaviour, however.

"The thing about a really good private spy," he tells me, "is that you'll never know he's around and he'll never get caught.

"The fact you can't see them ... it means nothing at all."

Discussion and Writing Questions

1. How effectively does Armstrong construct his argument for a reader who may never have been involved in any form of protest? How does he make the issue seem important for all Americans, whether you agree with him or not?

2. In a world at war with terrorism, must our expectations of governmental surveillance of nonviolent, legal protest organizations change? Is greater governmental involvement a necessary component of safety? In an essay, describe your own experiences with—or thoughts about—a specific protest group. How would your feelings and/or experiences with this group be changed if one or more members were, in fact, "spies"?

Intertextual Question

3. Consider the arguments about online gaming made by Clive Thompson (Chapter 1) and Steve Tilley (Chapter 1). Would it be right for the same "spies" who infiltrate real-world protest organizations to infiltrate virtual-world

groups, too? If a collection of Avatars in Second Life come together to organize against Bank of America or federal support for Head Start programs or whatever, and no laws are broken, is it reasonable for an Avatar representing a real-world governmental agent to spy on the gathering and report officially on its virtual doings?

Call It Slavery
JOHN MILLER

John R. Miller is a public policy scholar at the Wilson Center, a nonpartisan institution concerned with policy and scholarship in national and world affairs. Miller has served as the U.S. ambassador-at-large on modern day slavery (2004–2006) and as a U.S. representative in Congress from the state of Washington (1985–1993). He was a member of the Congressional Human Rights Caucus. He is a fellow of the Women and Public Policy Program at the John F. Kennedy School of Government at Harvard and a senior fellow of the Discovery Institute in Seattle. In "Call It Slavery," Miller explores the effects of the silence and misnomers regarding modern slavery.

Prereading Question

Does slavery still exist? If it does, what does slavery look like in the twenty-first century?

———————— ✦ ————————

The abolition of slavery was the great cause of 19th-century humanitarians. In the 21st century, it needs new champions.

"So YOU'RE GOING TO RUN THE STATE DEPARTMENT'S trafficking office!" a friend exclaimed when he heard the news. "What qualifications do you have to run a motor pool?" That was back in 2002, and despite a history of involvement in human rights issues as a congressman from the state of Washington, I was almost as much in the dark about human trafficking as my friend. Like most Americans, I assumed that slavery had ended in the 19th century. As I was to learn during the next four years, slavery may be illegal, but it still flourishes around the world, even in the United States. Despite the phenomenal increase in worldwide humanitarian concern, it remains one of the most curiously neglected issues of our time.

During my years as director of the U.S. State Department's Office to Monitor and Combat Trafficking in Persons, and later as ambassador at large on modern slavery, I met with many survivors of slavery: sex slaves; farm, factory, and domestic servitude slaves; child soldier slaves; even children enslaved as camel jockeys in the Persian Gulf states.

In an Amsterdam hospital I encountered Katya, who recalled how, as a Czech teenager with a disintegrating marriage and a two-year-old daughter, she was told by a "friend of the family" that she could make good money waiting on tables in Amsterdam. A Czech trafficker drove Katya and four other girls to the Netherlands, where he linked up with a Dutch counterpart. After they took the girls' passports for "safekeeping," the men drove Katya to a brothel in Amsterdam's red-light district. When Katya said that she had come to work in a restaurant, she was told that she owed the traffickers thousands of euros for transporting her across Europe. When Katya continued to resist, she was told she must do the men's bidding if she hoped to see her daughter alive. She was freed only after several years, through the efforts of a friendly taxi driver who enlisted a gang to intimidate her captors.

In Bangkok, I met a teenager named Lord at a Catholic shelter. She told me that her parents in the hills of Laos had sold her at the age of 11 to a woman who promised to educate her. She was then resold to a Bangkok embroidery factory, where she was forced to sew 14 hours a day without pay. When Lord protested the first time, she was beaten; the second time, she was shot in the face with a BB gun. She was locked in a closet; her captors poured industrial chemicals on her face. Bars across windows and doors kept Lord and other girls from leaving. They were finally rescued in a government raid.

In Uganda I talked with Nancy, who had been abducted at gunpoint along with her sister from their family's garden by the Lord's Resistance Army, then forced to march to a remote camp where she was trained to kill. (I did not have the heart to ask if she had been forced to kill relatives and friends, a common practice.) Nancy tried to escape, was caught and beaten, then was turned over to a rebel commander to serve as his concubine. Nancy escaped only when her jaw was shot off in a clash with government soldiers and she was left behind to die.

In the United States I met with Susan, an African-American woman in her twenties who had been terrorized since her teens by her Minneapolis pimp. He exerted such control over her that she didn't know how to buy groceries, take a bus, or interact with people outside "the business."

It is not a coincidence that the vast majority of the former slaves I met were women and girls. Sex and domestic servitude slaves are the largest discrete categories in human trafficking across international borders. As many as 80 percent of all slaves are women or girls, making human trafficking, as antislavery activist Michael Horowitz calls it, "the great immediate women's issue of our time." Not surprisingly, feminists, along with faith-based groups, have become the biggest advocates of abolition.

Because slavery is universally illegal—though it was banned in Saudi Arabia only in 1962 and in Mauritania in 1981—its existence is subterranean. There are no reliable estimates of the number of people held in bondage. The U.S. State Department and the International Labor Organization put the figure in the millions. The State Department estimates that as many as 17,500 slaves are brought into the United States every year, from many different countries, and it is likely that trafficking within the United States involves several times as many people. As is the case elsewhere in the world, most American slaves toil in brothels, massage parlors, and other sex businesses, or as domestic servants. A large proportion of those who come from abroad arrive by perfectly legal means, often in the company of "handlers" who help them obtain tourist or business visas.

As I grappled with the enormity of the crimes I encountered and the near silence that surrounded them, I turned to history for insight, and especially to the example of William Wilberforce (1759–1833), the great British reformer who led the 20-year campaign in Parliament to abolish the slave trade in the British Atlantic. In 1807, Parliament officially outlawed the horrible trade that every year saw thousands of human beings carried off from Africa to sugar plantations in the West Indies and to other British outposts in the Americas. Even so, slavery was not abolished in the British Empire until 1833, the year of Wilberforce's death.

In modern parlance, Wilberforce was a "values" politician. He was an evangelical Christian who confronted centuries of institutional support for slavery, even within organized religion.

Evangelicals and their Quaker allies took on the task of making Britain see that the long-accepted and rarely questioned institution of slavery was an abomination. Wilberforce had more than moral force at his command; he was a masterful strategist and orator. Edmund Burke compared him to Demosthenes. Even James Boswell, who maliciously described the stooped, five foot one British parliamentarian as a "dwarf," expressed amazement after watching him deliver a speech: "I saw what seemed a mere shrimp mount upon the table; but as I listened, he grew, and grew, until the shrimp became a whale."

For today's antislavery activists, I realized, much of the task is the same as it was in Wilberforce's time: to awaken others to an abomination that most people barely recognize. It is a measure of the challenge that remains that activists still need to persuade human rights organizations and other groups to pay attention to slavery. Freedom House, for example, does not weigh slavery in Freedom in the World, its respected country-by-country annual survey of human rights around the world. One reason is that victims of slavery tend to be isolated, relatively poor, and badly educated. They don't hold press conferences. But people deprived of their political and religious rights are often educated and articulate. If they can't speak for themselves, they have spokespersons who can.

Clarity about what is going on before our eyes, I discovered, can be a potent weapon. On a visit to Japan in 2004, I held a press conference to highlight the peculiar fact that Tokyo had issued 85,000 visas to female "entertainers" from the Philippines in 2003. The Japanese government quickly responded, and by 2006 the number of visas was down to 5,700. Not all governments are as sensitive to American opinion as Japan's, but the State Department's annual Trafficking in Persons Report, which rates the efforts of 170 countries to suppress slavery, has been a useful attention getter on many occasions.

In Wilberforce's day, slavery was shrouded in euphemism by its defenders: "field hand," "laborer" and "houseboy." Today, the news media and academics unthinkingly use words—"forced laborer," "child soldier," and "sex worker"—that have their own anesthetic effect, and along with others I have insisted on calling slavery by its right name. I have never understood why we constantly use the bloodless, bureaucratic term "human trafficking."

Today's slaves are not dragged off in chains, but they are just as effectively deprived of their freedom by force or threats. They are bought, sold, and leased. For years during the Bosnian civil war a sex slave auction operated in Belgrade, and many auction sites thinly disguised as sex tourism sites have functioned on the Web. Slaves may receive some pay for their work, but their wages amount to no more than the subsistence provided to people in bondage in the past. Because it is illegal, the trade is dominated by organized crime. It takes a network of workers to persuade a woman like Katya to leave her home country, to sell and transport her, and to keep her terrorized for years. Some law enforcement officials believe that the trade in humans is the third-largest source of profits for organized crime, after drugs and arms.

Unlike the slaves of yesterday, those of today are not captured in raids or warfare, but usually are either deceived into or in some cases willingly enter into slave status, then find themselves trapped. Yet, as in the past, the slave trade is defined by greed, sexual exploitation, beatings, and rape. Race is still a factor. In Mauritania, lighter-skinned descendants of Arab invaders sometimes ensnare darker-skinned Africans in slavery as shepherds or domestics. In India, the survivors of sex and agricultural slavery I met tended to be darker-skinned members of lower castes.

In most countries, what distinguishes the victims is not their color but their foreignness or otherness. Most of the survivors I talked to were attracted by the promise of a job in a distant land. Once there, they found themselves in unfamiliar surroundings and unable to escape. It is difficult to flee when you know neither the local language nor the geography, and when you have no friends or family outside your small world to turn to for help. I rarely met survivors who had been enslaved in their own community. Moldovan women are enslaved in Dutch brothels, Indonesian men on Malaysian construction sites, and Filipinas in Saudi Arabian homes.

Poverty often propels people into slavery, causing families, for example, to sell their children. But the equation is not always simple. In Indonesia, Save the Children found that some impoverished villages produced many slavery victims while similar villages nearby produced very few. A study in Nigeria showed that the villages that sent the most victims to Italy were not the poorest ones but those where television was available. As that study suggests, visions of opportunity drive many victims into the hands of modern slave traders, and often these slaves are people with some resources of their own. An Indonesian woman named Nour whom I met in Saudi Arabia paid a recruiting agency thousands of dollars to obtain work as a maid in Saudi Arabia, where she hoped to earn far greater sums to send home. But her masters confined Nour to a house, and beat her until gangrene forced the amputation of several fingers and toes.

As Wilberforce saw, well-intentioned reformers rob the abolitionist cause of some of its power by seeking to improve the conditions of slavery rather than end the institution itself. In the 18th century, the high-minded Dutch boasted of having the cleanest slave ships. Today's reformers call for better ventilation in factories for coerced workers and condoms and health inspections for those who may be enslaved in prostitution. The 21st-century Dutch are leading exponents of the idea that legalizing and regulating prostitution can reduce sex slavery. But as they have discovered, it is hard to promote a legalized sex trade, with its inevitable links to organized crime, without becoming a magnet for slave traders, and city officials in Amsterdam are now working to shrink the city's famous red-light district. Germany, which has also embraced legalization, has almost 10 times the number of people engaged in prostitution as neighboring France, and, correspondingly, more trafficking victims.

There is no dearth of multinational agreements designed to address trafficking, including the United Nations' Protocol to Prevent, Suppress, and Punish Trafficking in Persons, Especially Women and Children (2003). But in all my travels, I never encountered a government that attributed a specific action to an international covenant. Indeed, some of the governments with the worst reputations for non-enforcement, such as Mexico and Equatorial Guinea, were among the first to ratify the UN protocol. The UN's own moral authority in this area has been compromised by the fact, documented in a 2004 report to the organization by Prince Zeid Ra'ad al-Hussein of Jordan, that UN peacekeeping troops in the Democratic Republic of the Congo and other countries have been guilty of rape and of using food and money to entice children into sex.

There is no substitute for solid national laws and vigorous enforcement, and obtaining both requires moral suasion from abroad and, most of all, constant effort by nongovernmental organizations in each country. Prosecutors convicted more than 3,000 slave owners and traders around the world in 2007, up from just hundreds seven years ago. But far too many countries still treat slave trading lightly. In Germany and other European nations, convicted traffickers often get only suspended sentences or probation. Near Chennai, India, I met members of three generations of a lower-caste family—a boy, his father, and his grandfather—who had been freed by the government after many years of servitude as bonded laborers, working to pay off a debt to a local businessman who ensured that the debt grew ever larger. (With their millions of victims, India and Pakistan are the great exceptions to the rule that most modern slaves travel across national borders.) Just when I was feeling pleased with the provincial government's efforts, the father pointed to the rice mill where they had toiled. It was still operating, and the owner had not been punished—he was bringing in more slaves to replace those who had been released.

A situation in which the educational stakes are higher is difficult to imagine. Preventive education is vital, especially in alerting potential victims to the risks they face in traveling abroad in pursuit of opportunity. Efforts on the demand side can also be effective. In San Francisco, a mandatory "John school" for men caught soliciting prostitutes that showed them the link between the sex industry and slavery and other ills produced a dramatic drop in recidivism rates; the program has been replicated in other cities. A final imperative is to rescue and protect victims. Most countries summarily deport rescued slaves, but the burden of shame often prevents them from returning to their home villages. Toward the end of my tour as ambassador I saw more shelters being opened, but much more assistance is needed to help these traumatized and poorly educated people make new lives.

When Britain turned against slavery, it threw its military power against human traffickers. After Parliament passed the Slave Trade Act in 1807, Wilberforce and others prodded the British Admiralty into using part of the British navy to seize slave ships traveling to the Americas, regardless of which country's flag they flew. Britain sacrificed the lives of 600 sailors, but it liberated hundreds of thousands of slaves on the high seas.

There is no military solution for modern slavery. But the United States can continue to campaign for clarity, for action, and for abolition. Our own record bears blemishes and deep stains—both historic and modern—but we have probably done more than almost any other country to eradicate this scourge at home and abroad. Even before the Slave Trade Act, critics argued that Britain had no right to impose its moral values on the world. Wilberforce rightly replied that freedom is a universal value. And when critics insisted that Britain should not act unilaterally—it tried without success to enlist other European nations—his friend and ally, Prime Minister William Pitt, responded, "This miserable argument, if persevered in, would be an eternal bar to the annihilation of evil. How is it ever to be eradicated if every nation is thus prudentially to wait until the concurrence of all the world should be obtained?"

Thus, more than 200 years ago in facing Britain's own moral quandary, Pitt and Wilberforce posed the abolitionist challenge to all nations in all times. Today we need hundreds of Wilberforces in more than a hundred countries to finish the abolitionist revolution.

Discussion and Writing Questions

1. Miller claims that much like the antislavery movement of the late 1700s and early 1800s, today's antislavery advocates must create an awareness of slavery, its victims, and atrocities. What do you think is the best way to spread awareness about modern slavery?
2. Miller states that in the modern slave trade, many people are tricked into situations of forced slavery. The enticement of better pay for jobs often lures people to travel to foreign countries where control is more easily asserted over the victims. How do you think that countries can cooperate to reduce slave trafficking? Should countries have a shared obligation to fight against slavery? Consider the international relationship America has with one other nation; how might the "slave" trade between the United States and this nation be stopped?

Intertextual Question

3. How is the slavery described by Miller similar to the situations described in Struby's "A Fist Full of Dollars"? How does the lure of the financial reward of a "big fight" compare to the false promises described by Miller?

A Virtual World but Real Money
RICHARD SIKLOS

Across his career as a writer, Richard Siklos has worked for publications as diverse as the Globe and Mail, *Ontario's* London Free Press, *and Toronto's* Financial Times. *His work frequently focuses upon the news business, including articles on media barons such as Rupert Murdoch and Conrad Black, the focus of Siklos's book,*

Shades of Black. *In the following article, Siklos considers the real money to be made in unreal cyberspaces.*

Prereading Question

While poker and porn are both significant pieces of the virtual economy, the online opportunities to spend and earn real-world money are legion. Consider your own online experiences and those of your family and close friends. From this circle of relations and acquaintances, who makes money online and how? How do these same people spend money online?

———————— ✦ ————————

It has a population of a million. The "people" there make friends, build homes and run businesses. They also play sports, watch movies and do a lot of other familiar things. They even have their own currency, convertible into American dollars.

But residents also fly around, walk underwater and make themselves look beautiful, or like furry animals, dragons, or practically anything—or anyone—they wish.

This parallel universe, an online service called Second Life that allows computer users to create a new and improved digital version of themselves, began in 1999 as a kind of online video game.

But now, the budding fake world is not only attracting a lot more people, it is taking on a real world twist: big business interests are intruding on digital utopia. The Second Life online service is fast becoming a three-dimensional test bed for corporate marketers, including Sony BMG Music Entertainment, Sun Microsystems, Nissan, Adidas/Reebok, Toyota and Starwood Hotels.

The sudden rush of real companies into so-called virtual worlds mirrors the evolution of the Internet itself, which moved beyond an educational and research network in the 1990's to become a commercial proposition—but not without complaints from some quarters that the medium's purity would be lost.

Already, the Internet is the fastest-growing advertising medium, as traditional forms of marketing like television commercials and print advertising slow. For businesses, these early forays into virtual worlds could be the next frontier in the blurring of advertising and entertainment.

Unlike other popular online video games like World of Warcraft that are competitive fantasy games, these sites meld elements of the most popular forms of new media: chat rooms, video games, online stores, user-generated content sites like YouTube.com and social networking sites like MySpace.com.

Philip Rosedale, the chief executive of Linden Labs, the San Francisco company that operates Second Life, said that until a few months ago only one or two real world companies had dipped their toes in the synthetic water. Now, more than 30 companies are working on projects there, and dozens more are considering them. "It's taken off in a way that is kind of surreal," Mr. Rosedale said, with no trace of irony.

Beginning a promotional venture in a virtual world is still a relatively inexpensive proposition compared with the millions spent on other media. In Second Life, a company like Nissan or its advertising agency could buy an "island" for a one-time fee of $1,250 and a monthly rate of $195 a month. For its new campaign built around its Sentra car, the company then needed to hire some computer programmers to create a gigantic driving course and design digital cars that people "in world" could actually drive, as well as some billboards and other promotional spots throughout the virtual world that would encourage people to visit Nissan Island.

Virtual world proponents—including a roster of Linden Labs investors that includes Jeffrey P. Bezos, the founder of Amazon.com; Mitchell D. Kapor, the software pioneer; and Pierre Omidyar, the eBay founder—say that the entire Internet is moving toward being a three-dimensional experience that will become more realistic as computing technology advances.

Entering Second Life, people's digital alter-egos—known as avatars—are able to move around and do everything they do in the physical world, but without such bothers as the laws of physics. "When you are at Amazon.com you are actually there with 10,000 concurrent other people, but you cannot see them or talk to them," Mr. Rosedale said. "At Second Life, everything you experience is inherently experienced with others."

Second Life is the largest and best known of several virtual worlds created to attract a crowd. The cable TV network MTV, for example, just began Virtual Laguna Beach, where fans of its show, "Laguna Beach: The Real O.C.," can fashion themselves after the show's characters and hang out in their faux settings.

Unlike Second Life, which emphasizes a hands-off approach and has little say over who sets up shop inside its simulated world, MTV's approach is to bring in advertisers as partners.

In Second Life, retailers like Reebok, Nike, Amazon and American Apparel have all set up shops to sell digital as well as real world versions of their products. Last week, Sun Microsystems unveiled a new pavilion promoting its products, and IBM alumni held a virtual world reunion.

This week, the performer Ben Folds is to promote a new album with two virtual appearances. At one, he will play the opening party for Aloft, an elaborate digital prototype for a new chain of hotels planned by Starwood Hotels and Resorts. The same day, Mr. Folds will also "appear" at a new facility his music label's parent company, Sony BMG, is opening at a complex called Media Island.

Meanwhile, Nissan is introducing its Nissan promotion, featuring a gigantic vending machine dispensing cars people can "drive" around.

And some of this is likely to be covered for the outside world by such business news outlets as CNET and Reuters, which now have reporters embedded full-time in the virtual realm.

All this attention has some Second Lifers concerned that their digital paradise will never be the same, like a Wal-Mart coming to town or a Starbucks opening in the neighborhood. "The phase it is in now is just using it as a hype and marketing thing," said Catherine A. Fitzpatrick, 50, a member of Second Life who in the real world is a Russian translator in Manhattan.

In her second life, Ms. Fitzpatrick's digital alter-ego is a figure well-known to other participants called Prokofy Neva, who runs a business renting "real estate" to other players. "The next phase," she said, "will be they try to compete with other domestic products—the people who made sneakers in the world are now in danger of being crushed by Adidas."

Mr. Rosedale says such concerns are overstated, because there are no advantages from economies of scale for big corporations in Second Life, and people can avoid places like Nissan Island as easily as they can avoid going to Nissan's Web site. There is no limit to what can be built in Second Life, just as there is no limit to how many Web sites populate the Internet.

Linden Labs makes most of its money leasing "land" to tenants, Mr. Rosedale said, at an average of roughly $20 per month per "acre" or $195 a month for a private "island." The land mass of Second Life is growing about 8 percent a month, a spokeswoman said, and now totals "60,000 acres," the equivalent of about 95 square miles in the physical world. Linden Labs, a private company, does not disclose its revenue.

Despite the surge of outside business activity in Second Life, Linden Labs said corporate interests still owned less than 5 percent of the virtual world's real estate.

As many as 10,000 people are in the virtual world at a time, and they are engaged in a gamut of ventures: everything from holding charity fund-raisers to selling virtual helicopters to operating sex clubs. Linden also makes money on exchanging United States dollars for what it calls Linden dollars for around 400 Linden dollars for $1 (people can load up on them with a credit card). A typical article of clothing—say a shirt—would cost around 200 Linden dollars, or 50 cents. As evidence of the growth of its "economy," Second Life's Web site tracks how much money changes hands each day. It recently reached as much as $500,000 a day and is growing as much as 15 percent a month.

On Tuesday, a Congressional committee said it was investigating whether virtual assets and incomes should be taxed.

But many inhabitants simply hang out for free. For advertisers worried about the effectiveness of the 30-second TV spot and the clutter of real world billboards and Internet pop-up ads, Second Life is appealing because it is a place where people literally immerse themselves in their products.

Steve F. Kerho, director of interactive marketing and media for Nissan USA, said the Second Life campaign was part of a growing interest in online video games. "We're just trying to follow our consumer, that's where they're spending their time," Mr. Kerho said. "But there has to be something in it for them—it's got to be fun; it's got to be playful."

Projects like the Aloft hotel, an offshoot of Starwood's W Hotels brand, are designed to promote the venture but also to give its designers feedback from prospective guests before the first real hotel opens in 2008.

The new Sony BMG building has rooms devoted to popular musicians like Justin Timberlake and DMX, allowing fans to mingle, listen to tunes or watch videos. Sony BMG is also toying with renting residences in the complex, as well as selling music downloads that people can listen to throughout the simulated world.

Sibley Verbeck, chief executive of the Electric Sheep Company, a consultancy that designed the Aloft and Sony BMG projects, said the flurry of corporate interest stemmed from the 10 to 20 percent growth in the number of people who had gone into virtual worlds each month for the last three years. Though exact numbers are difficult to come by, the figure should top a few million by next year, he said.

The spread of these worlds, however, is limited by access to high-speed Internet connections and, in Second Life's case, software that is challenging to master and only runs on certain models of computers.

"If it doesn't crash and burn then it will become real," he said. "So now's the time to start experimenting and learning ahead of your competition."

As part of that process, businesses are learning that different rules apply when they venture into an arena where audiences are in control. "Users are the content—that's the thing that everybody has a hard time getting over," said Michael Wilson, the chief executive of Makena Technologies, which operates the virtual world There.com and helped build Virtual Laguna Beach.

For example, Sun Microsystems kicked off the opening of its Second Life venue with a press conference online hosted by executives and Mr. Rosedale of Linden Labs. But by the time the event was in full swing, several members of the audience had either walked or flown onto the stage, where they were running roughshod over the proceedings.

Even Mr. Rosedale got in on the act: he conjured a pair of sunglasses that he superimposed on a video image of a Sun representative talking on a screen behind the stage. (In virtual world lingo, such high jinks are known as "griefing.")

Some corporate events have been met with protests by placard-waving avatars. And there is even a group called the Second Life Liberation Army that has staged faux "attacks" on Reebok and American Apparel stores. (The S.L.L.A. says it is fighting for voting rights for avatars—as well as stock in Linden Labs.)

Companies in this new environment have to get used to the idea that they may never know exactly who they are dealing with. Most of those in Second Life have chosen their names from a whimsical menu of supplied surnames, resulting in monikers like Snoopybrown Zamboni and Bitmason Pimpernel; males posing as female avatars and vice versa are not uncommon.

Another issue companies have to contend with is that their brands may already be in these virtual worlds, but illegally. Henry Jenkins, a professor at the Massachusetts Institute of Technology Media Lab, said one Second Life habitué created a virtual reproduction of the Ikea catalog to help people decorate their digital pads.

Mr. Verbeck of Electric Sheep said copyright infringement was rampant. His company runs an online boutique where Second Life residents sell each other pixelized creations of everything from body parts to home furnishings to roller skates—many of them unauthorized knockoffs.

So far, the boutique has not had many requests to stop selling fake products. But "we did have a request from the Salvador Dali Museum—which was great," Mr. Verbeck said. "Second Life is so surreal that it was perfect."

Discussion and Writing Questions

1. How effectively does Siklos describe the phenomenon of Second Life for readers who may be entirely ignorant of this—and other—online gaming and interacting venues? What could make his description of this aspect of modern technological life more engaging for these unaware but interested readers?

2. Siklos alternates between very short paragraphs and (comparatively) very long paragraphs. As a reader, what effect does this style of organization have on the way you read his argument? Would it be easier to process the information if it were presented in larger or smaller paragraphs? Why? Copy one of Siklos's long paragraphs and then show where you would break the piece into three or more separate paragraphs. What other revisions would you make to the paragraph to improve on it, once it was divided into separate chunks of text?

Intertextual Question

3. How does this argument by Siklos compare and contrast with the argument made by Steve Tilley in "And Now a Game from Our Sponsor" (Chapter 5)?

What the Country Needs? A Fiscal Triple Play

DAVID M. WALKER

David M. Walker is former comptroller general of the United States and president and CEO of the Peter G. Peterson Foundation, which promotes public awareness of the nation's economic challenges. In the following article, Walker proposes a plan to pull the economy out of the recession that began circa September 2008.

Prereading Question

Do you think the federal bailouts of 2008 and 2009 were able to stimulate the economy? Why do you think these bailouts were or were not successful?

—————————— ✦ ——————————

N ot only is our country in a deep recession, but our federal financial condition is deteriorating rapidly. We need to pull a triple play, and soon, to avoid a "super subprime crisis."

First, to get our economy back on track, we need a fiscal stimulus package that is timely, targeted and temporary—large enough to make a difference but not so large as to guarantee significant waste. Its provisions should be designed to stimulate short-term consumption and create or save jobs—within this calendar year. While it may involve temporary time extensions of unemployment and other federal benefits, benefit expansions should be avoided until we get our fiscal house in order.

The stimulus being considered by the Congress is very large. Many believe that we could achieve much more stimulus with a lower price tag if a vast majority of the legislation's provisions met the above criteria. Only time will tell whether the bill that goes to President Obama's desk is modified to better meet these standards.

The federal government has engaged in a number of major "bailout" or "assistance" efforts already. More will undoubtedly occur, and we need to learn from past mistakes to increase the chance of future success.

The Troubled Asset Relief Program (TARP), for example, has been a major disappointment. This should not be surprising since it was enacted in a crisis atmosphere without clearly defined and transparent objectives and conditions to be met before the "funds flowed." As a result, it is difficult to assess the benefit of the first $350 billion in taxpayer funds. Proponents assert how much worse it would have been had they not acted, but the absence of any clear positive accomplishment is telling.

Second, the federal government needs an independent and professional person or board (e.g., three persons) who would serve as a gatekeeper and help ensure that any proposed federal assistance is consistent with the program's objectives and meets certain criteria before the funds flow. Once the funds flow, the person or board would ensure transparency and accountability.

Having been on the front lines of fighting waste and abuse for almost 10 years as comptroller general of the United States and head of the U.S. Government Accountability Office (GAO), I have concluded that the traditional transparency and accountability mechanisms are not enough to protect the taxpayers' interests when huge incremental spending amounts are involved.

Third, while turning the economy around is the priority now, we also need to take steps to put an extraordinary process in place to put our nation's finances in order and maintain investor confidence. President Obama was right when he said in January that we need to achieve a "grand bargain" during his presidency. But we need to start now—our fiscal clock is ticking, and time is not working in our favor.

As a former head of three federal agencies and a public trustee of Social Security and Medicare, I have learned that the process that one employs is critically important when transformational changes are needed. It has also led me to the conclusion that the "regular order" in Congress is broken and that achieving progress on multiple fronts within a relatively short time frame is not possible on a piecemeal basis.

What does this mean? The president and the Congress need to work together to establish a "Fiscal Future Commission" (or Task Force) that, unlike most Washington commissions, would be designed to accelerate action and get the ball across the goal line rather than punt it down the field. Ideally, this commission would be created by statute to ensure buy-in from both the Congress and the president. It should include selected congressional members and administration and non-governmental officials. It should engage the American people outside Washington's Beltway while also leveraging digital technology and the Web. After engaging the public and key stakeholders, it would make a range of budget control, entitlement, other spending and tax reform recommendations that would be subject to an "up or down" vote in Congress, with limitations on amendments so they would not undercut the fiscal "bottom line" of the commission's recommendations.

To achieve initial success and gain both enhanced credibility and momentum, the commission could be tasked with reporting on selected issues in an expedited manner—for example, Social Security reforms. Hopefully, action would be taken on any such interim recommendations. But if it weren't, then any related recommendations would be included in the group's final report. This approach would serve to provide a fail-safe mechanism to help ensure that the commission's recommendations are given appropriate consideration by the Congress.

We can and must come to grips with our current and structural fiscal challenges. Employing this three-pronged approach would enable the Obama administration and the Congress to focus on our immediate challenges while putting a credible process in place to help put our nation's financial house in order. The time for action is now.

Discussion and Writing Questions

1. Walker says that the Troubled Asset Relief Program (TARP) has been a disappointment because of the lack of oversight. He uses the TARP example to suggest an independent "gatekeeper" to monitor any other bailout monies. Do you think a single person could effectively monitor the use of billions of dollars of federal monies?

2. Walker suggests that bailout monies should be used for quick and temporary creation of jobs and a stimulus to consumption. Do you think that President Obama's plan achieved those objectives? Explain your answer in a brief essay.

Intertextual Question

3. Walker discusses the three necessary steps needed to make the federal bailouts effective. How might Walker respond to Joelle Fraser's description of Susanville, California, after the prison industry came to town?

CHAPTER 5

Business of/and Class

Previous chapters covered a range of business-related topics, from the cultural costs of pleasure to the financial fallout from unethical labor practices. You considered effects—on individuals, small towns, and nations—and traced the chain of logic and narration back to likely causes. The readings in Chapter 5 will challenge you to put these critical thinking and reading skills to further tests, in part by considering not only the complexity of some issues but also their socioeconomic contexts. An example illustrates the point.

When the American financial industry tottered on the brink of collapse, beginning late in 2008, the U.S. government rushed to act, passing sweeping legislation and spending $700 billion in a matter of weeks—an unprecedented spending measure in an almost unthinkably short time for deliberation and debate. When the automotive industry tottered on the brink of its own collapse, however, the governmental rush to help these corporations was considerably slower and less enthusiastic. The CEOs of the Big Three automakers, desperate for immediate support to keep their companies afloat, flew to Washington to lobby Congress; they were publicly criticized and humiliated for flying to DC in private corporate jets, a criticism not raised with representatives of the financial corporations in need of support only months before. The chastened CEOs were sent home to develop clear plans for how governmental support would be used (a demand also not made previously of the financial industry CEOs), and all returned to Congress by more economical and humble means—one driving hundreds of miles in a hybrid vehicle, even.

Pundits on radio and cable television were furious with this treatment of one group of CEOs versus the treatment of another. This fury was heightened in mid-2009 when huge bonuses were paid to financial corporation executives because those bonuses were legally promised by contracts that preceded governmental intervention, while blue-collar union workers within the auto industry were told to consider their contracts neither sacred nor binding, as the demands of the new economy would lead to new demands on workers. A popular line was repeated as a way to summarize this seeming discrepancy in the value of white-collar versus blue-collar workers: "You matter if you take a shower before work, but you don't matter if you take a shower after work." The implications were clear and unflattering: Workers who spend their days in clean offices have important contracts that must be honored, while workers who sweat and stand on factory assembly lines need to understand that their contracts are potentially not worth the paper upon which they are printed. The seeming discrepancy in treatment led to discussions of class, upper versus middle and working, and to discussions of race, with virtually all of the corporate, white-collar workers thought to be white and male, while the blue-collar workers were often women and minorities. None of these arguments were necessarily right or fair or even based on solid reality rather than simple perception.

The readings in Chapter 5 challenge you to consider your own thoughts on issues of race and class and your own place in these economies of race and class. White-collar work—in management and finance—is examined, as are traditionally blue-collar jobs in manufacturing. Pink-collar work, particularly domestic labor, is examined, as is a final contrast—both implicit and explicit—between the middle-class lives of American and Chinese citizens, representatives of two of the world's largest economies—both heavily influenced by matters of race and class.

The Color of Money
ANDREW ADAM NEWMAN

Andrew Adam Newman is a frequent contributor to the New York Times' *business, arts, and style sections. His articles have appeared in* New York *magazine,* Salon.com, Portfolio.com, Babble.com, *and* Bark *magazine. In the following article from* Adweek, *Newman examines the lack of diversity in the advertising workforce and the changes that are being instigated by Cyrus Mehri, a civil rights lawyer.*

Prereading Question

Should industries, such as advertising, specifically recruit minorities? What is the role that diversity should play in hiring practices?

———————— ✦ ————————

WILL THE THREAT OF A CLASS-ACTION LAWSUIT FORCE ADVERTISING TO FINALLY SOLVE ITS DIVERSITY PROBLEM?

Black athletes, musicians and actors figure more prominently in ad campaigns than ever, but the chances that African Americans actually created those ads are pretty slim.

According to Bureau of Labor Statistics data from January 2008, the advertising field—defined as advertising and PR agencies, as well as media, direct mail and other operations exclusively devoted to creating and delivering ads—is just 5 percent African American, 3 percent Asian and 8 percent Hispanic or Latino. Those numbers are particularly stark considering that New York, the city with the highest concentration of ad agencies, is only 45 percent white, according to U.S. Census data. *USA Today* recently dubbed the ad industry "a poster child for a dearth of diversity."

For more than four decades, civil rights groups have accused the ad business of violating equal-opportunity hiring laws. In 2006, the New York City Commission on Human Rights (NYCCHR), acting on a complaint from Sanford Moore, an African American who had worked at agencies including BBDO, launched an investigation of 16 prominent New York firms, including BBDO, DDB, Ogilvy & Mather, Saatchi & Saatchi and Young & Rubicam. The agencies settled with the commission, committing to increase diversity over three years.

In the wake of that settlement, some agencies have increased the number of minorities working in their shops. And the industry as a whole is making progress, according to Nancy Hill, who became the American Association of Advertising Agencies' first female CEO this year, and whose commitment to diversity has been lauded by Moore and others. "I know the industry still has a long way to go," Hill says. "But a lot of things are starting to come together."

But the data suggest that some shops have merely donned a fig leaf—offering bromides about how their hiring process is "colorblind," doing pro bono work for minority causes, but still hiring only those who look like them.

Soon, those shops could be in for a day of reckoning, as Cyrus Mehri, the civil rights lawyer behind several landmark racial discrimination suits—including those against Coca-Cola (which settled for $193 million) and Texaco (which settled for $176 million)—is now targeting the advertising business. The result could be the dropping of so many fig leaves that the industry will need a rake.

Mehri says he has been contacted by "people from inside the industry who have suffered discrimination" and that his firm will soon issue a report on African Americans in advertising. (Critics agree that the situation with African Americans is unique, since they have been confronting both racial stereotypes in advertising and the lack of professional opportunities for more than a half century.) Using Census and Equal Employment Opportunity Commission data, the report will benchmark advertising against 28 other "persuasion" industries.

Among the findings in a preliminary report obtained by *Adweek*: African Americans make up only 3.2 percent of advertising's upper management in the U.S., well under half of the average of 7.2 percent in similar professions.

Mehri won't say whether he's preparing a class-action suit against agencies, but even if he isn't, he will likely leave the industry more diverse than he found it. Based on the remedies he and the late Johnnie Cochran prescribed in a study about the lack of black head coaches in the NFL, for example, the league adopted new hiring policies and more than tripled their ranks within four years.

Luke Visconti, co-founder of the magazine *DiversityInc*, who describes the ad industry's diversity efforts as "laughable," says advertising pros should take note that Mehri "can use the legal system to grind you to bits," but that he is reasonable in crafting constructive solutions.

As Mehri turns over rocks, there's no telling what he'll find. It behooves industry insiders to know what to expect from his efforts, how some of his prior targets have responded, and how certain companies—some of them the ad industry's biggest clients—have embedded diversity deep in their hiring and management practices.

MEHRI'S TRACK RECORD

"I've yet to see an industry that has such a consistent record of indifference to minority involvement," Mehri says of the ad business on the phone from his Washington law firm, Mehri & Skalet. "It has a history of purposeful discrimination. They've been on notice a long time, but they just go through the motions and allow a discriminatory climate to continue. They're real laggards, and it's hard to understand why."

One of Mehri's best-known cases, originally launched in 1996 on behalf of two management-level employees against Texaco, and which expanded into a class-action colossus representing 1,400 aggrieved black Texaco employees, alleged that in hiring and promotion the company had regularly chosen less-experienced whites over African Americans. Texaco fought the suit for more than two years, but after testimony that claimed managers had referred to workers as "niggers" and "porch monkeys," and a recording emerged of an executive referring to African Americans as "black jelly beans," Texaco sat down in 1997 to settle.

Along with $115 million that Texaco agreed to pay employees, it promised $35 million to fund an Equality and Tolerance Task Force—consisting of civil rights lawyers, scholars, retired judges and executives—that would increase diversity at the company. It also set aside $26 million to administer salary raises over five years to black employees.

In 1999, Mehri's suit on behalf of 2,200 former and then-current employees against Coca-Cola claimed that blacks at the company were widely overlooked for promotions.

Coke's settlement of $193 million the following year was unprecedented in its heft. It was also noteworthy because Coke agreed to fund a task force, which would include a former secretary of labor and a former chair of the Equal Employment Opportunity Commission, to overhaul hiring practices. The company also agreed to tie executive compensation to diversity hiring goals and issue four yearly progress reports to the court.

Coke even asked the court to oversee its progress for a fifth year.

From 2000 to 2006, among senior executives—the ranks which industries have struggled hardest to diversify—Coke increased minority representation from 8 percent to 21 percent. For "pipeline" jobs a tier below, from 2002 to 2006, Coke increased the proportion of minorities from 21 percent to 27 percent.

"The work that we do and the decisions that we make all focus on inclusive and fair behavior," Steve Bucherati, chief diversity officer at Coca-Cola, wrote in response to questions from *Adweek*. Bucherati also noted that 29 percent of Coke's North America marketing and advertising division are minorities, as is the leader of the advertising team.

These settlements are emblematic of how vast class-action discrimination suits, by Mehri and others, gained popularity in the 1990s not just to recompense plaintiffs, but also to reshape hiring policies.

As Nancy Levit, a law professor at the University of Missouri's Kansas City School of Law, wrote recently in the *Boston College Law Review*, cases like Texaco's "have encouraged greater use of litigation to address deeply entrenched corporate practices." The goal often "is not damages but transformation of the company's treatment of employees" and the opportunity to "make a difference in workplace inclusivity."

Mehri's impact on the NFL was just as striking. In 2002, he and Cochran issued a report called "Black Coaches in the National Football League: Superior Performance, Inferior Opportunities." Though more than two-thirds of the players in the league are black, no team had hired a black head coach until 1989. When Mehri and Cochran issued their report, only two of the league's 32 teams had black head coaches.

The report recommended requiring team owners to conduct a face-to-face interview with at least one minority candidate when hiring in the future. The NFL agreed to adopt the rule, which became known as the Rooney Rule, after Dan Rooney, the Pittsburgh Steelers owner who chaired the league's Workplace Diversity Committee.

In 2003, Detroit Lions GM Matt Millen hired Steve Mariucci, who is white, as head coach without interviewing any candidates of color. The NFL slapped Millen with a $200,000 fine. Other team owners complied with the rule after that and while doing so might seem merely symbolic, the results were dramatic. Four years after the Rooney Rule took effect, the NFL reached an all-time high of seven African-American head coaches. (Today, there are six.) Before 2007, no African-American head coach had reached the Super Bowl, but both coaches that year—Lovie Smith of the Chicago Bears and Tony Dungy of the Indianapolis Colts— were black.

"What is done in the NFL is really transferable to the business world, because at base the process ensures that those who are making decisions sit down with candidates and have a conversation about the position," says Jeremi Duru, a law professor at Temple University's James E. Beasley School of Law, who worked for Mehri's firm when it issued the NFL report. "If you sit down face to face and talk about issues of shared concern, racial biases tend to be diminished."

WHERE TOP MARKETERS STAND

One thing that often happens when Mehri gets involved in a case is that Weldon Latham's phone rings. Both Texaco and Coke hired Latham—a partner in the Washington, D.C., law firm of Davis Wright Tremaine and chair of its Diversity Counseling Group—to iron out a settlement with Mehri.

When it comes to the ad industry, though, Latham actually was on the scene before Mehri. Omnicom Group hired him when its agencies BBDO, DDB, Merkley + Partners and PHD were among the 16 shops named two years ago in the investigation by New York's human-rights commission.

Latham, who has worked with numerous Fortune 500 companies not just to defend them against suits, but to help proactively develop multicultural initiatives, says business-to-business industries like advertising have been slow to adapt to diversity.

"Consumer products companies that interact with the public directly are usually a lot better about recognizing the value of diversity than a business-to-business company," he says.

DiversityInc's Visconti says, "If you believe people are created equally, then talent is distributed equally. If it's all white men in your executive committee, something went wrong."

Visconti's magazine has been compiling a Top 50 Companies for Diversity list for eight years. This year, 352 firms were evaluated on factors including the racial makeup of their workforce,

CEO diversity policies and the use of minority- and women-owned suppliers.

Iconic companies crowd the list: The top five this year, in order, were Verizon, Coca-Cola, Bank of America, PricewaterhouseCoopers and Procter & Gamble.

Conspicuously absent from the list is an advertising agency, and in eight years an agency has never appeared. (Full disclosure: *Adweek* currently does not employ a single person of color among the 16 members of its editorial and design staffs.)

Adweek cross-referenced the 2008 list with the top 100 U.S. ad spenders for the first seven months of 2008, and found that four of the top five diversity companies are also top ad spenders. In all, 22 of the top diversity companies—nearly half—were among this year's 100 top ad spenders.

P&G, the largest ad spender, has a unit within its so-called "talent supply" team that "solely focuses on diversity recruiting," according to Maxine Brown Davis, the company's chief diversity officer, who responded to questions from *Adweek* in an e mail. The company, she wrote, attends professional conferences held by groups with "high-potential diverse candidates," like the National Society of Black Engineers.

Verizon, the fourth-biggest ad spender, provided a statement in response to *Adweek*'s questions, saying the company is committed to looking like America because "customers and constituents are increasingly diverse and require diverse employee experiences." The company ties 5 percent of upper management's pay to diversity: half for promoting minorities and the other half for contracting with diverse suppliers.

HOW AGENCIES ARE RESPONDING

Clients increasingly are inquiring about diversity on the agency side, according to Heide Gardner, chief diversity officer for Interpublic Group. "They're pushing their values along the supply chain and they are interested in our progress," she says. "More clients are including questions about workforce and supplier diversity in RFPs. I would guesstimate that at least a third of all RFPs include questions about supplier and workforce diversity."

Agencies, however, are not keeping up in certain areas.

As part of their settlement with New York's human-rights commission, the 15 agencies (down from 16, after Draft and FCB merged) reported their minority hiring numbers for 2007 to the commission, and the results appeared impressive: As a group, they committed to have 18 percent of new hires be minorities, and on average they actually hired 25 percent.

But according to data from the NYCCHR as reported in *Advertising Age*, the number of African Americans hired—which had been the original issue—were still paltry. Moore, who brought the complaint to the commission, said he was discouraged by the African-American numbers and unswayed by the bright spots elsewhere. "Blacks are not the minority of choice" for those doing the hiring, he says. And he adds that he's seen minority hiring spurts before, only to see people of color leave the industry after bumping up against glass ceilings.

The NYCCHR was not able to provide data about those agencies' 2007 hiring results to *Adweek* by press time.

"You don't let someone off the hook for decades of blatant discrimination because they hire a few people," Moore says. "Madison Avenue has been about supporting, subsidizing and propagating a value system that marginalizes blacks, black media institutions, black creativity and black culture."

And advertising, he says, requires neither special degrees nor a particularly keen intellect: "Madison Avenue is one of the last places where undereducated whites can still make big money." White executives for decades, he adds, have told him that diversity was "the moral issue of our time" and that their own shops had a "level playing field." To which he counters, "If it were a level playing field, black people wouldn't be rolling off the playing field."

This is not to say there haven't been concerted efforts to diversify. Over the last few years, a handful of ad agencies have hired diversity officers whose primary focus is to increase recruitment, and to structure mentoring programs and affinity groups within the agencies. The programs build a supportive culture within firms that, consciously or not, have not always supported people of color, and in so doing may be beginning to crack the glass ceiling.

Gardner was named director of diversity for IPG in 2003 and, in 2007, was promoted to svp and chief diversity officer, marking the first time a person of color has served as an officer in the company. (Last year, IPG appointed its sole African-American board member, Jocelyn Miller-Carter, who owns a Florida technology company.)

According to Gardner, a major challenge involves not just hiring minorities, but keeping them on board, since turnover with minorities is 30 percent higher than whites at IPG. "This really speaks to the issue of sustainability," Gardner says. "We have done a much better job of recruiting" for entry-level jobs, she says, "but now we have to focus on the mid- and senior levels."

Today, 20 percent of the company's junior staff are minorities, but of the nearly 100 agencies that Interpublic owns outright or partly, only two are headed by African Americans: Larry Harris in 2007 was named president of the newly formed Ansible, a mobile marketing agency that is a joint venture between IPG and mobile technology provider Velti; and Steve Stoute is founder of Translation Consultation + Brand Imaging.

Gardner says the company does not go so far as the NFL and require a diverse candidate slate, but it "recommends" it.

She also says that some, but not all, of IPG's companies tie bonuses to diversity goals, a practice some experts say is a key to achieving diversity. For a senior executive, it can account for 10 percent to 15 percent of a bonus, or $40,000–60,000, according to Gardner.

Tiffany Warren, vp and director of multicultural programs and community outreach at Arnold, says the company has achieved its level of 31 percent non-white employees without tying executive pay to diversity goals, since "what works for a Fortune 500 company doesn't necessarily work for us."

AN OLD PROBLEM

In his recent book *Madison Avenue and the Color Line*, about African-Americans' role in advertising over the last century, professor and advertising consultant Jason Chambers links the historically negative depictions of black people in ads to their limited opportunities in the industry.

"If one looks at advertisements as documentaries, then the world for much of the 20th century was one in which whites enjoyed the fruits of consumption and blacks, if visible at all, contentedly served them from the margins," Chambers writes.

The book, among other things, details how civil rights groups and the NYCCHR have decried the lack of representation in the industry—and how agencies have vowed to remedy the situation—for more than four decades.

In 1963, the Urban League of New York released a study that found of the more than 20,000 employees in the city's largest ad agencies, only 25 African Americans were in "creative or executive positions." Five years later, a report from the NYCCHR said the scarcity of African Americans and Puerto Ricans employed at ad agencies was "a state of de facto segregation strongly suggesting discrimination."

In the wake of that report, writes Chambers, virtually every major agency instituted recruitment and mentoring programs and diversified, but the programs were expensive and disappeared because of the recession in the early 1970s.

Reached at his office at the University of Illinois at Urbana-Champaign, Chambers puzzles at why ad executives seem to see diversity as a do-gooder issue rather than a bottom-line one. The firms' leaders, he says, should be asking themselves these questions: "Why aren't we as mediators between manufacturers and consumers, pushing hardest for diversity? What level of insight creativity are we not getting because of that insularity?"

LEADING A HORSE TO WATER

After the NYCCHR began its latest investigation of the industry, the 4A's assembled a task force that culminated in a handbook, *Principles & Best Practices for Diversity and Inclusion in Advertising Agencies*. It recommends establishing diversity goals and timetables, tying executive compensation to those goals, focusing recruiting both on minority universities and minority executive recruiters, increasing retention of minority employees through mentoring programs, and hiring more minority businesses as vendors.

Adonis Hoffman, the staff lawyer for the 4A's who wrote the handbook, says the trade group can only lead horses to water. "We can provide guidance and leadership and give them all the resources," says Hoffman, "but it becomes a matter of individual corporate will."

As for the forthcoming report—and possible legal action—from Mehri, Hoffman says agencies should accept his recommendations. "I wouldn't advise the companies to hunker down," he says. "I'd advise them to face this head-on and see what they can do, because it's an issue that has been bouncing around this industry for a long, long time."

Hill, the 4A's CEO, says the association is doing what it can. This includes the continuation of its AAAA Foundation, which has created a number of scholarships for multicultural aspirants, including the Bill Bernbach Minority Scholarship, the John Mack Carter Scholarship and Operation JumpStart. In January, the association announced a partnership with Howard University to place multicultural talent in management at ad agencies, help African Americans transition from other industries into advertising and work with traditional black colleges to highlight the industry.

Also, Hill serves on the board of Together Our Resources Can Help (TORCH), which provides underserved New York City public high school students with exposure to career training and opportunities in communications and the arts. (*Adweek* publisher and editorial director Alison Fahey serves on the same board.)

On another front, Arnold's Warren hires interns to help out with the AdColor Awards, an initiative she co-founded last year to recognize creative achievement in five categories for multicultural talent both within agencies and at marketing departments in general-market companies.

One of those interns, Andy Deaza, is now 20 and recently moved to South Beach to study at the Miami Ad School. But Deaza, who is Dominican and Puerto Rican, did not find the ad business so much as the ad business found him. When he was a sophomore at Washington Irving High School in Manhattan, "I wasn't the best student and was kind of getting into trouble," he says. Deaza, whose favorite subject was art, was introduced to TORCH by his art teacher.

He threw himself into the program, was chosen to host its annual talent program (twice), attended an expenses-paid conference in San Francisco, and interned with JWT Director of Trendspotting Ann Mack and then Warren. Along the way, he says, he improved his grades and stayed out of trouble.

"There were definitely people helping guide the way," says Deaza. "If it wasn't for Debi [Deutsch, executive director of TORCH] and Tiffany, I wouldn't know about the industry. For whatever reason, white people know about the industry, but we don't—I don't know why."

Hill met Deaza not long ago.

"The night I met this kid and heard his story, the hair on my arms stood up," Hill says. "What it says to me is that you have to attack this problem from many different angles and when you see the programs come together in one individual like Andy, you know our efforts are worth it."

Asked if he had a dream client he'd like to work for one day, Deaza does not even have to think about it.

"Nike," he says. "I've been a Jordan fan all my life and I'm too young to have seen him play growing up. But those Spike Lee commercials—man, things like that are the reason I love this industry. To be able now to be so close to making something like that is surreal—that gives me the chills. If I ever got to put a swoosh on the end of something, I'd be a happy man."

Discussion and Writing Questions

1. The article focuses on the lack of diversity in the advertising workforce. What relationships does the lack of diversity have with social class? What examples does Newman provide that illustrate these relationships? Can you think of other examples of ethnic and social class connections? What effects do these relationships have on business practices?

2. Does the advertising industry have an obligation to diversify its workforce? Who would benefit from diversification? Write an essay that addresses these questions.

Intertextual Question

3. Both Newman and Larry Copeland address the issue of industry's responsibility to diversity. Do you think they are accurate in their explanations of how diversity should be treated within business contexts? Can the advertising industry learn anything from the auto industry regarding diversity.

Maid to Order—The Politics of Other Women's Work

Barbara Ehrenreich

Barbara Ehrenreich holds a PhD in cell biology from Rockefeller University but chose political activism over a scientific career. During the 1990s, she wrote a regular column for Time *magazine. Ehrenreich has written for the* New York Times, Mother Jones, *the* Atlantic Monthly, Ms., *the* New Republic, Z Magazine, In These Times, *Salon.com, and others. She has taught at the Graduate School of Journalism at the University of California, Berkeley. Ehrenreich is the author of* Nickel and Dimed: On (Not) Getting By in America. *In the following essay, Ehrenreich describes her experiences as a maid and examines the consequences of hiring out domestic chores.*

Prereading Question

Ehrenreich explores the reasons that people outsource domestic chores and the consequences for those who end up having to do the work. Who do you think should be responsible for household chores, such as house cleaning? Who was/is responsible for such duties in your household? Why?

———————— ✦ ————————

In line with growing class polarization, the classic posture of submission is making a stealthy comeback. "We scrub your floors the old-fashioned way," boasts the brochure from Merry Maids, the largest of the residential-cleaning services that have sprung up in the last two decades, "on our hands and knees." This is not a posture that independent "cleaning ladies" willingly assume—preferring, like most people who clean their own homes, the sponge mop wielded from a standing position. In her comprehensive 1999 guide to homemaking, *Home Comforts,* Cheryl Mendelson warns: "Never ask hired housecleaners to clean your floors on their hands and knees; the request is likely to be regarded as degrading." But in a society in which 40 percent of the wealth is owned by 10 percent of households while the bottom 20 percent reports negative assets, the degradation of others is readily purchased. Kneepads entered American political discourse as a tool of the sexually subservient, but employees of Merry Maids, The Maids International, and other corporate cleaning services spend hours every day on these kinky devices, wiping up the drippings of the affluent.

I spent three weeks in September 1999 as an employee of The Maids International in Portland, Maine, cleaning, along with my fellow team members, approximately 60 houses containing a total of about 250 scrubbable floors—bathrooms, kitchens, and entryways requiring the hands-and-knees treatment. It's a different world down there below knee level, one that few adults voluntarily enter. Here you find elaborate dust structures held together by a scaffolding of dog hair; dried bits of pasta glued to the floor by their sauce; the congealed remains of gravies, jellies, contraceptive creams, vomit, and urine. Sometimes, too, you encounter some fragment of a human being: a child's legs, stamping by in disgust because the maids are still present when he gets home from school; more commonly, the Joan & David–clad feet and electrolyzed calves of the female homeowner. Look up and you may find this person staring at you, arms folded, in anticipation of an overlooked stain. In rare instances she may try to help in some vague, symbolic way, by moving the cockatoo's cage, for example, or apologizing for the leaves shed by a miniature indoor tree. Mostly, though, she will not see you at all and may even sit down with her mail at a table in the very room you are cleaning, where she would remain completely unaware of your existence unless you were to crawl under that table and start gnawing away at her ankles.

Housework, as you may recall from the feminist theories of the Sixties and Seventies, was supposed to be the great equalizer of women. Whatever else women did—jobs, school, child care— we also did housework, and if there were some women who hired others to do it for them, they seemed too privileged and rare to include in the theoretical calculus. All women were workers, and the home was their workplace—unpaid and unsupervised, to be sure, but a workplace no less than the offices and factories men repaired to every morning. If men thought of the home as a site of leisure and recreation—a "haven in a heartless world"—this was to ignore the invisible female proletariat that kept it cozy and humming. We were on the march now, or so we imagined, united against a society that devalued our labor even as it waxed mawk-ish over "the family" and "the home." Shoulder to shoulder and arm-in-arm, women were finally getting up off the floor.

In the most eye-catching elaboration of the home-as-workplace theme, Marxist feminists Maria Rosa Dallacosta and Selma James proposed in 1972 that the home was in fact an eco-nomically productive and significant workplace, an extension of the actual factory, since housework served to "reproduce the labor power" of others; particularly men. The male worker would hardly be in shape to punch in for his shift, after all, if some woman had not fed him, laundered his clothes, and cared for the children who were his contribution to the next generation of workers. If the home was a quasi-industrial workplace staffed by women for the ultimate benefit of the capitalists, then it followed that "wages for housework" was the obvious demand.

But when most American feminists, Marxist or otherwise, asked the Marxist question *cui bono?* they tended to come up with a far simpler answer—men. If women were the domestic proletariat, then men made up the class of domestic exploiters, free to lounge while their mates scrubbed. In consciousness-raising groups, we railed against husbands and boyfriends who refused to pick up after themselves, who were unaware of housework at all, unless of course it hadn't been done. The "dropped socks," left by a man for a woman to gather up and launder, joined lipstick and spike heels as emblems of gender oppression. And if, somewhere, a man had actually dropped a sock in the calm expectation that his wife would retrieve it, it was a sock heard round the world. Wherever second-wave feminism took root, battles broke out between lovers and spouses over sticky countertops, piled-up laundry, and whose turn it was to do the dishes.

The radical new idea was that housework was not only a relationship between a woman and a dust bunny or an unmade bed; it also defined a relationship between human beings, typically husbands and wives. This represented a marked departure from the more conservative Betty Friedan, who, in *The Feminine Mystique,* had never thought to enter the male sex into the equation, as either part of the housework problem or part of an eventual solution. She raged against a society that consigned its educated women to what she saw as essentially janitorial chores, beneath "the abilities of a woman of average or normal human intelligence," and, according to unidentified studies she cited, "peculiarly suited to the capacities of feeble-minded girls." But men are virtually exempt from housework in *The Feminine Mystique—* why drag them down, too? At one point she even disparages a "Mrs. G.," who "somehow couldn't get her housework done before her husband came home at night and was so tired then that he had to do it." Educated women would just have to become more efficient so that housework could no longer "expand to fill the time available."

Or they could hire other women to do it—an option approved by Friedan in *The Feminine Mystique* as well as by the National Organization for Women, which she had helped launch. At the 1973 congressional hearings on whether to extend the Fair Labor Standards Act to household workers, NOW testified on the affirmative side, arguing that improved wages and working conditions would attract more women to the field, and offering the seemingly self-contradictory prediction that "the demand for household help inside the home will continue to increase as more women seek occupations outside the home." One NOW member added, on a personal note: "Like many young women today, I am in school in order to develop a rewarding career for myself. I also have a home to run and can fully conceive of the need for household help as my free time at home becomes more and more restricted. Women know [that] housework is dirty, tedious work, and they are willing to pay to have it done. . . ." On the aspirations of the women paid to do it, assuming that at least some of them were bright enough to entertain a few, neither Friedan nor these members of NOW had, at the time, a word to say.

So the insight that distinguished the more radical, post-Friedan cohort of feminists was that when we talk about housework, we are really talking, yet again, about power. Housework was not degrading because it was manual labor, as Friedan thought, but because it was embedded in degrading relationships and inevitably served to reinforce them. To make a mess that another person will have to deal with—the dropped socks, the toothpaste sprayed on the bathroom mirror, the dirty dishes left from a late-night snack—is to exert domination in one of its more silent and intimate forms. One person's arrogance—or indifference, or hurry—becomes another person's occasion for toil. And when the person who is cleaned up after is consistently male, while the person who cleans up is consistently female, you have a formula for reproducing male domination from one generation to the next.

Hence the feminist perception of housework as one more way by which men exploit women or, more neutrally stated, as "a symbolic enactment of gender relations." An early German women's liberation cartoon depicted a woman scrubbing on her hands and knees while her husband, apparently excited by this pose, approaches from behind, unzipping his fly. Hence, too, the second-wave feminists' revulsion at the hiring of maids, especially when they were women of color: At a feminist conference I attended in 1980, poet Audre Lorde chose to insult the all-too-white audience by accusing them of being present only because they had black housekeepers to look after their children at home. She had the wrong crowd; most of the assembled radical feminists would no sooner have employed a black maid than they would have attached Confederate flag stickers to the rear windows of their cars. But accusations like hers, repeated in countless conferences and meetings, reinforced our rejection of the servant option. There already were at least two able-bodied adults in the average home—a man and a woman—and the hope was that, after a few initial skirmishes, they would learn to share the housework graciously.

A couple of decades later, however, the average household still falls far short of that goal. True, women do less housework than they did before the feminist revolution and the rise of the two-income family: down from an average of 30 hours per week in 1965 to 17.5 hours in 1995, according to a July 1999 study by the University of Maryland. Some of that decline reflects a relaxation of standards rather than a redistribution of chores; women still do two thirds of whatever housework—including bill paying, pet care, tidying, and lawn care—gets done. The inequity is sharpest for the most despised of household chores, cleaning: in the thirty years between 1965 and 1995, men increased the time they spent scrubbing, vacuuming, and sweeping by 240 percent—all the way up to 1.7 hours per week—while women decreased their cleaning time by only 7 percent, to 6.7 hours per week. The averages conceal a variety of arrangements, of course, from minutely negotiated sharing to the most clichéd division of labor, as described by one woman to the *Washington Post:* "I take care of the inside, he takes care of the outside." But perhaps the most disturbing finding is that almost the entire increase in male participation took place between the 1970s and the mid-1980s. Fifteen years after the apparent cessation of hostilities, it is probably not too soon to announce the score: in the "chore wars" of the Seventies and Eighties, women gained a little ground, but overall, and after a few strategic concessions, men won.

Enter then, the cleaning lady as *dea ex machina*, restoring tranquillity as well as order to the home. Marriage counselors recommend her as an alternative to squabbling, as do many within the cleaning industry itself. A Chicago cleaning woman quotes one of her clients as saying that if she gives up the service, "my husband and I will be divorced in six months." When the trend toward hiring out was just beginning to take off, in 1988, the owner of a Merry Maids franchise in Arlington, Massachusetts, told *The Christian Science Monitor*, "I kid some women. I say, 'We even save marriages. In this new eighties period you expect more from the male partner, but very often you don't get the cooperation you would like to have. The alternative is to pay somebody to come in. . . .'" Another Merry Maids franchise owner has learned to capitalize more directly on housework-related spats; he closes between 30 and 35 percent of his sales by making follow-up calls Saturday mornings, which is "prime time for arguing over the fact that the house is a mess." The micro-defeat of feminism in the household opened a new door for women, only this time it was the servants' entrance.

In 1999, somewhere between 14 and 18 percent of households employed an outsider to do the cleaning, and the numbers have been rising dramatically. Mediamark Research reports a 53 percent increase, between 1995 and 1999, in the number of households using a hired cleaner or service once a month or more, and Maritz Marketing finds that 3o percent of the people who hired help in 1999 did so for the first time that year. Among my middle-class, professional women friends and acquaintances, including some who made important contributions to the early feminist analysis of housework, the employment of a maid is now nearly universal. This sudden emergence of a servant class is consistent with what some economists have called the "Brazilianization" of the American economy: We are dividing along the lines of traditional Latin American societies—into a tiny overclass and a huge underclass, with the latter available to perform intimate household services for the former. Or, to put it another way, the home, or at least the affluent home, is finally becoming what radical feminists in the Seventies only imagined it was—a true "workplace" for women and a tiny, though increasingly visible, part of the capitalist economy. And the question is: As the home becomes a workplace for someone else, is it still a place where you would want to live?

Strangely, or perhaps not so strangely at all, no one talks about the "politics of housework" anymore. The demand for "wages for housework" has sunk to the status of a curio, along with the consciousness-raising groups in which women once rallied support in their struggles with messy men. In the academy, according to the feminist sociologists I interviewed, housework has lost much of its former cachet—in part, I suspect, because fewer sociologists actually do it. Most Americans, over 80 percent, still clean their homes, but the minority who do not include a sizable faction of the nation's opinion-makers and culture-producers—professors, writers, editors, politicians, talking heads, and celebrities of all sorts. In their homes, the politics of housework is becoming a politics not only of gender but of race and class—and these are subjects that the opinion-making elite, if not most Americans, generally prefer to avoid.

Even the number of paid houseworkers is hard to pin down. The Census Bureau reports that there were 549,000 domestic workers in 1998, up 9 percent since 1996, but this may be a considerable underestimate, since so much of the servant economy is still underground. In 1995, two years after Zoe Baird lost her chance to be attorney general for paying her undocumented nanny off the books, the *Los Angeles Times* reported that fewer than 10 percent of those Americans who paid a housecleaner reported those payments to the IRS. Sociologist Mary Romero, one of the few academics who retain an active interest in housework and the women who do it for pay, offers an example of how severe the undercounting can be: the 1980 Census found only 1,063 "private household workers" in El Paso, Texas, though the city estimated their numbers at 13,400 and local bus drivers estimated that half of the 28,300 daily bus trips were taken by maids going to and from work. The honesty of employers has increased since the Baird scandal, but most experts believe that household workers remain, in large part, uncounted and invisible to the larger economy.

One thing you can say with certainty about the population of household workers is that they are disproportionately women of color: "lower" kinds of people for a "lower" kind of work. Of the "private household cleaners and servants" it managed to locate in 1998, the Bureau of Labor Statistics reports that 36.8 were Hispanic, 15.8 percent black, and 2.7 percent "other." Certainly the association between housecleaning and minority status is well established in the psyches of the white employing class. When my daughter, Rosa, was introduced to the wealthy father of a Harvard classmate, he ventured that she must have been named for a favorite maid. And Audre Lorde can perhaps be forgiven for her intemperate accusation at the feminist conference mentioned above when we consider an experience she had in 1967: "I wheel my two-year-old daughter in a shopping cart through a supermarket . . . and a little white girl riding past in her mother's cart calls out excitedly, 'Oh look, Mommy, a baby maid.'" But the composition of the household workforce is hardly fixed and has changed with the life chances of the different ethnic groups. In the late nineteenth century, Irish and German immigrants served the northern upper and middle classes, then left for the factories as soon as they could. Black women replaced them, accounting for 60 percent of all domestics in the 1940s, and dominated the field until other occupations began to open up to them. Similarly, West Coast maids were disproportionately Japanese American until that group, too, found more congenial options. Today, the color of the hand that pushes the sponge varies from region to region: Chicanas in the Southwest, Caribbeans in New York, native Hawaiians in Hawaii, whites, many of recent rural extraction, in Maine.

The great majority—though again, no one knows exact numbers—of paid housekeepers are freelancers, or "independents," who find their clients through agencies or networks of already employed friends and relatives. To my acquaintances in the employing class, the freelance housekeeper seems to be a fairly privileged and prosperous type of worker, a veritable aristocrat of labor—sometimes paid $15 an hour or more and usually said to be viewed as a friend or even treated as "one of the family." But the shifting ethnic composition of the workforce tells another story: this is a kind of work that many have been trapped in—by racism, imperfect English skills, immigration status, or lack of education—but few have happily chosen. Interviews with independent maids collected by Romero and by sociologist Judith Rollins, who herself worked as a maid in the Boston area in the early Eighties, confirm that the work is undesirable to those who perform it. Even when the pay is deemed acceptable, the hours may be long and unpredictable; there are usually no health benefits, no job security, and, if the employer has failed to pay Social Security taxes (in some cases because the maid herself prefers to be paid off the books), no retirement benefits. And the pay is often far from acceptable. The BLS found full-time "private household cleaners and servants" earning a median annual income of $12,220 in 1998, which is $1,092 below the poverty level for a family of three. Recall that in 1993 Zoe Baird paid her undocumented household workers about $5 an hour out of her earnings of $507,000 a year.

At the most lurid extreme there is slavery. A few cases of forced labor pop up in the press every year, most recently—in some nightmare version of globalization—of undocumented women held in servitude by high-ranking staff members of the United Nations, the World Bank, and the International Monetary Fund. Consider the suit brought by Elizabeth Senghor, a Senegalese woman who alleged that she was forced to work fourteen-hour days for her employers in Manhattan, without any regular pay, and was given no accommodations beyond a pull-out bed in her employers' living room. Hers is not a particularly startling instance of domestic slavery; no beatings or sexual assaults were charged, and Ms. Senghor was apparently fed. What gives this case a certain rueful poignancy is that her employer, former U.N.

employee Marie Angelique Savane, is one of Senegal's leading women's rights advocates and had told *The Christian Science Monitor* in 1986 about her efforts to get the Senegalese to "realize that being a woman can mean other things than simply having children, taking care of the house."

Mostly, though, independent maids—and sometimes the women who employ them—complain about the peculiar intimacy of the employer-employee relationship. Domestic service is an occupation that predates the refreshing impersonality of capitalism by several thousand years, conditions of work being still largely defined by the idiosyncrasies of the employers. Some of them seek friendship and even what their maids describe as "therapy," though they are usually quick to redraw the lines once the maid is perceived as overstepping. Others demand deference bordering on servility, while a growing fraction of the nouveau riche is simply out of control. In August 1999, *The New York Times* reported on the growing problem of dinner parties being disrupted by hostesses screaming at their help. To the verbal abuse add published reports of sexual and physical assaults—a young teenage boy, for example, kicking a live-in nanny for refusing to make sandwiches for him and his friends after school.

But for better or worse, capitalist rationality is finally making some headway into this weird preindustrial backwater. Corporate cleaning services now control 25 to 30 percent of the $1.4 billion housecleaning business, and perhaps their greatest innovation has been to abolish the mistress-maid relationship, with all its quirks and dependencies. The customer hires the service, not the maid, who has been replaced anyway by a team of two to four uniformed people, only one of whom—the team leader—is usually authorized to speak to the customer about the work at hand. The maids' wages, their Social Security taxes, their green cards, backaches, and child-care problems—all these are the sole concern of the company, meaning the local franchise owner. If there are complaints on either side, they are addressed to the franchise owner; the customer and the actual workers need never interact. Since the franchise owner is usually a middle-class white person, cleaning services are the ideal solution for anyone still sensitive enough to find the traditional employer-maid relationship morally vexing.

In a 1997 article about Merry Maids, *Franchise Times* reported tersely that the "category is booming, [the] niche is hot, too, as Americans look to outsource work even at home." Not all cleaning services do well, and there is a high rate of failure among informal, mom-and-pop services. The "boom" is concentrated among the national and international chains—outfits like Merry Maids, Molly Maids, Mini Maids, Maid Brigade, and The Maids International—all named, curiously enough, to highlight the more antique aspects of the industry, though the "maid" may occasionally be male. Merry Maids claimed to be growing at 15 to 20 percent a year in 1996, and spokesmen for both Molly Maids and The Maids International told me that their firms' sales are growing by 25 percent a year; local franchisers are equally bullish. Dan Libby, my boss at The Maids, confided to me that he could double his business overnight if only he could find enough reliable employees. To this end, The Maids offers a week's paid vacation, health insurance after 90 days, and a free breakfast every morning consisting—at least where I worked—of coffee, doughnuts, bagels, and bananas. Some franchises have dealt with the tight labor market by participating in welfare-to-work projects that not only funnel employees to them but often subsidize their paychecks with public money, at least for the first few months of work (which doesn't mean the newly minted maid earns more, only that the company has to pay her less). The Merry Maids franchise in the city where I worked is conveniently located a block away from the city's welfare office.

Among the women I worked with at The Maids, only one said she had previously worked as an independent, and she professed to be pleased with her new status as a cleaning-service employee. She no longer needed a car to get her from house to house and could take a day off—unpaid of course—to stay home with a sick child without risking the loss of a customer. I myself could see the advantage of not having to deal directly with the customers, who were sometimes at home while we worked and eager to make use of their supervisory skills: criticisms of our methods, and demands that we perform unscheduled tasks, could simply be referred to the franchise owner.

But there are inevitable losses for the workers as any industry moves from the entrepreneurial to the industrial phase, probably most strikingly, in this case, in the matter of pay. At Merry Maids, I was promised $200 for a forty hour week, the manager hastening to add that "you can't calculate it in dollars per hour" since the forty hours include all the time spent traveling from house to house—up to five houses a day—which is unpaid. The Maids International, with its straightforward starting rate of $6.63 an hour, seemed preferable, though this rate was conditional on per-fect attendance. Miss one day and your wage dropped to $6 an hour for two weeks, a rule that weighed particularly heavily on those who had young children. In addition, I soon learned that management had ways of shaving off nearly an hour's worth of wages a day. We were told to arrive at 7:30 in the morning, but our billable hours began only after we had been teamed up, given our list of houses for the day, and packed off in the company car at about 8:00 A.M. At the end of the day, we were no longer paid from the moment we left the car, though as much as fifteen minutes of work—refilling cleaning-fluid bottles, etc.—remained to be done. So for a standard nine-hour day, the actual pay amounted to about $6.10 an hour, unless you were still being punished for an absence, in which case it came out to $5.50 an hour.

Nor are cleaning-service employees likely to receive any of the perks or tips familiar to independents—free lunches and coffee, cast-off clothing, or a Christmas gift of cash. When I asked, only one of my coworkers could recall ever receiving a tip, and that was a voucher for a free meal at a downtown restaurant owned by a customer. The customers of cleaning services are probably no stingier than the employers of independents; they just don't know their cleaning people and probably wouldn't even recognize them on the street. Plus, customers probably assume that the fee they pay the service—$25 per person-hour in the case of The Maids franchise I worked for—goes largely to the workers who do the actual cleaning.

But the most interesting feature of the cleaning-service chains, at least from an abstract, historical perspective, is that they are finally transforming the home into a fully capitalist-style work-place, and in ways that the old wages-for-housework advocates could never have imagined. A house is an innately difficult work-place to control, especially a house with ten or more rooms like so many of those we cleaned; workers may remain out of one another's sight for as much as an hour at a time. For independents, the ungovernable nature of the home-as-workplace means a certain amount of autonomy. They can take breaks (though this is proba-bly ill-advised if the homeowner is on the premises); they can ease the monotony by listening to the radio or TV while they work. But cleaning services lay down rules meant to enforce a factorylike—or even conventlike—discipline on their far-flung employees. At The Maids, there were no breaks except for a daily ten-minute stop at a convenience store for coffee or "lunch"—meaning something like a slice of pizza. Otherwise, the time spent driving between houses was considered our "break" and the only chance to eat, drink, or (although this was also officially forbidden) smoke a cigarette. When the houses were spaced well apart, I could eat my sandwich in one sitting; otherwise it would have to be divided into as many as three separate, hasty snacks.

Within a customer's house, nothing was to touch our lips at all, not even water—a rule that, on hot days, I sometimes broke by drinking from a bathroom faucet. TVs and radios were off-limits, and we were never, ever, to curse out loud, even in an ostensibly deserted house. There might be a homeowner secreted in some locked room, we were told, ear pressed to the door, or, more likely, a tape recorder or video camera running. At the time, I dismissed this as a scare story, but I have since come across ads for devices like the Tech-7 "incredible coin-sized camera" designed to "get a visual record of your babysitter's actions" and "watch employees to prevent theft." It was the threat or rumor of hidden recording devices that provided the final capitalist-industrial touch—supervision.

What makes the work most factorylike, though, is the intense Taylorization imposed by the companies. An independent, or a person cleaning his or her own home, chooses where she will start and, within each room, probably tackles the most egregious dirt first. Or she may plan her work more or less ergonomically, first doing whatever can be done from a standing position and then squatting or crouching to reach the lower levels. But with the special "systems" devised by the cleaning services and imparted to employees via training videos, there are no such decisions to make. In The Maids' "healthy touch" system, which is similar to what I saw of the Merry Maids' system on the training tape I was shown during my interview, all cleaning is divided into four task areas—dusting, vacuuming, kitchens, and bathrooms—which are in turn divided among the team members. For each task area other than vacuuming, there is a bucket containing rags and the appropriate cleaning fluids, so the biggest decision an employee has to make is which fluid and scrubbing instrument to deploy on which kind of surface; almost everything else has been choreographed in advance. When vacuuming, you begin with the master bedroom; when dusting, with the first room off of the kitchen; then you move through the rooms going left to right. When entering each room, you proceed from left to right and top to bottom, and the same with each surface—top to bottom, left to right.

Deviations are subject to rebuke, as I discovered when a team leader caught me moving my arm from right to left, then left to right, while wiping Windex over a French door.

It's not easy for anyone with extensive cleaning experience—and I include myself in this category—to accept this loss of autonomy. But I came to love the system: First, because if you hadn't always been traveling rigorously from left to right it would have been easy to lose your way in some of the larger houses and omit or redo a room. Second, some of the houses were already clean when we started, at least by any normal standards, thanks probably to a housekeeper who kept things up between our visits; but the absence of visible dirt did not mean there was less work to do, for no surface could ever be neglected, so it was important to have "the system" to remind you of where you had been and what you had already "cleaned." No doubt the biggest advantage of the system, though, is that it helps you achieve the speed demanded by the company, which allots only so many minutes per house. After a week or two on the job, I found myself moving robotlike from surface to surface, grateful to have been relieved of the thinking process.

The irony, which I was often exhausted enough to derive a certain malicious satisfaction from, is that "the system" is not very sanitary. When I saw the training videos on "Kitchens" and "Bathrooms," I was at first baffled, and it took me several minutes to realize why: There is no water, or almost no water, involved. I had been taught to clean by my mother, a compulsive house-keeper who employed water so hot you needed rubber gloves to get into it and in such Niagara like quantities that most microbes were probably crushed by the force of it before the soap suds had a chance to rupture their cell walls. But germs are never mentioned in the videos provided by The Maids. Our antagonists existed entirely in the visible world—soap scum, dust, counter crud, dog hair, stains, and smears—and were attacked by damp rag or, in hardcore cases, by a scouring pad. We scrubbed only to remove impurities that might be detectable to a customer by hand or by eye; otherwise our only job was to wipe. Nothing was ever said, in the videos or in person, about the possibility of transport-ing bacteria, by rag or by hand, from bathroom to kitchen or even from one house to the next. Instead, it is the "cosmetic touches" that the videos emphasize and to which my trainer continually directed by eye. Fluff out all throw pillows and arrange them sym-metrically. Brighten up stainless steel sinks with baby oil. Leave all spice jars, shampoos, etc., with their labels facing outward. Comb out the fringes of Persian carpets with a pick. Use the vacuum to create a special, fernlike pattern in the carpets. The loose ends of toilet paper and paper towel rolls have to be given a special fold. Finally, the house is sprayed with the service's signature air freshener—a cloying floral scent in our case, "baby fresh" in the case of the Mini Maids.

When I described the "methods" employed to housecleaning expert Cheryl Mendelson, she was incredulous. A rag moistened with disinfectant will not get a countertop clean, she told me, because most disinfectants are inactivated by contact with organic matter—i.e., dirt—so their effectiveness declines with each swipe of the rag. What you need is a detergent and hot water, followed by a rinse. As for floors, she judged the amount of water we used—one half of a small bucket—to be grossly inadequate, and, in fact, the water I wiped around on floors was often an unsavory gray. I also ran The Maids' cleaning methods by Don Aslett, author of numerous books on cleaning techniques and self-styled "number-one cleaner in America." He was hesitant to criticize The Maids directly, perhaps because he is, or told me he is, a frequent speaker at conventions of cleaning-service franchise holders, but he did tell me how he would clean a countertop: first, spray it thoroughly with an all-purpose cleaner, then let it sit for three to four minutes of "kill time," and finally wipe it dry with a clean cloth. Merely wiping the surface with a damp cloth, he said, just spreads the dirt around. But the point at The Maids, apparently, is not to clean so much as it is to create the appearance of having been cleaned, not to sanitize but to create a kind of stage setting for family life. And the stage setting Americans seem to prefer is sterile only in the metaphorical sense, like a motel room or the fake interiors in which soap operas and sitcoms take place.

But even ritual work takes its toll on those assigned to perform it. Turnover is dizzyingly high in the cleaning-service industry, and not only because of the usual challenges that confront the working poor—child-care problems, unreliable transportation, evictions and prior health problems. As my long-winded interviewer at Merry Maids warned me, and my coworkers at The Maids confirmed, this is a physically punishing occupation, something to tide you over for a few months, not year after year. The hands-and-knees posture damages knees, with or without pads; vacuuming strains the back; constant wiping and scrubbing invite repetitive stress injuries even in the very young. In my three weeks as a maid, I suffered nothing more than a persistent muscle spasm in the right forearm but the damage would have been far worse if I'd had to go home every day to my own housework and children, as most of my coworkers did, instead of returning to my motel and indulging in a daily after-work regimen of ice packs and stretches. Chores that seem effortless at home, even almost recreational when undertaken at will for twenty minutes or so at a time, quickly turn nasty when performed hour after hour, with few or no breaks and under relentless time pressure.

So far, the independent, entrepreneurial housecleaner is holding her own, but there are reasons to think that corporate cleaning services will eventually dominate the industry. New users often prefer the impersonal, standardized service offered by the chains, and, in a fast-growing industry, new users make up a sizable chunk of the total clientele. Government regulation also favors the corporate chains, whose spokesmen speak gratefully of the "Zoe Baird effect," referring to customers' worries about being caught paying an independent off the books. But the future of housecleaning may depend on the entry of even bigger players into the industry. Merry Maids, the largest of the chains, has the advantage of being a unit within the $6.4 billion ServiceMaster conglomerate, which includes such related businesses as TruGreen-ChemLawn, Terminix, Rescue Rooter, and Furniture Medic. Swisher International, best known as an industrial toilet-cleaning service, operates Swisher Maids in Georgia and North Carolina, and Sears may be feeling its way into the business. If large multinational firms establish a foothold in the industry, mobile professionals will be able to find the same branded and standardized product wherever they relocate. For the actual workers, the change will, in all likelihood, mean a more standardized and speeded-up approach to the work—less freedom of motion and fewer changes to pause.

The trend toward outsourcing the work of the home seems, at the moment, unstoppable. Two hundred years ago women often manufactured soap, candles, cloth, and clothing in their own homes, and the complaints of some women at the turn of the twentieth century that they had been "robbed by the removal of creative work" from the home sound pointlessly reactionary today. Not only have the skilled crafts, like sewing and cooking from scratch, left the home but many of the "white collar" tasks arc on their way out, too. For a fee, new firms such as the San Francisco–based Les Concierges and Cross It Off Your List in

Manhattan will pick up dry cleaning, baby-sit pets, buy groceries, deliver dinner, even do the Christmas shopping. With other firms and individuals offering to buy your clothes, organize your financial files, straighten out your closets, and wait around in your home for the plumber to show up, why would anyone want to hold on to the toilet cleaning?

Absent a major souring of the economy, there is every reason to think that Americans will become increasingly reliant on paid housekeepers and that this reliance will extend ever further down into the middle class. For one thing, the "time bind" on working parents shows no sign of loosening; people are willing to work longer hours at the office to pay for the people—housecleaners and baby-sitters—who are filling in for them at home. Children, once a handy source of household help, are now off at soccer practice or SAT prep classes; grandmother has relocated to a warmer climate or taken up a second career. Furthermore, despite the fact that people spend less time at home than ever, the square footage of new homes swelled by 33 percent between 1975 and 1998, to include "family rooms," home entertainment rooms, home offices, bedrooms, and often bathrooms for each family member. By the third quarter of 1999, 17 percent of new homes were larger than 3,000 square feet, which is usually considered the size threshold for household help, or the point at which a house becomes unmanageable to the people who live in it.

One more trend impels people to hire outside help, according to cleaning experts such as Aslett and Mendelson: fewer Americans know how to clean or even to "straighten up." I hear this from professional women defending their decision to hire a maid: "I'm just not very good at it myself" or "I wouldn't really know where to begin." Since most of us learn to clean from our parents (usually our mothers), any diminution of cleaning skills is transmitted from one generation to another, like a gene that can, in the appropriate environment, turn out to be disabling or lethal. Upper-middle-class children raised in the servant economy of the Nineties are bound to grow up as domestically incompetent as their parents and no less dependent on people to clean up after them. Mendelson sees this as a metaphysical loss, a "matter of no longer being physically centered in your environment." Having cleaned the rooms of many overly privileged teenagers in my stint with The Maids, I think the problem is a little more urgent than that. The American overclass is raising a generation of young people who will, without constant assistance, suffocate in their own detritus.

If there are moral losses, too, as Americans increasingly rely on paid household help, no one has been tactless enough to raise them. Almost everything we buy, after all, is the product of some other person's suffering and miserably underpaid labor. I clean my own house (though—full disclosure—I recently hired someone else to ready it for a short-term tenant), but I can hardly claim purity in any other area of consumption. I buy my jeans at The Gap, which is reputed to subcontract to sweatshops. I tend to favor decorative objects no doubt ripped off, by their purveyors, from scantily paid Third World craftspersons. Like everyone else, I eat salad greens just picked by migrant farm workers, some of them possibly children. And so on. We can try to minimize the pain that goes into feeding, clothing, and otherwise provisioning ourselves—by observing boycotts, checking for a union label, etc.—but there is no way to avoid it altogether without living in the wilderness on berries. Why should housework, among all the goods and services we consume, arouse any special angst?

And it does, as I have found in conversations with liberal-minded employers of maids, perhaps because we all sense that there are ways in which housework is different from other products and services. First, in its inevitable proximity to the activities that compose "private" life. The home that becomes a workplace for other people remains a home, even when that workplace has been minutely regulated by the corporate cleaning chains. Someone who has no qualms about purchasing rugs woven by child slaves in India or coffee picked by impoverished peasants in Guatemala might still hesitate to tell dinner guests that, surprisingly enough, his or her lovely home doubles as a sweatshop during the day. You can eschew the chain cleaning service of course, hire an independent cleaner at a generous hourly wage, and even encourage, at least in spirit, the unionization of the housecleaning industry. But this does not change the fact that someone is working in your home at a job she would almost certainly never have chosen for herself—if she'd had a college education, for example, or a little better luck along the way—and the place where she works, however enthusiastically or resentfully, is the same as the place where you sleep.

It is also the place where your children are raised, and what they learn pretty quickly is that some people are less worthy than others. Even better wages and working conditions won't erase the hierarchy between an employer and his or her domestic help, because the help is usually there only because the employer has "something better" to do with her time, as one report on the growth of cleaning services puts it, not noticing the obvious implication that the cleaning person herself has nothing better to do with her time. In a merely middle-class home, the message may be reinforced by a warning to the children that that's what they'll end up doing if they don't try harder in school. Housework, as radical feminists once proposed, defines a human relationship and, when unequally divided among social groups, reinforces preexisting inequalities. Dirt, in other words, tends to attach to the people who remove it—"garbagemen" and "cleaning ladies." Or, as cleaning entrepreneur Don Aslett told me with some bitterness—and this is a successful man, chairman of the board of an industrial cleaning service and frequent television guest—"The whole mentality out there is that if you clean, you're a scumball."

One of the "better" things employers of maids often want to do with their time is, of course, spend it with the children. But an underlying problem with post-nineteenth-century child-raising, as Deirdre English and I argued in our book *For Her Own Good* years ago, is precisely that it is unmoored in any kind of purposeful pursuit. Once "parenting" meant instructing the children in necessary chores; today it's more likely to center on one-sided conversations beginning with "So how was school today?" No one wants to put the kids to work again weeding and stitching; but in the void that is the modern home, relationships with children are often strained. A little "low-quality time" spent washing dishes or folding clothes together can provide a comfortable space for confidences—and give a child the dignity of knowing that he or she is a participant in, and not just the product of, the work of the house.

There is another lesson the servant economy teaches its beneficiaries and, most troublingly, the children among them. To be cleaned up after is to achieve a certain magical weightlessness and immateriality. Almost everyone complains about violent video games, but paid housecleaning has the same consequence-abolishing effect: you blast the villain into a mist of blood droplets and move right along; you drop the socks knowing they will eventually levitate, laundered and folded, back to their normal dwelling place. The result is a kind of virtual existence, in which the trail of litter that follows you seems to evaporate all by itself. Spill syrup on the floor and the cleaning person will scrub it off when she comes on Wednesday. Leave *The Wall Street*

Journal scattered around your airplane seat and the flight attendants will deal with it after you've deplaned. Spray toxins into the atmosphere from your factory's smokestacks and they will be filtered out eventually by the lungs of the breathing public. A servant economy breeds callousness and solipsism in the served, and it does so all the more effectively when the service is performed close up and routinely in the place where they live and reproduce.

Individual situations vary, of course, in ways that elude blanket judgment. Some people—the elderly and disabled, parents of new babies, asthmatics who require an allergen-free environment—may well need help performing what nursing-home staff call the "ADLs," or activities of daily living, and no shame should be attached to their dependency. In a more generous social order, housekeeping services would be subsidized for those who have health-related reasons to need them—a measure that would generate a surfeit of new jobs for the low-skilled people who now clean the homes of the affluent. And in a less gender-divided social order, husbands and boyfriends would more readily do their share of the chores.

However we resolve the issue in our individual homes, the moral challenge is, put simply, to make work visible again: not only the scrubbing and vacuuming but all the hoeing, stacking, hammering, drilling, bending, and lifting that goes into creating and maintaining a livable habitat. In an ever more economically unequal culture, where so many of the affluent devote their lives to such ghostly pursuits as stock-trading, image-making, and opinion-polling, real work—in the old-fashioned sense of labor that engages hand as well as eye, that tires the body and directly alters the physical world—tends to vanish from sight. The feminists of my generation tried to bring some of it into the light of day, but, like busy professional women fleeing the house in the morning, they left the project unfinished, the debate broken off in midsentence, the noble intentions unfulfilled. Sooner or later, someone else will have to finish the job.

Discussion and Writing Questions

1. At one point, Ehrenreich says that the feminist perception is that housework is a way that men exploit women. Do you agree with this statement? If women choose to outsource housework, does it then become a situation of women exploiting other women?

2. At the end of her article, Ehrenreich proposes some potential consequences for outsourcing housework. In an essay explain what you think the consequences of raising generations of children in homes where the housework is outsourced might be. What are the differences in values that children might experience in homes where the work is completed by family members rather than low-salary employees?

Intertextual Question

3. Ehrenreich implies that outsourcing domestic chores teaches children not to be responsible for themselves. How does this argument compare with that of Brian Stelter (Chapter 3), even though he and Ehrenreich write on very different topics?

The Men We Carry in Our Minds
SCOTT RUSSELL SANDERS

Scott Russell Sanders is a Distinguished Professor of English at Indiana University. He has won numerous awards for his fiction and nonfiction works. He has written twenty books and is regularly cited in anthologies. In the following essay from his essay collection The Paradise of Bombs, *Sanders describes the working-class men of his childhood and the differences between classes and genders he witnessed as a scholarship student at Brown University in the 1960s.*

Prereading Question

What are the differences between workers and bosses? What are long-term physical and financial effects of blue-collar labor compared to those of white-collar employment?

───────────── ✦ ─────────────

The first men, besides my father, I remember seeing were black convicts and white guards, in the cotton field across the road from our farm on the outskirts of Memphis. I must have been three or four. The prisoners wore dingy gray-and-black zebra suits, heavy as canvas, sodden with sweat. Hatless, stooped, they chopped weeds in the fierce heat, row after row, breathing the acrid dust of boll-weevil poison. The overseers wore dazzling white shirts and broad shadowy hats. The oiled barrels of their shotguns flashed in the sunlight. Their faces in memory are utterly blank. Of course those men, white and black, have become for me an emblem of racial hatred. But they have also come to stand for the twin poles of my early vision of manhood—the brute toiling animal and the boss.

When I was a boy, the men I knew labored with their bodies. They were marginal farmers, just scraping by, or welders, steel workers, carpenters; they swept floors, dug ditches, mined coal, or drove trucks, their forearms ropy with muscle; they trained horses, stoked furnaces, built tires, stood on assembly lines wrestling parts onto cars and refrigerators. They got up before light, worked all day long whatever the weather, and when they came home at night they looked as though somebody had been whipping them. In the evenings and on weekends they worked on their own places, tilling gardens that were lumpy with clay, fixing broken-down cars, hammering on houses that were always too drafty, too leaky, too small.

The bodies of the men I knew were twisted and maimed in ways visible and invisible. The nails of their hands were black and split, the hands tattooed with scars. Some had lost fingers. Heavy lifting had given many of them finicky backs and guts weak from hernias. Racing against conveyor belts had given them ulcers. Their ankles and knees ached from years of standing on concrete. Anyone who had worked for long around machines was hard of hearing. They squinted, and the skin of their faces was creased like the leather of old work gloves. There were times, studying them, when I dreaded growing up. Most of them coughed, from dust or cigarettes, and most of them drank cheap wine or whiskey, so their eyes looked bloodshot and bruised. The fathers of my friends always seemed older than the mothers. Men wore out sooner. Only women lived into old age.

As a boy I also knew another sort of men, who did not sweat and break down like mules. They were soldiers, and so far as I could tell they scarcely worked at all. During my early school years we lived on a military base, an arsenal in Ohio, and every day I saw GIs in the guard shacks, on the stoops of barracks, at the wheels of olive drab Chevrolets. The chief fact of their lives was boredom. Long after I left the Arsenal I came to recognize the sour smell the soldiers gave off as that of souls in limbo. They were all waiting—for wars, for transfers, for leaves, for promotions, for the end of their hitch—like so many braves waiting for the hunt to begin. Unlike the warriors of older tribes, however, they would have no say about when the battle would start or how it would be waged. Their waiting was broken only when they practiced for war. They fired guns at targets, drove tanks across the churned-up fields of the military reservation, set off bombs in the wrecks of old fighter planes. I knew this was all play. But I also felt certain that when the hour for killing arrived, they would kill. When the real shooting started, many of them would die. This was what soldiers were *for*, just as a hammer was for driving nails.

Warriors and toilers: those seemed, in my boyhood vision, to be the chief destinies for men. They weren't the only destinies, as I learned from having a few male teachers, from reading books, and from watching television. But the men on television—the politicians, the astronauts, the generals, the savvy lawyers, the philosophical doctors, the bosses who gave orders to both soldiers and laborers—seemed as remote and unreal to me as the figures in tapestries. I could no more imagine growing up to become one of these cool, potent creatures than I could imagine becoming a prince.

A nearer and more hopeful example was that of my father, who had escaped from a red-dirt farm to a tire factory, and from the assembly line to the front office. Eventually he dressed in a white shirt and tie. He carried himself as if he had been born to work with his mind. But his body, remembering the earlier years of slogging work, began to give out on him in his fifties, and it quit on him entirely before he turned sixty-five. Even such a partial escape from man's fate as he had accomplished did not seem possible for most of the boys I knew. They joined the Army, stood in line for jobs in the smoky plants, helped build highways. They were bound to work as their fathers had worked, killing themselves or preparing to kill others.

A scholarship enabled me not only to attend college, a rare enough feat in my circle, but even to study in a university meant for the children of the rich. Here I met for the first time young men who had assumed from birth that they would lead lives of comfort and power. And for the first time I met women who told me that men were guilty of having kept all the joys and privileges of the earth for themselves. I was baffled. What privileges? What joys? I thought about the maimed, dismal lives of most of the men back home. What had they stolen from their wives and daughters? The right to go five days a week, twelve months a year, for thirty or forty years to a steel mill or a coal mine? The right to drop bombs and die in war? The right to feel every leak in the roof, every gap in the fence, every cough in the engine, as a wound they must mend? The right to feel, when the layoff comes or the plant shuts down, not only afraid but ashamed?

I was slow to understand the deep grievances of women. This was because, as a boy, I had envied them. Before college, the only people I had ever known who were interested in art or music or literature, the only ones who read books, the only ones who ever seemed to enjoy a sense of ease and grace were the mothers and daughters. Like the menfolk, they fretted about money, they scrimped and made-do. But, when the pay stopped coming in, they were not the ones who had failed. Nor did they have to go to war, and that seemed to me a blessed fact. By comparison with the narrow, ironclad days of fathers, there was an expansiveness, I thought, in the days of mothers. They went to see neighbors, to shop in town, to run errands at school, at the library, at church. No doubt, had I looked harder at their lives, I would have envied them less. It was not my fate to become a woman, so it was easier for me to see the graces. Few of them held jobs outside the home, and those who did filled thankless roles as clerks and waitresses. I didn't see, then, what a prison a house could be, since houses seemed to me brighter, handsomer places than any factory. I didn't realize—because such things were never spoken of—how often women suffered from men's bullying. I did learn about the wretchedness of abandoned wives, single mothers, widows; but I also learned about the wretchedness of lone men. Even then I could see how exhausting it was for a mother to cater all day to the needs of young children. But if I had been asked, as a boy, to choose between tending a baby and tending a machine, I think I would have chosen the baby. (Having now tended both, I know I would choose the baby.)

So I was baffled when the women at college accused me and my sex of having cornered the world's pleasures. I think something like my bafflement has been felt by other boys (and by girls as well) who grew up in dirt-poor farm country, in mining country, in black ghettos, in Hispanic barrios, in the shadows of factories, in Third World nations—any place where the fate of men is as grim and bleak as the fate of women. Toilers and warriors,

I realize now how ancient these identities are, how deep the tug they exert on men, the undertow of a thousand generations. The miseries I saw, as a boy, in the lives of nearly all men I continue to see in the lives of many—the body-breaking toil, the tedium, the call to be tough, the humiliating powerlessness, the battle for a living and for territory.

When the women I met at college thought about the joys and privileges of men, they did not carry in their minds the sort of men I had known in my childhood. They thought of their fathers, who were bankers, physicians, architects, stockbrokers, the big wheels of the big cities. These fathers rode the train to work or drove cars that cost more than any of my childhood houses. They were attended from morning to night by female helpers, wives and nurses and secretaries. They were never laid off, never short of cash at month's end, never lined up for welfare. These fathers made decisions that mattered. They ran the world.

The daughters of such men wanted to share in this power, this glory. So did I. They yearned for a say over their future, for jobs worthy of their abilities, for the right to live at peace, unmolested, whole. Yes, I thought, yes yes. The difference between me and these daughters was that they saw me, because of my sex, as destined from birth to become like their fathers, and therefore as an enemy to their desires. But I knew better. I wasn't an enemy, in fact or in feeling. I was an ally. If I had known, then, how to tell them so, would they have believed me? Would they now?

Discussion and Writing Questions

1. Sanders talks about the differences in the work of the men and the women he observed growing up. Do you think that men's perceptions of women's work, either inside or outside the home, have changed over time? Do women have an accurate perception of men's work outside the home?

2. What is the perception of personal control and power of different segments of workers (e.g., working class, management, stay-at-home parent)? Examine your own experiences or interview a relative, friend, or colleague and describe how perceptions of power are related to the person's job.

Intertextual Question

3. Sanders talks about the struggle of the working class. How does Sanders' description of working men compare to Ehrenreich's description of women working as maids? What similarities and differences can you identify that are related to gender and the working class?

African Americans Feel Auto Industry's Pain

LARRY COPELAND

Larry Copeland is a writer for USA Today. *He frequently reports on the auto industry. In the following article, Copeland examines the effects of the economic downturn on African Americans employed in the auto industry.*

Prereading Question

What role do you think the American auto industry plays in the economy of the United States? Who do you think would be most affected by changes in the American auto industry?

——————————— ✦ ———————————

Gregory Baranco, a new car dealer in Atlanta for 30 years, and George McGregor, a longtime union shop steward in Detroit, don't know each other. But their lives have a shared theme.

The men, both African American, built and sustained lives of middle-class success in the nation's domestic automobile industry, and both took a route to prosperity increasingly unavailable to others.

The financial crisis in the auto industry has been more devastating for African Americans than any other community, threatening a half-century's economic gains by the black middle class. From blacks who left behind subsistence jobs in the South for high-paying factory jobs in the North during the Great Migration, to entrepreneurs who translated hard work and the gift of selling into their own businesses—they're all getting hammered.

"One of the engines of the black middle class has been the auto sector," says John Schmitt, an economist who studies the issue at the Center for Economic and Policy Research, a liberal Washington think tank. In the late 1970s, "one of every 50 African Americans in the U.S. was working in the auto sector. These jobs were the best jobs. Particularly for African Americans who had migrated from the South, these were the culmination of a long upward trajectory of economic mobility."

General Motors and Chrysler made it into the new year, however, only with $17.4 billion in federal loans and have asked for more after March. Whether to risk more taxpayer money or let them face bankruptcy filings now falls to the administration of President Obama.

From 1979 to 2007, black employment in the auto industry fell from about one in 50 African Americans to about one in 100, Schmitt says. The trend continued last year: He estimates that the number of African Americans in the auto industry fell from about 140,000 at the end of 2007 to about 110,000 at the end of 2008.

The auto sector job losses have hit blacks harder than whites or Hispanics because the percentage of African Americans in the industry—14.2%—still is higher than their share of the labor force overall—11.2%—says Robert E. Scott, senior international economist at the liberal Economic Policy Institute in Washington. "This is an industry that offers particularly good wages for workers, especially for those who do not have a college degree," a group with a higher proportion of African Americans, says Scott. He says 21.9% of black workers have four-year college degrees, vs. 33.7% of whites.

An Economic Policy Institute report last month said African Americans have been especially hard-hit in this recession, with a jobless rate that rose to 11.2% in November, up 2.8 percentage points from a year earlier. The national jobless rate that month rose 2 points, to 6.7%, from a year earlier. "The consequences of an auto industry collapse ... would be nothing less than catastrophic for African Americans," the report said.

The impact goes far beyond factory workers and others employed in the industry, says Randi Payton, president and CEO of On Wheels media, which publishes magazines and produces websites about the auto industry for minority audiences.

"The Big Three are leaders in philanthropy in the African-American community," he says. "They are major contributors to education through historically black colleges and universities, and to non-profits such as the NAACP, National Urban League and National Council of Negro Women.

"The auto industry also is one of the largest advertisers in African-American media," he says. "And if you're a business dependent on the auto industry, such as supplier, you're facing the same problems the auto companies are. Banks won't finance us, and in many cases, they're withdrawing lines of credit."

Detroit's struggles are reverberating among the nation's 60 or so African-American automotive suppliers, which have annual sales of about $4 billion and employ some 8,000 people, about

70% of them black, says Leon Richardson, chairman of the National Association of Black Automotive Suppliers. "This is going to be a very difficult time for African-American automotive suppliers," he says. "We have probably lost close to five (in the past 18 months) but are braced for many more."

ACCESS TO CAPITAL AN ISSUE

The picture is also bleak for black auto dealers. According to Damon Lester, president of the National Association of Minority Automobile Dealers, 150 to 200 minority dealers were among the about 800 U.S. auto stores that closed last year, and 300 more could shutter their doors this year.

Lester says most minority dealers are first-generation owners, with more limited access to capital than more established dealers. He says the federal bailout of General Motors and Chrysler won't help black dealers—or any dealers. "It gives another survival line to the manufacturers, but it does not assist the dealers in gaining access to capital," he says.

Baranco, 60, opened his General Motors dealership in Atlanta on April 4, 1978, with his wife, Juanita. By 1989, he was listed as the fourth-largest black auto dealer in the nation by *Fortune* magazine.

He has cut his staff from 83 to 30 in the past year and a half, and says the Buick-Pontiac-GMC facility is likely to close this year. "I'm trying to hold on while GM is going through really challenging times," he says. "They're trying to figure out what their future is going to look like and whether Baranco is going to be part of it.

"There has been nothing of this magnitude in my years in the business, because it encompasses not only the increased (foreign) competition but the credit issue," Baranco says. "I've got customers that I could have gotten financed a year and a half ago that I can't get financed now.

"I don't really think I'm going to make it," Baranco says of his GM dealership.

He'll still be selling cars—for a foreign automaker. Five years ago, he opened a Mercedes-Benz dealership. Though Mercedes' sales have been hit by the recession, too, parent Daimler has the financial resources to survive it. But it can't replace what the Detroit companies have meant to the U.S. economy and society.

BUILDING BLOCK

It's difficult to overstate the importance of the domestic auto industry in creating the nation's black middle class, says Thomas Sugrue, professor of history and sociology at the University of Pennsylvania. "The auto industry became a magnet for African-American migrants from the South because it offered relatively well-paying, relatively secure jobs with excellent benefits," he says.

"Ford began recruiting black workers in the South in the 1920s, and became known as one of the more generous employers for African Americans. Black workers got equal pay for equal work, although they were confined mostly to unskilled jobs. Ford was well ahead of the curve in providing employment for black workers."

During the late 1920s and 1930s, the United Auto Workers union worked with civil rights activists to challenge racial bias in the industry and opened up jobs that had been closed to blacks, Sugrue says. The percentage of black workers in the auto industry skyrocketed during World War II, from 4% at the start of the war to 15% by 1945, and to 16% by 1960.

"That opening of auto employment created a black working class that had a degree of security unprecedented for most folks coming from the rural South," Sugrue says. "That opened up a whole area of upward mobility for black workers."

McGregor, 62, left Memphis for Detroit in 1968 after a stint in Vietnam. He'd heard from a fellow soldier that autoworkers in the Motor City were pulling down two or three times what he'd been making before he was drafted. "When I got out, I went home and stayed exactly one week," he says. "I got on the Greyhound bus and came straight to Detroit."

McGregor had an uncle working at Ford, another at Chrysler. He applied at GM on his first Saturday in Detroit, and was hired on Monday. "When I got the telegram that they wanted me to come out, I was standing in line at Ford. They offered me a job, too, but in order to get to the Ford job, I would have to go past the GM plant. So I took the GM job."

He started at $3.28 an hour, more than double the $1.25 he'd been making in Memphis. "It felt like 50 times more. I still have that check. I have it framed."

Discussion and Writing Questions

1. Why does Copeland claim that changes in the auto industry would greatly impact African Americans?

2. What other industries do you think would be affected by changes in the American auto industry? Are there other segments of the population who would be specifically affected by these changes in industry? In an essay, explain how one industry other than the automotive will be affected.

Intertextual Question

3. How does the description of the effects of the auto industry on the lifestyles of African Americans compare to the description of the benefits of boxing in Struby's essay in Chapter 1?

Understanding China's Middle Class
ALLISON CUI AND KHEEHONG SONG

Allison Cui is a senior consultant, based in Shanghai, for the global management consulting company Monitor Group. She holds an MBA from Stanford Graduate School of Business. She has worked as a senior project manager and as a software engineer. Kheehong Song is partner of Monitor Group, head of M2C (Monitor's marketing practice) Asia, and managing director of Monitor's Shanghai office. The China Business Review *is the official magazine of the U.S.-China Business Council. In this article, Cui and Song examine the changing middle class of China and the approaches that will be necessary for targeting this growing consumer population.*

Prereading Question

What consumer role does the middle class play in the United States? How important is it for businesses to understand the middle class of other countries?

———————— ✦ ————————

Gone are the days when companies looked at China as a monolithic land of 1 billion potential customers. Companies are now focusing on how to capture small segments of China's giant market, and none of these segments is as attractive or as full of potential as the country's rapidly growing—and multifaceted—middle class. As China's economy continues to grow, more people will migrate to China's booming metropolises to find better-paying jobs. These working consumers, once among the country's poorest, will steadily climb the income ladder and join the new middle class. Companies that can effectively understand the composition and needs of this diverse group will be positioned to reap massive rewards.

WHY THE MIDDLE CLASS?

Though many foreign companies have remarked on the importance of China's middle class as a consumer segment, few realize just how dramatic its ascendance is. From 1995 to 2005, the population of China's middle class—defined here as households with annual incomes ranging from $6,000 to $25,000—grew from close to zero in 1995 to an estimated 87 million in 2005, according to MasterCard Worldwide, Asia Pacific. China's middle class will jump to 340 million by 2016. The purchasing power—disposable income minus savings—of China's middle class is also growing. In 2006, around 39 percent of urban households were middle class. By 2016, that percentage will likely rise to 60 percent. At present, the middle class accounts for 27 percent of China's total urban disposable income. By 2015, that percentage is expected to rise to more than 40 percent. Considering its swelling numbers, purchasing power, and trajectory, China's middle class presents marketing opportunities that companies cannot afford to miss.

WHAT DOES IT MEAN TO BE MIDDLE CLASS?

Different types of companies have different concepts of exactly what it means to be middle class in China. For example, HSBC Holdings plc and Deutsche Bank AG have used income to differentiate the middle class from the affluent and laboring classes in China. From an investment bank's perspective, using income level as the defining criterion makes sense. But simply judging a group by income is far from sufficient for marketers of consumer goods. Such marketers trying to reach the middle class have to know more than their salaries: They must know what makes middle class consumers tick.

Income plays a powerful role in most purchasing decisions for any consumer segment, but other elements play a role that is sometimes greater than income. When products are relatively inexpensive, income has little influence on a consumer's decisionmaking process. Deciding to buy chocolate, for example, depends significantly more on consumers' emotion and shopping experience—a store's ambience, for example—than it does on how much money they make. Using income as the only indicator of spending habits allows much information to slip through the cracks. In addition, income is a difficult variable to act upon, in part because the data on income in China tends to be either unavailable or unreliable. Thus, companies must find meaningful alternatives to predict what consumers can afford and what they are willing to pay for certain goods and services. Studies by the Monitor Group indicate that scores of non-income-related hooks—including age, the stage in a consumer's career, and location of purchase—influence purchase decisions.

The Chinese badminton industry is a good example. Most Chinese school kids who play badminton do so in an outdoor playground with a group of friends, wear non-professional badminton sportswear, and purchase a relatively inexpensive racket in a sports stadium or shop near school. Professionals and businesspeople, however, usually play badminton in indoor badminton clubs, gyms, or stadiums. One of the major reasons they play badminton is to make friends or develop business relationships. They are aware of racket brands and wear professional sportswear to display social status.

The differences between school kids and professionals are mainly due to their disparate life stages and buying power. If a sports equipment and apparel company understands the differences between these two segments, it will use varying products and prices to target them through different channels. Nonetheless, even within the professional segments, consumers exhibit distinct buying behavior based on their occupation and level of career development. For example, engineers usually exhibit different buying behavior from marketing professionals, and senior managers may not care as much about brands as junior managers, who tend to buy famous brands to show their emerging social status.

PURCHASING POWER AND HOW THE MIDDLE CLASS BUYS

Of all the challenges that the middle class presents to marketers, understanding the specific needs and purchasing power of the group is of utmost importance. Though middle class consumers have rising purchasing power and are increasingly willing to pay more for higher quality, brand names, and differentiated features, they are still price sensitive. Recognizing differences in behavior within middle class segments is essential to success in the Chinese marketplace.

When Inter IKEA Systems B.V. first entered China in 1998, its strategy was to offer stylish furniture at premium prices. The strategy was a flop. Middle class customers filled IKEA's stores to look around but bought less than expected.

In the last few years, however, IKEA has repositioned itself as a brand targeting segments with annual household incomes above ¥40,000 ($5,857). Thanks to achievements in localization, the company has been able to cut prices by an average of 54 percent in more than 1,000 categories since 2005. IKEA broke the bottleneck and succeeded in China because it recognized that middle class consumers wanted and would pay for high-quality products, but not at the same premiums as the affluent class.

MEET THE MIDDLE CLASS

China's relatively new middle class consists of a rapidly shifting, diverse population. At present, China's lower middle class accounts for 44 percent of the total middle class. As the middle class matures, however, the number of people in the upper middle class—households that earn $12,000 to $25,000—will spike dramatically. Companies must prepare for the different shopping behaviors of each sub-segment within the middle class. Lower middle class shoppers, for example, tend to buy top-tier products that can display their wealth and status. These middle class consumers sometimes spend a large portion of their income on expensive goods. By contrast, upper middle class shoppers, who are more experienced with different types of brands, will seek out relatively high-quality products without paying as much attention to brands or will pick out products that merely reflect personal tastes.

To differentiate customer segments, Monitor Group has used "action segmentation," a market analysis strategy that draws on statistical data from a customer survey with several thousand samples and wide coverage. This methodology identifies multiple consumer segments to help companies address core organizational issues, achieve a well-designed marketing mix, reach growth targets, and more effectively engage their market. In the case of China's middle class, Monitor focused on purchasing behavior and demographic features, rather than income, as the key measures for understanding the middle class.

In one case, Monitor examined the correlation between consumer occupation and purchasing decisions within the tourism industry, the results of which allowed companies to customize their tourist packages more effectively. Monitor found three distinct segments of Chinese tourists: business, leisure, and backpacking travelers. Business travelers have fairly stable travel schedules throughout the year. They are reimbursed for some expenses and tend to spend more than leisure travelers. Leisure travelers enjoy sightseeing and recreational activities and tend to be more cost-conscious and self-organized. Chinese backpackers are willing to spend more and care most about uniqueness and experience. They want more personalized services, such as global positioning systems and specially trained tour guides. Unlike US backpackers, they have money and time and backpack mainly to be fashionable and gain new experiences.

In another case, an examination of the different levels of daily exercise among men and women revealed that although men tend to exercise at a more or less constant rate throughout their lives, women exercise less after marriage and still less after having children. This information helped sportswear companies identify which demographic segments were most profitable to target.

Applying the action segmentation methodology to the Chinese middle class, Monitor identified six sub-segments within the group, each with its own unique needs and consumption patterns. These include Early Heavy Buyers, the Smarts, the Quality-Oriented, Trend Followers, Driven Businesspeople, and Value Seekers.

To serve the specific needs of China's diverse middle class, companies must understand the desires of these six sub-segments and learn how to reach them. Early Heavy Buyers are energetic consumers, consisting primarily of professionals in tertiary industries and junior managers at multinational corporations. They tend to be young and well-educated, with an interest in and exposure to the world outside China. As consumers, they are early adopters of the latest products and aggressively seek out fashion that can help them stand out from their peers. Because they serve as trendsetters, members of this group actively search for information online and share that information with peers. They predominantly make purchases online or by mail order and have a high willingness to spend, especially on discretionary goods such as fashion items and lifestyle products and services. This group of trendsetters stands out from Trend Followers, who attempt to emulate Early Heavy Buyers in certain ways but approach purchasing decisions differently. Trend Followers tend to be junior white-collar workers and civil servants who have some leisure time and a stable salary but are new to the middle class and have less room for discretionary spending. They are less well-informed than Early Heavy Buyers and consequently place more emphasis on the shopping experience. They are also more price sensitive. Though Early Heavy Buyers may be more concerned with being the first to get a new product, Trend Followers will wait for discounts and tend to take advantage of promotions.

Like Trend Followers, Value Seekers are usually junior white-collar office workers or government employees. As their incomes rise, they increasingly demand better quality and service, but remain sensitive to price. Though they purchase some goods from relatively inexpensive luxury brands to help show their status, they remain more concerned about value than other middle class segments. Trend Followers may choose products that are in fashion, while Value Seekers tend to look for the best quality-to-price ratio regardless of how popular the item may be at the time.

The final three—the Smarts, the Quality-Oriented, and Driven Businesspeople—tend to be older and to have been in the middle class longer. The Smarts are usually more sophisticated shoppers who prefer to buy from specialty stores and boutiques instead of major outlets. They regularly order business and fashion magazines to stay on top of trends but also rely on word of mouth.

Like the Smarts, Driven Businesspeople are willing to pay premiums for convenience. Driven Businesspeople are relatively wealthy and lead extremely busy lives. They do not have much time to gather information and compare different brands or clothes, but they have higher purchasing power. They usually trust friends' recommendations, develop brand preferences before they buy, and are not price sensitive. They are experienced consumers with high degrees of brand loyalty, especially in fashion. For this group, product and service quality are much more important than price. The Quality-Oriented share much in common with the Smarts and Driven Businesspeople but tend to have more leisure time. More than either of those groups, family is a priority for the Quality-Oriented and has a strong influence on their purchasing decisions. For example, large markets and department stores that carry a range of products important to a family are the major purchasing channels for the Quality-Oriented, and television is their dominant information resource for new products.

Monitor helped a sportswear client target two of the six middle-class segments—Driven Businesspeople and Value Seekers—by understanding different buying habits. To better target Driven Businesspeople, Monitor recommended that its client market products in mid-range to high-end gyms and fitness clubs, where many businesspeople usually go, to develop brand awareness and attract customers. Monitor also recommended that its client place mid-to-high-end products in department stores and flagship shops, where Driven Businesspeople usually go to buy sportswear. By contrast, to target Value Seekers, Monitor recommended that the client become more aware of Value Seekers' tendency to spend time comparing products, shopping at hypermarkets, and buying less expensive products.

Discussion and Writing Questions

1. Do you think the six segments of the Chinese middle class have correlations in the American middle class? What segments would you divide the American middle class into? Can you characterize each segment's consumer patterns as Cui and Song did?

2. Cui and Song claim that not only income level but also occupation affects buying behavior. Interview business people who represent a specific occupation regarding their buying behavior. Does the level of their career development affect their buying behavior? Do they buy brands to "show their emerging social status," or do brands play an insignificant role in their consumer choices? Analyze the responses you gather and compare them to the information presented in Cui and Song's article.

Intertextual Question

3. How does Cui and Song's examination of the Chinese middle class compare to Andrew Newman's discussion of the insularity of the advertising industry? Would a more diverse staff help advertising agencies to target population segments more effectively?

CREDITS

CHAPTER 1

"A Fist Full of Dollars" by Tim Struby, from *Maxim* (March, 2007). Used by permission of the author.

"The Sims: Suburban Rhapsody" by Clive Thomson from *Psychology Today* (Nov. 1, 2003). Reprinted with permission from Psychology Today Magazine. Copyright © 2003 Sussex Publishers, LLC.

"Tiger Woods" by Roger O. Crockett, reprinted from the October 13, 2008 issue of *BusinessWeek* by special permission. Copyright © 2008 The McGraw-Hill Companies, Inc.

"The Adult Film Industry: Time to Regulate?" by Corita R. Grudzen and Peter R. Kerndt from PLoS Med 4(6): e126. Published online June 19, 2007. doi:10.1371/journal.pmed.0040126. © 2007 C.R. Grudzen and P.R. Kerndt.

"And Now a Game from Our Sponsor" by Steve Tilley from *Official Xbox Magazine*, Dec. 28, 2007. Reprinted by permission.

CHAPTER 2

"The Student Loan Scandal" by William Beaver from *Society*, 45(3), pp. 216–221 (2008). © Springer Science and Business Media, LLC 2008. Reprinted with kind permission from Springer Science and Business Media.

"Starbucks Cutting More Jobs, Closing Stores" by Bruce Horovitz, published Jan. 29, 2009 in *USA Today*, a division of Gannett Co., Inc. Reprinted with permission.

CHAPTER 3

CHAPTER 4

"The New Spies" by Stephen Armstrong from *New Statesman,* Aug. 7, 2008. Copyright 2008 New Statesman, Ltd. Reprinted by permission of the publisher.

"Call It Slavery" by John R. Miller from *The Wilson Quarterly,* Summer 2008. Reprinted by permission of the author.

"A Virtual World but Real Money" by Richard Siklos, from the *New York Times,* Oct. 19, 2006. © 2006 The New York Times. All rights reserved. Used by permission and protected by the Copyright Laws of the United States. The printing, copying, redistribution, or retransmission of the Material without express written permission is prohibited.

"What the Country Needs? A Fiscal Triple Play" by David M. Walker, published Feb. 5, 2009 in *USA Today,* a division of Gannett Co., Inc. Reprinted with permission.

CHAPTER 5

"The Color of Money," originally published in *Adweek,* Vol. 49, Issue 35, Dec. 1, 2008 as "The Minority Report" by Andrew Adam Newman. Used with permission of e5 Global Media, LLC.

"Maid to Order" by Barbara Ehrenreich. Reprinted by permission of International Creative Management, Inc. Copyright © 2000 by Barbara Ehrenreich for *Harper's Magazine.*

"The Men We Carry in Our Minds" by Scott Russell Sanders. Copyright © 1984 by Scott Russell Sanders. First appeared in *Milkweed Chronicle;* from THE PARADISE OF BOMBS, reprinted by permission of the author and the author's agents, the Virginia Kidd Agency, Inc.

"African Americans Feel Auto Industry's Pain" by Larry Copeland, published Jan. 20, 2009 in *USA Today,* a division of Gannett Co., Inc. Reprinted with permission.

"Understanding China's Middle Class" by Allison Cui and Kheehong Song. Originally published in the January–February 2009 issue of the *China Business Review.* Reprinted with the permission of the US-China Business Council, Washington, DC.